The Ethos of the Christian Heart

Other Books of Interest from St. Augustine's Press

Adrian Reimers, *The Good Is Love: The Body and Human Acts in Humanae Vitae and John Paul II*

George Gänswein, *Who Believes Is Not Alone: My Life Beside Benedict XVI*

Roberto Regoli, *Beyond the Crises: The Pontificate of Benedict XVI*

Marin Schlag, editor, , *Holiness through Work: Commemorating the Encyclical Laborem Exercens*

Donald S. Prudlo, *Governing Perfection*

Richard Schaefer, *Devotional Activism: Public Religion, Innovation and Culture in the Nineteenth-Century*

John Tanyi Nquah Lebui, *The Cross and the Flag: Papal Diplomacy and John Paul II's Struggle Against the Tyranny of the Possible*

Michael Franz (editor), *Eric Voegelin's Late Meditations and Essays: Critical Commentary Companions*

Peter Kreeft, *The Philosophy of Jesus*

Peter Kreeft, *Socratic Logic (3rd Edition)*

Pete Fraser, *Twelve Films about Love and Heaven*

Jean-Luc Marion, *Descartes's Grey Ontology: Cartesian Science and Aristotelian Thought in the Regulae*

Josef Pieper, *In Tune with the World*

Sister M. Pascalina Lehnert, *His Humble Servant: Sister M. Pascalina Lehnert's Memoirs of Her Years of Service to Eugenio Pacelli, Pope Pius XII*

John Paull II, *John Paul II LifeGuide: Words to Live By*

Roger Scruton, *The Meaning of Conservatism: Revised 3rd Edition*

Roger Scruton, *The Politics of Culture and Other Essays*

Joseph Bottum, *Spending the Winter: A Poetry Collection*

D. C. Schindler, *God and the City*

The Ethos of the Christian Heart

Reading *Veritatis Splendor*

Adrian Reimers

St. Augustine's Press
South Bend, Indiana

Manufactured in the United States of America.

1 2 3 4 5 6 30 29 28 27 26 25

Library of Congress Control Number: 2024939400

Paperback ISBN: 978-1-58731-242-7

∞ The paper used in this publication meets the minimum requirements of the American National Standard for Information Sciences – Permanence of Paper for Printed Materials, ANSI Z39.48-1984.

St. Augustine's Press
www.staugustine.net

TABLE OF CONTENTS

PREFACE

Moral theology, teaching, and practice within the Catholic Church today are in flux. Increasingly we hear of the need for a *new paradigm* or new standards for doing moral theology. In a recent address to moral theologians, Pope Francis offered generalized direction for those working in moral theology, ethics, and related fields, warning against an attitude and approach that works "so much evil to the Church."[1] The Pope continued,

> [...] it is like a "going back," whether from fear or from lack of genius or lack of courage. It is true that we theologians, even Christians, should turn to the roots; this is true. Without the roots we cannot take a step forward. From the roots we draw inspiration, but in order to go forward. This is different than turning backward. Turning backward is not Christian. [...] The Christian cannot turn back. Return to the roots to gain inspiration, to proceed. Yes. But to turn back is to return to have a defense, a security that avoids the risk of going forward, the Christian risk to carry the faith, the Christian risk to take the way with Jesus Christ.

Turning back, "tornare indietro," is a serious problem for Pope Francis. He has condemned the "indietrismo" ("backwardness")

1 Francis, Discorso del Santo Padre Francesco ai Partecipanti ai Convegno Internazionale di Teologia Morale, 13 Maggio 2022. Downloaded (October 2023 from https://www.vatican.va/content/francesco/it/speeches/2022/may/documents/20220513-convegno-teologia-morale.html. Author's translation.

of many American voices in the Church who are seen to be too "conservative." In the address just cited, he gives a partial answer to his meaning. He encourages a turning to the roots of theology, and he gives as an example his own approach in the Apostolic Exhortation *Amoris Laetitia*, in which he relies on the thought of St. Thomas Aquinas and, of course, Holy Scripture. To judge from this one address as well as from other comments that the Holy Father has made, this "turning back," the *indietrismo*, consists largely in the reliance of Catholic scholars, especially in the years preceding the Second Vatican Council, on manuals that provide sharp, clear-cut answers to theological questions—particularly to moral questions. This approach tended to look to the law as expressed in or derived from the Ten Commandments and then to arrive at specific conclusions by casuistic reasoning. Such an approach could indeed arrive at the objective truth, but in a way that obscured the work of the Holy Spirit and the law of love.[2] At the time of the Second Vatican Council, many thinkers besides Pinckaers realized that a new approach was needed.

Among these was philosopher Karol Wojtyła, who in his philosophical writings and especially in his pontifical work as John Paul II, addressed the bases of philosophical ethics and the Church's moral teachings. Indeed, as Pope Francis was later to urge so warmly, Karol Wojtyła/Pope John Paul II turned to the roots of Christian teaching in the Scriptures and in the writings of Saints Augustine, Thomas Aquinas, John of the Cross, and others to draw out an account of the human heart, its call to communion with God, and its sinful resistance to that call. In his encyclicals on Christ's redeeming work (*Redemptor Hominis*), on God's mercy (*Dives in Misericordia*), and the mission of the Holy Spirit to human hearts (*Dominum et Vivificantem*), as well as those on human work, suffering, economic relations, and the impending Third Millennium, he turned to the roots of the Church's faith

2 On this see Servais Pinckaers, *Morality: The Catholic View* (South Bend, Indiana: St Augustine's Press, 2001), which presents an excellent analysis of this issue.

to go forward and present to the Church a vision of the life of those redeemed by Jesus Christ.

Especially noteworthy in this respect was his extended series of public audiences on the theology of the body.[3] Relying on a close and deep reading of the Scriptures, he developed an acute analysis of the human heart, its call to communion in love and its deformation by sinful concupiscence. There he developed an account of the feminine genius (which he later amplified in *Mulieris Dignitatem*) and masculine responsibility. Furthermore, to a Church internally befuddled by widespread rejection of Pope Paul VI's encyclical on the transmission of human life, *Humanae Vitae,* John Paul II presented a humanly sensitive and Scriptural explanation of the ethos of Christian marriage and the harm to love incurred by recourse to artificial contraceptives.[4] This work went far beyond a rigid appeal to natural law or to proof-texting from the Scriptures. The focus of this work, as expressed in the subtitle of the original Polish manuscript, is the redemption of the body and the sacramentality of marriage.[5] Then in 1993, John Paul II addressed the Scriptural, theological, and philosophical bases of the moral law in his encyclical *Veritatis Splendor,* an encyclical that was opposed furiously when it appeared and which continues to find resistance within the Church, even in circles close to the current pontiff.

The impetus for this current work was the invitation by the John Paul II Catholic University of Lublin (KUL) to present the Karol Wojtyła Memorial Lectures on Pope John Paul II and the encyclical *Veritatis Splendor* in the spring of 2020. The focus of the lectures was to be on Karol Wojtyła's engagement with modern philosophy and its impact on the encyclical. Because of the

3 John Paul II, *Man and Woman He Created Them: A Theology of the Body* (Boston: Pauline Books & Media, 2006).

4 On this see Adrian J. Reimers, *The Good Is Love: The Body and Human Acts in Humanae Vitae and John Paul II* (South Bend, Indiana: St Augustine's Press, 2020).

5 John Paul II, *Mężczyzna i niewiastą stworzył ich: Odkupienia ciała a sakramentalność małżeństwa* (Lublin: Wydawnictwo KUL, 2008).

COVID pandemic, these lectures were postponed until 2022, but the two lost years provided an opportunity to deepen my investigation of and reflection on that encyclical. I offer this current work as the fruit of that engagement with my colleagues at the KUL.

INTRODUCTION

> "You shall love the Lord your God with all your heart, and with all your soul, and with all your mind." This is the greatest and first commandment. And a second is like it: "You shall love your neighbor as yourself." (Matt 22:37–39)

The twofold purpose of Pope Saint John Paul II's encyclical *Veritatis Splendor* is:

> [...] to set forth, with regard to the problems being discussed, the principles of a moral teaching based upon Sacred Scripture and the living Apostolic Tradition, and at the same time to shed light on the presuppositions and consequences of the dissent which that teaching has met.[1]

Most of the critical and interpretative attention has focused on this second purpose, to address the contemporary dissent to Catholic moral teaching. Indeed, in its second chapter the encyclical identifies and critically addresses problematic conceptions concerning the moral life. However, the Encyclical's first purpose is to "set forth [...] the principles of a moral teaching based upon Sacred Scripture and the living Apostolic Tradition." In other words, *Veritatis Splendor* is far more than an examination and refutation of errors in moral theology. On this Servais Pinckaers writes concerning his own study on *Veritatis Splendor*:

1 John Paul II, Encyclical *Veritatis Splendor* (Vatican City: Libreria Editrice Vaticana, 1993), §5.

> We would like to show, among other things, that the Encyclical is more innovative than it looks. It is not content to defend the traditional positions; it traces the paths of a profound renewal in the presentation of Catholic morality. We would gladly say that it performs a kind of discreet revolution in the conception of Christian morality, affecting the very bases that support it.[2]

This encyclical is a treatise about love, God's love for us and our loving response to the love of the Creator and Redeemer. The encyclical begins with Christ's challenge to the rich young man who asks him about the way to eternal life and concludes with a discussion of the call to the holiness evidenced in martyrdom. John Paul II presents the cross of Christ as the ultimate standard of Christian love and hence morality.

Since Plato and Aristotle, philosophers have reflected on human nature and the requirements of the good life. The modern era has seen the emergence of empirical sciences of human nature, from medicine and anthropology to psychology and sociology—disciplined, rigorous studies of every aspect of the human being. However, the Second Vatican Council teaches that there is more that lies beyond the unaided powers of human reason.

> The truth is that only in the mystery of the incarnate Word does the mystery of man take on light. For Adam, the first man, was a figure of Him Who was to come, namely Christ the Lord. Christ, the final Adam, by the revelation of the mystery of the Father and His love, fully reveals man to man himself and makes his supreme calling clear.[3]

2 Servaise-Th. Pinckaers, O.P., *Pour une lecture de VERITATIS SPLENDOR* (Paris: Éditions Mame, 1995), 7–8 (my translation).

3 Second Vatican Council. Pastoral Constitution on the Church in the Modern World *Gaudium et Spes* (Boston: Pauline Books & Media, 1965), §22.

This implies that the various sciences and even philosophy cannot suffice to explain our human nature and its ethical requirements. We cannot fully grasp the mystery of our own being as human persons without the light of Christ, the Incarnate Word. Only in Christ can we grasp our supreme calling, a calling from the Father. This implies, of course, that as human beings we *have* a calling, a destiny, and that this vocation is one that is fully realized only in Christ. Elsewhere in that Conciliar document we read:

> The root reason for human dignity lies in man's call to communion with God. From the very circumstance of his origin man is already invited to converse with God. For man would not exist were he not created by God's love and constantly preserved in it; and he cannot live fully according to truth unless he freely acknowledges that love and devotes himself to his Creator.[4]

As the Supreme Pastor of the Church, Pope John Paul II sought at length to address how the followers of Christ can and must respond to the invitation of the God who created them and invites them into his friendship. The scope, therefore, of Pope John Paul II's project in *Veritatis Splendor* is far broader than to critique certain moral theories. What he presents is an extended account of the nature and demands of the moral life.

Using the tools of human reason, of philosophy and theology, we explore the demands of morality. From Plato to Kant, to John Stuart Mill and the present, thinkers have reflected on what it means to act morally, to be good human beings. For its part, moral theology studies the roots of moral good and evil in Christian Revelation and by doing so seeks to help the Church's Magisterium in its pastoral work of leading her members—and indeed all men—to salvation. In *Veritatis Splendor* John Paul II sought to address this fundamental issue of moral goodness and evil, devoting close attention to certain theories of morality being widely

4 *Gaudium et Spes*, §19.

discussed in the Catholic Church, especially in the years following the Second Vatican Council. At stake in these discussions is much more than the validity or acceptability of different theories of morality and human acts. Unfortunately, many of the relevant theories neglect the transcendence of the human person, his "call to communion with God," accepting this-worldly premises of post-Enlightenment thought. According to these premises, the Church's judgment of some human acts becomes unintelligible. Many of the acts under discussion—most prominently the use of contraceptives—had been identified by the Magisterium as intrinsically evil, incompatible with God's love. Such acts are condemned as evil, and those who engage in them risk God's judgment unless they repent and seek his forgiveness. Pope John Paul II's concern was the widespread dissent from the Church's moral teachings and the serious effects of such dissent on the salvation of souls.

The problem of dissent

Dissent from magisterial teaching about moral theology was particularly evident in the wake of Pope Paul VI's Encyclical *Humanae Vitae,*[5] when Catholic moral theologians sought to evade or at least "soften" the encyclical's determination that contraception is contrary to God's law and therefore morally evil. Because many Catholics, especially in the West, felt they could not accept Pope St. Paul VI's judgment that contraceptive acts are morally wrong, moral theologians sought to alleviate to the apparent conflict between the Church's formal teaching and the experience of these lay persons.[6] These issues are surfacing again with renewed vigor, as moral theologians question the appropriateness of

5 Paul VI, Encyclical *Humanae Vitae* (Vatican City: Libreria Editrice Vaticana, 1968).

6 Adrian J. Reimers, *The Good Is Love; The Body and Human Acts in Humanae Vitae and John Paul II* (South Bend, IN: St. Augustine's Press, 2020), 46–49.

definitive magisterial interventions on moral issues.[7] Of course, these analyses had to do not only with the issue of contraception but also matters involving medical ethics and the end of life, as well as the indissolubility of marriage, sexual orientation, and abortion. Implicit in many of these studies was a rejection of the Church's authority to pronounce definitively on the moral value of human acts. What was sought was an approach that, without denying Catholic doctrine, allowed for *pastoral* approaches that allowed for at least a private dissent in conscience from the Church's formal teaching. Consequently, the publication of *Veritatis Splendor* met with vigorous opposition and even rejection within the Catholic theological community. At the time of this writing, these concerns and objections have found new life, as it were, first with the publication of Pope Francis's Post-Synodal Apostolic Exhortation *Amoris Laetitia*[8] and subsequently with proposals arising from within the theological academy.[9] Indeed, encouraged by a flawed reading of *Amoris Laetitia*, Pope Saint Paul VI's encyclical *Humanae Vitae* and *Veritatis Splendor* have come under renewed criticism and reevaluation within the community of moral theologians.[10]

In *Veritatis Splendor* John Paul II addresses these contemporary conceptions, coming to grips with the roots of the modern errors that have resulted in the loss of transcendence. However, the scope of *Veritatis Splendor* is far broader than evil and judgment of sin. The fundamental structure of the encyclical—and the

7 See Jarosław Kupczak, O.P. (translated by Grzegorz Ignatik), *Before Amoris Laetitia: Sources of the Controversy* (Washington, DC: Catholic University of America Press, 2018), 128–35.

8 Francis, Post-Synodal Apostolic Exhortation *Amoris Laetities* (Vatican City: Libreria Editrice Vaticana, 2016).

9 See V. Paglia (ed.), *Etica teológica della vita: Scrittura, tradizione, sfide practiche* (Vatican City: Librería Editrice Vaticana, 2022).

10 See Gerard O'Connell, "Spanish priest: 'Amoris Laetitia' allows the Church to 'untie the knots' in Catholic morality since 'Humanae Vitae,'" *America Magazine*, May 27, 2022; also the "Dubia" submitted by four Cardinals in the wake of *Amoris Laetitia*.

proper concern of Catholic moral theology as such—is founded on love. God's judgment is not like that of a human judge in an earthly court, who evaluates the evidence in relation to the law to determine whether the defendant has complied with or violated the law. Jesus says, "If any one hears my sayings and does not keep them, I do not judge him; for I did not come to judge the world but to save the world" (John 12:47). In saying this, Jesus does not deny the reality of judgment, as the subsequent verses make clear. The primary reality is the salvation that he realizes by his gift of himself on the cross. The logic underlying *Veritatis Splendor* is the logic of love, whose perfect model is the love of Christ, in which the Christian is invited to participate by making of himself a gift in love.

The project of this work

Until his elevation to the papacy in 1978, Karol Wojtyła taught philosophical ethics at the Catholic University of Lublin (KUL) beginning in 1954. As the only Catholic university in the Eastern Bloc, the KUL became an energetic hotbed of creative Christian philosophy as philosophers such as M. A. Krąpiec, S. Swieżawski, J. Kalinowski, and Karol Wojtyła sought to form an "island" in Poland, an "oasis [in the Communist bloc] to save philosophy from the deluge of Marxist philosophy."[11] As a practicing philosopher, Wojtyła participated in academic conferences, both within and beyond Poland, and contributed to philosophical literature; he was a practicing philosopher. His teaching and writing engaged modern philosophers, especially those of the phenomenological school, as well as the ancient and medieval traditions. His lectures on philosophy at the Catholic University of Lublin have been collected and published under the title of *The Lublin Lectures*, which give a valuable insight into Wojtyła's analysis and understanding

11 Mieczysław Krąpiec, O.P. and Andrzej Maryniarczyk S.D.B., *The Lublin Philosophical School* (Lublin: Polskie Towarzystwo Tomasza z Akwinu, 2010), 5 ff.

of key figures in the history of philosophy.[12] Another series of lectures delivered in Kraków in 1949 has been published under the title *Considerations on the Essence of Man*.[13] These lectures, which manifest the fundamental Thomistic character of Wojtyła's thought, intend to present an understanding of man to a Catholic audience living in a totalitarian Marxist environment. In the publisher's introduction to the work, Fr. Andrzej Maryniarczyk writes,

> This work finds itself in the midst of its author's immense concern for a comprehensive understanding of man which, achieved on the basis of philosophical understanding and supplemented by theological reflection, becomes a "personalistic norm" for every ethical, political, and social system, as well as for the whole of culture.[14]

Indeed, the constant theme of Karol Wojtyła's work was the human person regarded not only from a theoretical perspective but out of a pastoral concern.[15] He was acutely aware of the harm caused by European post-Enlightenment thought from which God the Creator had been largely expelled, in which salvation history had gone lost, and philosophers proposed that man must live as though God does not exist.[16]

At the heart of *Veritatis Splendor* lies the issue of the relationship between freedom and truth, and consequent upon that, the

12 Karol Wojtyła, *The Lublin Lectures/Wykłady Lubelski* (Lublin: Polskie Towarzystwo Tomasza z Akwinu, 2020).

13 Karol Wojtyła, *Considerations on the Essence of Man – Rozważania o istocie człowieka* (Lubin-Rome: Polskie Towarzystwo Tomasza z Akwinu, 2016).

14 Andrzej Maryniarczyk, S.D.B. in K. Wojtyła, *Considerations on the Essence of Man*, 13.

15 John Paul II. *Crossing the Threshold of Hope* (edited by Vittorio Messori) (New York: Alfred A. Knopf, 1994), 201.

16 Ibid., 53; also John Paul II, *Memory and Identity* (New York: Rizzoli, 2005), 7, 10.

relationship between freedom and law. The nexus of freedom, truth, and law underlies the controversies addressed in the controversial (among moral theologians, at least) second chapter of the encyclical. There the pope addresses such issues as conscience, intrinsically evil acts, and the theory of fundamental freedom. Inevitably, these discussions revolve around how to conceive the nature of the human act and the conception of natural law. This present work examines this encyclical against the backdrop of the philosophers with whom Karol Wojtyła engaged in his own philosophical project. Of central concern to Wojtyła throughout his career were the nature and prerogatives of the human person. Among his most frequent modern interlocutors were David Hume, Immanuel Kant, the utilitarian school, and Max Scheler. The program of Wojtyła's philosophical corpus is to present an alternative account of the human person to that which has marked the post-Enlightenment world. Having shared in the sufferings of his native Poland under the Nazi occupation and then as a scholar working in Communist Poland, Wojtyła was keenly aware of the forms of materialism which formed the environment of his own life and work. He offers not only his own analyses but also provides a model for engaging with the contemporary culture.

After examining Karol Wojtyła's engagement with the post-Enlightenment thinkers, we turn to his own works, most notably his book *Person and Act* (*Osoba i czyn*) which appeared in 1969. There, as well as in other works, we will find the close affinities with the encyclical. Indeed, his philosophical corpus can be read as a philosophical preparation for his subsequent papal writings, such as the theology of the body, his social encyclicals, and in particular *Veritatis Splendor*, in which the author portrays what kind of being a person must be to be able to give himself in love. After its publication, some objected that John Paul II could not have written its second chapter of *Veritatis Splendor.* They argued that John Paul II did not think in the ways expressed in its more technical second chapter, that the language was not his own.[17] We shall see that this criticism is not well founded.

We will then turn to an examination of some key issues of contention surrounding *Veritatis Splendor*, such as natural law, conscience, fundamental option, and intrinsically evil acts with an eye to understanding how John Paul II understood these concepts and uses them in *Veritatis Splendor*.

Reading the encyclical only as a critique of dissent in moral theology, some seem to have seen the pope as an authoritarian scold, jealous of his pontifical prerogatives and power laying down the law for his flock to obey.[18] The truth is quite to the contrary. He was a very modern thinker seriously engaged with the ancient and modern thinkers who have shaped the Western culture that had fallen so grievously into destructive nihilism in the 20th century. This is the central thrust of his papal corpus and is notably true of *Veritatis Splendor*.

17 Richard A. McCormick, "Some Early Reactions to *Veritatis Splendor*" in C. Curran and R. McCormick (eds.), *John Paul II and Moral Theology* (Mahwah, NJ: Paulist Press, 1998), 9–10.

18 For example, Bernard Häring, "A Distrust that Wounds," in C. Curran and R McCormick (eds.), *John Paul II and Moral Theology* (Mahwah, NJ: Paulist Press, 1998), 42.

THE GOOD

A brief overview of the vanishing good

Contemporary Western civilization arguably has no use for the concept of ultimate good, nor does such a concept play a role in contemporary ethics. With the scientific revolution and philosophical reflection based on science, the ultimate good—indeed, good itself—has largely disappeared from Western scientific thought.

René Descartes provided the tools to show all physical reality can be represented mathematically. The mathematical representation of things in space and time, combined with Newton's laws of motion and gravitation (and a few others), suggested that the universe can, at least in principle, be described with mathematical precision. Even the overthrow of the neat Newtonian structure by relativity and quantum theory did not undermine the fundamental vision of a universe ruled by invariant mathematical laws. So, in Descartes's philosophy we find hardly a trace of moral reflection, except for his attribution of error to moral fault. The British Empiricists, especially Hume, picked up on this, and good became disconnected from the physical world. Kant was concerned for morality, but—significantly—no moral categories appear in his *Critique of Pure Reason*, which addresses the conditions and structure of knowledge of the world. Morality is attributed only to a will that is disconnected from the realm of *noumena*, that is, the realm of cause and effect. For this reason, Karol Wojtyła will argue that Kant has failed to address the truth about the good.[1] In the mathematized universe there is no place for good. Indeed, the

1 Karol Wojtyła, *The Lublin Lectures/Wykłady Lubelskie*, 381.

good—the notion of teleology—has disappeared even from biology. This has been an admittedly slow achievement, which came to fulfillment only in the 20th century. According to contemporary Neo-Darwinism, evolution is never toward the better nor higher; there is no better, only survival success.[2] And so, because of their ubiquity and the enormous range of sub-species, the most successful species on earth is not the human being, but the bacterium.

At the root of this loss of the teleology is Descartes's dualism of mind and body. In distinguishing sharply between himself as a "thinking thing" and his body as an "extended thing," Descartes removed his own body and, indeed, everything outside his mind from the realm of meaning. The world of bodies, if we may speak this way, is not a world of "things," much less of substances, that interact with other things according to their natures. Rather they are bodies in the mathematical sense, three-dimensional solids occupying determined locations in space, from which every other body is excluded. Every body, occupying and moving within its spatial-temporal parameters, interacts with other such bodies according to the applicable physical laws. Comparably to the image consisting of pixels on the television screen, each of which has its own location and color-value, every physical point in space is a kind of three-dimensional pixel characterized by its gravitational mass, color, electromagnetic charge, "spin," and whatever else physicists may discover. Consequently, if the drama of good and evil on the television screen occurs only in the minds of the viewers, it may well be—as Hume will eventually argue—that the evil we find in human acts is located only in the mind.[3] The world in which we live is thus conceived only as a four-dimensional space-time continuum in which individual points (pixels) have their changing physical values which are unrelated to any standard of good.

2 John R. Searle, *The Rediscovery of the Mind* (Cambridge, MA / London: MIT Press, 1992), 51–52.

3 David Hume, "An Enquiry concerning the Principles of Morals," in *Hume's Ethical Writings* (London: Collier Books, 1965), 109, 118.

Therefore, human morality is not a matter of attaining any properly human excellence or of meeting some preestablished moral standard (such as the moral law). Darwin, in the *Descent of Man*, attributes our moral sense to the need of our species to survive and to our individual desire for acceptance within the group, which includes the approbation of our fellows. He concludes: "As all men desire their own happiness, praise or blame is bestowed on actions and motives, according as they lead to this end; and as happiness is an essential part of the general good, the greatest-happiness principle indirectly serves as a nearly safe standard of right and wrong."[4]

This "greatest happiness principle" is, of course, the basis for the philosophy of utilitarianism, to which we now turn. Karol Wojtyła observed that Jeremy Bentham firmly and sternly repudiates all metaphysical claims relevant to morality.[5] In this respect, his utilitarian successor, John Stuart Mill, carries forward, albeit less abrasively, Bentham's anti-metaphysical perspective. Mill repeatedly affirms that metaphysical and theological truth claims are irrelevant to his arguments, which are founded ultimately on the experiences of pleasure broadly understood. Mill presents not so much a hedonistic philosophy as a philosophy for the contemporary free-market economy under enlightened democratic institutions. The basis of a well-ordered society is not mere survival but happy or pleasant survival. Mill's utilitarianism envisions no transcendence, but rather a progressive civilization with (effectively) a compelling "civil religion" to instill public-spiritedness manifest in a concern for the well-being of all.[6] Mill's social concerns notwithstanding, however, the bases of utilitarianism are inherently and irredeemably subjective. Happiness is a *feeling* of pleasure. For Mill, utilitarianism is divinely sanctioned because

4 Charles Darwin, *The Descent of Man* (Princeton: Princeton University Press, 1981), 393.

5 *Lublin Lectures*, 529.

6 John Stuart Mill, *Utilitarianism* (Cambridge, Indianapolis: Hackett, 2001), 33.

God wants his creatures to be happy.[7] In fact, however, the bases of his utilitarianism are totally immanentist and hence subjective.

From the foregoing sketch of Enlightenment conceptions, we see that neither science nor human experience can found an objective conception of good. The most we can hope for is a widely accepted consensus of what a given population regards as good. Most decent Americans think that education is good and child pornography is evil. *The good* as such, however, disappears. Furthermore, the conception of an ultimate or highest good has become impossible. Such a good is incomprehensible in the wake of the Enlightenment.

The meaning of life

The human person does not live from seminar room discussions, but in his existential encounter with reality in his own life. We may say that the question of the good is forced upon us by the very fact that we are forced to confront it. The human being has a limited lifespan, "seventy years or eighty for those who are strong" (Ps 90:10), and it falls to him to determine the direction he will take in those few decades. The question can be ignored, of course, but the reality of one's life remains. It is necessary to make sense of one's life. The meaning of the good is an existential issue. What is the good?

In *Veritatis Splendor* John Paul II takes as the only possible starting point Jesus's response to the rich young man who asks how he can have eternal life. Jesus responds, "Only God is good" (Matt 19:18). This is why John Paul II says, "*Only God can answer the question about what is good, because he is the Good itself.*"[8] The Pope's strategy here is reminiscent of St. Thomas Aquinas, who starts his discussion of morality with the discussion of happiness, of man's ultimate good. Pinckaers writes, "This is a clear invitation to place *at the beginning of morality the question of happiness*

7 Ibid., 22.
8 *Veritatis Splendor*, §9.

and of the purpose of life, as do the Fathers and Saint Thomas (cf. CCC n 1716–1729)."[9] In this, Thomas recalls Aristotle, who begins his *Nicomachean Ethics* with an investigation into the highest good for a human being.[10] Granting that the imperfect, but real, happiness that can be attained in this life requires temporal created good, the ultimate good can consist only in God.[11] Specifically, perfect happiness is the personal intellectual vision of the divine essence.[12] Thomas does not say simply that happiness *comes from* God. Nor does he claim that the supernatural happiness is something added onto the natural happiness to be attained in this life—to put it crudely, the happiness that Aristotle describes in his *Ethics* with heaven added on for those who are holy. Rather, according to St. Thomas, the object of our happiness—what happiness consists in—is God himself and not simply something that God gives. And so, as Pope John Paul II says, "*Only God can answer the question about what is good, because he is the Good itself.*" Furthermore, St. Thomas does not recognize, as some have maintained, two ends of human life, one natural and one supernatural.

Many—perhaps most—people consider Catholic morality to be a system of laws and rules—mostly prohibitions. By contrast, *Veritatis Splendor* offers a resuscitation of the earlier Christian conception of morality as founded ultimately not on laws but on the love of God. "*The moral life presents itself as the response* due to the many gratuitous initiatives taken by God out of love for man. It is a response of love [...]."[13] The First Great Commandment follows from this conception of the moral life as a loving response to God's gratuitous love: "And you shall love the Lord your God with all your heart, with all your soul, with all your

9 Pinckaers, op. cit., 18.

10 Aristotle, *Nicomachean Ethics,* trans. Hugh Tredennick (London: Penguin Books, 1976), I, 1093a, 18–27.

11 Thomas Aquinas, *Summa Theologiae* Ia, IIae q.2, aa. 4, 8.

12 Ibid., q. 3, a. 8.

13 *Veritatis Splendor*, §10.

mind, and with all your strength" (Mk 12:30; cf. Mt 22:37). If, as Karol Wojtyła maintains, a norm is some truth about the good,[14] then the fundamental norm is that God is the good and the source of every lesser good. This norm implies the moral imperative to love God above all things. Hence: "*Acknowledging the Lord as God is the very core, the heart of the Law,* from which the particular precepts flow and towards which they are ordered."[15] This commandment and indeed its underlying norm constitute a challenge to the contemporary notion that we must do ethics as if God does not exist ("*etsi Deus non daretur*"). Generally, belief in the existence and reality of God is no longer acknowledged as a "public fact" but rather as a personal predilection or choice. This is directly related to the disappearance of *good* from scientific and, effectively, social discourse. Yet, if it is possible that a man become somehow united to the good in itself so that the good is incorporated into his being, then the human person is necessarily a spiritual being.

Interiority

The ethics we find in *Veritatis Splendor* is an ethics of interiority and not simply of behavior. Contemporary ethics often finds itself wrestling with questions of advantageous choice, questions like the notorious "trolley problem," and with issues of fairness in business, social life, and interactions with the environment. Important as such issues may be, they do not concern the goodness or wickedness of the person as such. Indeed, some may wonder if the question of personal goodness, one's goodness or wickedness *as a person* is worth investigating. Interestingly, Immanuel Kant does require a certain interiority. He insists that it is not enough to do what is right; one must always act for the sake of

14 Karol Wojtyła, *Love and Responsibility* trans. Grzegorz Ignatik (Boston: Pauline Books & Media, 2013), 25. See also Adrian J. Reimers, *The Truth about the Good* (Ave Maria, FL: Sapientia Press, 2011), 148–49.

15 *Veritatis Splendor*, §11.

duty.[16] From the very start, *Veritatis Splendor* points to the interior. If a human being is spiritual, then his goodness cannot consist only in his attainment (or ability to achieve) of external goals. To be a good soldier, violinist, business manager, or the like is not to be a good person. In asking his question of Christ, the rich young man "senses that there is a connection between moral good and the fulfilment of his own destiny."[17] He is, insists John Paul II, seeking the meaning of his own life, a good that is worth living for, an eternal good.

Goods and kinds of goodness

If we conceive God as Giver-of-all-good-things, he need not be recognizably good unless we know what constitute "good things." Further, we know from social and political life that a giver of good things need not necessarily be a good being. St. Thomas Aquinas argued that God is the good from which all goods derive. Karol Wojtyła develops this notion further in his Lublin lectures.[18] Therefore the goodness of things derives from that of God, and it is in relation to God that they are good. More precisely, creatures have their goodness insofar as they participate in God's goodness, indeed, in God's very being. This implies that God cannot be judged by comparison with creatures. Strictly speaking, *God is good for nothing*. This is the lesson from *Job*. One loves God for his intrinsic goodness, not for the good that he brings. Since things derive their goodness from their participation in the Creator's goodness, there must be a sense in which things—bears and pears, pines and porcupines, planets, politicians, and children—have their own goodness. It remains, then, to sort out the kinds of goodness that things can have.

Following St. Thomas's Aristotelianism, Karol Wojtyła distinguishes among three senses of "good": the *bonum honestum*,

16 Immanuel Kant, *Grounding of the Metaphysics of Morals*, trans. James W. Ellington (Indianapolis: Hackett Publishing Co. 1993), 401–02.

17 *Veritatis Splendor*, §7.

18 *Lublin Lectures*, 244–305.

bonum delectabile, and *bonum utile*. Of these, the honest or fitting good is primary, the prime analogate. The delightful good is so in virtue of the delight or pleasure yielded by some fitting good. The useful is good in virtue of its capacity to cause some other good, be this a true or apparent good.

Since inanimate things do not govern their own behavior, they are more or less adaptable to human intentions. They can be used as tools, good for their utility or agreeableness, and by these criteria we evaluate them. By working with the natural instincts of some animals, human intelligence can use them to meet human needs and desires. Such beings are perceived as useful goods. However, it is not so with human beings. Repeatedly in his papal writings, Pope St. John Paul II cited this text from the Second Vatican Council.

> Indeed, the Lord Jesus, when he prayed to the Father, "that all may be one [...] as we are one" (John 17:21–22) opened up vistas closed to human reason, for he implied a certain likeness between the union of divine Persons, and the unity of God's sons in truth and charity. This likeness [to the Trinity] reveals that man, who is the only creature on earth which God willed for itself, cannot fully find himself except through a sincere gift of himself.[19]

Speaking to leaders of Polish culture after the fall of Communism, John Paul II drew their attention to this Conciliar text, which affirms first that the human being does not exist for the sake of any other creature on earth. No one is created as a slave, a tool, or a plaything for pleasure. Further, we read that personal fulfillment is found neither in acquiring nor enjoying, but only in "sincere gift of self." Later in that same document, we read: "A human being is more precious for what he is than for what he has."[20] In his address John Paul II continued:

19 *Gaudium et Spes,* §24.
20 Ibid., §35.

> The ideological system which conferred on us the tone of our existence during the period of the past decades, consonant with its materialistic premises, did indeed propose the primacy of "*having*." It tried ultimately to see the culture in terms of production-consumption. [...] Individuals habituated to seeing their own existence according to the primacy of "having" (and hence of the primacy of material values) are often found in the West where this primacy of human "*having*" is better consolidated. [...] In every case systematic materialism, in its dialectical form and again in this practice, sacrifices the human "*being*" in favor of "*having*."[21]

This comment proved to be controversial in both Poland and the West. Instead of celebrating the advent of capitalism and prosperity after years of Marxist domination, the Polish Pontiff warned against falling into a new and equally dangerous form of materialism. This is evident in the contrast between "having" and "being."

Having

"To have" is to possess, control, dispose of. One can have things (possessions) and experiences. We may consider "bucket lists" of experiences a person hopes to enjoy before "kicking the bucket," as though someone's life may be incomplete if he has died without seeing a Broadway play or jumped from an airplane with a parachute. Having is therefore external to the person. Whether one has what he wants—be it a thing, an experience, or a pleasure—is a matter of fate. Having obtained or attained what he wants does not change the person for the better. It simply satisfies a particular want. The capacity to *have* or to *enjoy* depends on

21 John Paul II, "Discourse to Representatives of the World of Culture," downloaded 28 May 2012 from https://www.vatican.va/content/john-paul-ii/it/speeches/1991/june/documents/hf_jp-ii_spe_19910608_mondo-cultura.html. Translation by the author.

accidental characteristics that may pertain to a person but which are not his *as a person*. Einstein's brain differed from most others by the number of folds in its cerebellum. Ted Williams and John McEnroe were gifted with extraordinary eyesight and reflexes. The brilliant operatic soprano begins to dread the loss of her vocal instrument's brilliance and agility. The capacity for athletic or artistic excellence depends on physical gifts that they *have*.

Being

"*Persona est rationalis naturae individua substantia.*" As such, the person is capable of self-possession and self-governance. To have a rational nature is to be able to possess the world under that aspect of *truth*. Intellect and the power to reason depend on the body for their exercise, which is why one person can be more intelligent or clever than another, but the power itself is independent of the body's features. So, very small children and mentally challenged persons can respond to humor and understand right and wrong, even if they are unable to work out quadratic equations or conjugate Latin verbs. The person makes contact with the world rationally, through the power of reason. Wojtyła writes, "The human person, as a distinctively definite subject, establishes contact with other beings precisely through his interiority."[22] That is to say, by the power of reason the person interiorizes the world around her. This, according to Wojtyła, is the most immediate contact one can have with reality.

Furthermore, because the human being is rational, to be is to stand in relation, which means that the person is social, political.[23] By its very nature the intellect is dialogical. The process of abstraction, which is the act of discerning the essences of things, requires the interaction with another mind or minds. Indeed, scientists and philosophers of science will speak of posing questions to nature.

22 Karol Wojtyła, *Love and Responsibility* (translated by G. Ignatik), (Boston: Pauline Books & Media, 2013), 5.

23 Jacques Maritain, *The Person and the Common Good* (Notre Dame, Indiana: University of Notre Dame Press, 1966), 47–89.

Anthropologists, historians, and police detectives ask themselves what some person or group of persons have in mind as they performed the acts that built a village, established a custom, or committed a crime. The human processes of thinking and of understanding are predicated on the notion that one is interacting with another mind. This is the case, even if one denies that there is such a mind behind the structures of nature. To be a person is to stand in relation, whether explicitly or implicitly, with another mind. To ask oneself about the true good is to question one's own mind and implicitly in relation to another mind. To ask whether this mushroom is good (safe to eat and tasty) is to acknowledge the existence of a mind—perhaps of a scientist or a master chef—that can determine the hidden properties of the plant. It is in virtue of her conception of the truth and the truth about the good that the person is *who she is*.

We tend to see sensual—or even more so—muscular contact with the world to be more direct than "mental" contact with it, but this is the result of a confusion. If by "mental" we refer simply to the thoughts, images, and sounds we make within our imaginative power—what St. Thomas called "phantasms"—then the person's mental contact with the world is less real than muscular, physical contact. However, this is not what Karol Wojtyła meant. Through the power of reason, the person conforms her mind to truth. Senses can possess the visual, aural, tactile properties of the world. Muscles can grasp or move physical objects in the world. In this way sensation and physical power can "have" real things. However, neither sensation nor physical interaction is the primary way of making contact with reality.

Reason is the power to grasp what things are, to grasp the essences of things. The intellect is not a data storehouse in the brain, a kind of physical memory in which images from the senses and internal feelings (such as sadness or a stomach ache) are stored for later access. Rather this intellect is the understanding of the world; or better, the intellect is the world-as-known in the mind of the person. As a spiritual being, the person relates to the world not simply as it affects him but as it is known. This is why a human person can disregard the senses in certain situations and follow what she believes to be truth. The world-as-known is structured according to laws known to the person. This is the point of science. We all recognize the danger of a growling dog with bared fangs, but we need scientists to tell us about the dangers of radiation near Chernobyl.

Similarly, reason can know the good, and we respond to the good intelligently. The meat in the kitchen looks good, and the dog might gladly eat it. The rational person may note that this same meat was bought two weeks ago and ask whether it may have gone bad. If it is Lent, the Catholic will ask whether it is Friday. The Jew will need to know if it is pork. Sense desire can long for the meat, but for the sake of a higher good reason turns away. In fact, it is the truth about the good that is the basis for decision and as such of the transcendence of the person in the act. This dependence on truth makes the human will independent of objects.[24] This means that the person's acts are formed not by circumstances but by his knowledge of the truth about the good.

The Truth about Good and Evil

Veritatis Splendor rests upon a dramatic conception of the human being as one destined for participation in the glory of God, who is also capable of entering into damnable evil so great as to effect his own eternal ruin. Indeed, we may even say that because the person is capable of such participation—he is *capax Dei*—he can incur damnation. To unfold this conception, we return to a text that Saint John Paul II frequently cited. "The truth is that only in the mystery of the incarnate Word does the mystery of man take on light."[25]

As we noted earlier, this is a disconcerting text, for it clearly implies that the complete understanding of the human person lies

24 Karol Wojtyła, "Person and Act." In K. Wojtyła, *Person and Act and Related Essays*. Translated by Grzegorz Ignatik (Washington, D.C.: The Catholic University of America Press, 2021), 237.

25 *Gaudium et Spes*, §22.

beyond the competence of any human science, including philosophy itself. The full truth about man can be found only in the mystery of Christ, the incarnate and eternal Word. But this mystery is accessible only by the theological virtue of faith in Jesus Christ. The Council goes on to explain.

> For Adam, the first man, was a figure of Him Who was to come, namely Christ the Lord.[26]

The reference to Adam is significant. Regardless of how one understands the historicity of the creation account in Genesis—even if we trace human origins to the rift valley in Africa more than 50,000 years ago[27]—the name "Adam" identifies that human being according to the Creator's intention at the beginning.[28] Man as such, according to the intention of the Creator God, is already a figure of the God-Man who was to come. Jesus is exactly like every other man, except for his sinlessness. The significance of this is that an ordinary human being, in this case a Middle Eastern Jew—a Semitic man—can be and indeed is God Incarnate. There was nothing about Jesus Christ in his humanity that does not pertain to any other human being.

> Christ, the final Adam, by the revelation of the mystery of the Father and His love, fully reveals man to man himself and makes his supreme calling clear.[29]

Furthermore, in faith—"by the revelation of the Father and His love"—we human beings can know who we really are intended

26 Ibid.

27 James Owne, "Modern Humans Came Out of Africa, Definitive Study Says," *National Geographic*, July 18, 2007. Accessed March 29, 2022 from https://www.nationalgeographic.com/history/article/modern-humans-came-out-of-africa-definitive-study-says.

28 John Paul II, *Man and Woman He Created Them* (henceforth Theology of the Body), Translation, Introduction, and Index by Michael Waldstein. (Boston: Pauline Books & Media, 2006) 132–33.

29 *Gaudium et Spes*, §22.

to be, and we can know the destiny to which we are called. That is, in Christ we find the one who reveals what we human beings, in all our diversity, are to be living for.

> He Who is "the image of the invisible God" (Col. 1:15) is Himself the perfect man. To the sons of Adam He restores the divine likeness which had been disfigured from the first sin onward. Since human nature as He assumed it was not annulled, by that very fact it has been raised up to a divine dignity in our respect too.[30]

At this point the Pastoral Constitution introduces the disfigurement wrought by the first sin, while reminding us of the fact that Adam was created in the image and likeness of God, which is the key to understanding the dignity and greatness of the human person.

The image of God

"Let us enter into the setting of the biblical "beginning." In it the revealed truth concerning man as "the image and likeness" of God constitutes the immutable *basis of all Christian anthropology*. [...] What makes man like God is the fact that—unlike the whole world of other living creatures, including those endowed with senses (*animalia*)—man is also a rational being (*animale rationale*)."[31]

If the image and likeness of God is the basis of Christian anthropology, we need to understand wherein this image consists and what it implies. In his *Republic* and *Phaedo*, Plato maintains

30 Ibid.

31 John Paul II, Apostolic Letter *Mulieris Dignitatem* (Vatican City: Libreria Editrice Vaticana, 1988) §6. It is important to note that the Latin term that is rendered "man" in English is "*homo*," which means "human being"; "*vir*" means "man" in the sense of "male human being." And John Paul II notes that this man was created as male and female, as Scripture affirms at Genesis 1:26–27.

that in some sense the rational part of the human being is divine[32] but this is far from maintaining that the human being is an image of God. Indeed, Plato had no concept of God as understood by the Hebrews or Christianity. However, in his mind—as well as in Aristotle's[33]—reason is a divine attribute. We can say that Plato and Aristotle (among others) glimpse the divinely revealed truth that, as a rational being, man bears in himself the image and likeness of God.

John Paul II develops this thought in his theology of the body audiences, where we read:

> In the cycle of the seven days of creation, a precise step-by-step progression is evident; man, by contrast, is not created according to a natural succession, but the Creator seems to halt before calling him into existence, as if he entered back into himself to make a decision, "Let us make man in our own image, in our likeness" (Gen 1:27). [...]
>
> Already in the light of the Bible's first sentences, man can neither be understood nor explained in his full depth with the categories taken from the "world," that is, from the visible totality of bodies.[34]

Implicit here is a discontinuity, an essential difference between the human being and other material beings, which implies that the human being must be understood in metaphysical and not only physical terms.[35] The *rational* animal is something more than simply an animal. Contrary to the accounts we find in materialism,

32 Plato, *Republic,* 518c and *Phaedo* 80a, in *Collected Dialogues of Plato* (Princeton: Princeton University Press, 1961).

33 Aristotle, *Metaphysics,* (translated by W. D. Ross) in Robert Maynard Hutchins (editor) *Great Books of the Western World,* Volume 1 (Chicago, London: Encyclopaedia Britannica, 1952) 983a10.

34 Theology of the Body, 135.

35 Ibid., 136.

the power of reason does not and cannot reduce to a nexus of survival mechanisms ordered to survival or competitive advantage.[36]

The metaphysics of reason

As rational animal, man can know and understand truth. Truth is intrinsically personal. Only persons can know truth, and by its nature truth profoundly touches the person. Pope John Paul II addressed this in a homily at the Catholic University of Lublin, where he had taught philosophy. Citing a maxim from Aristotle's *De Anima,* which Thomas Aquinas adopts, John Paul II said,[37]

> This orientation and this aspiration are strictly united to the man of every era, to the very nature of the human intellect. "*Intellectus est quodammodo omnia*—The intellect is, in a way, all things." Indeed, everything that exists in any way whatever is given to human knowledge, and hence to the human intellect, as a task.[38]

There are two parts to this saying. First the intellect *is* what it knows. To understand a thing is for the intellect or the mind to be formed by that thing. The essence of the object of knowledge becomes the form of the knowing intellect. Therefore, the chemist is not merely a person whose memory is a kind of databank filled with a catalogue of facts about elements and chemical compounds, the rules of bonding, and the like. He is, rather, chemistry-alive. The student, a prospective chemist, submits himself to the science faculty by entrusting himself to them. He not only

36 Charles Darwin, *The Descent of Man*, 385–91.

37 Aristotle, *De Anima and the Commentary of St. Thomas Aquinas* (New Haven: Yale University Press, 1951), III, 5 430a10 ff.

38 John Paul II, "Omelia di Giovanni Paolo II" June 1987, Lublin, Poland. Downloaded from http://w2.vatican.va/content/john-paul-ii/it/homilies/1987/documents/hf_jp-ii_hom_19870609_celebraz-parola-lublino.html. Accessed 24 April 2017. Author's translation into English.

learns individual facts about chemicals but follows the professors as they develop arguments and research strategies. He is given his own bench in the laboratory where he learns—partly by watching and largely by acting—how chemicals interact with each other. As he learns, he and his student colleagues increasingly become members of the community of chemists, where they come more and more to understand the common language, the priorities, and the ordinary practices of chemists. The rational mind "becomes all things" not by way of some physical mechanism, a biophysical structure that accurately interprets data received through the senses. Rather, the chemist's mind interiorizes the science according to the form of things and the logic of its principles.

Particularly important is the influence of other persons on the formation of the mind (and hence, of the intellect). As John Paul II notes, we learn and form our minds in dialogue with other persons.

> In believing we entrust ourselves to the knowledge acquired by other people. On the one hand, the knowledge acquired through belief can seem an imperfect form of knowledge, to be perfected gradually through personal accumulation of evidence; on the other hand, belief is often humanly richer than mere evidence, because it involves an interpersonal relationship and brings into play not only a person's capacity to know but also the deeper capacity to entrust oneself to others, to enter into a relationship with them which is intimate and enduring.[39]

Granting that knowledge by belief is imperfect compared to knowledge by scientific investigation and argument, knowledge by belief has this great value of necessarily involving an

39 John Paul II, Encyclical Letter *Fides et Ratio* (Vatican City: Libreria Editrice Vaticana, 1998), §32.

interpersonal relationship. Most of our knowledge is from others. Often it is verified by personal investigation as when one investigates further what one has learned in the classroom, but even more often it becomes the basis for one's understanding of the world, of the environment in which he lives. Such knowledge ordinarily comes from parent and relatives, teachers in school, friends, and the like. From infancy on, the human person's mind is formed by those older who are in some way authoritative. These introduce him to the world. Very early on, the child learns that if he lets go of his glass of milk it will fall and make a mess. Only much later will he learn Newton's law of gravity and eventually even Einstein's account of gravitational fields. However, it was father who taught the first lesson about gravity and falling objects and mother who introduced the concept of social responsibility and of cleaning up the messes one has made.

To believe another person is to enter her mind, as it were, and to interpret what she means. A belief is ordinarily presented in words, supplemented by other signs (hand gestures perhaps) and actions—"Watch me as I show you." Hearing (or reading) these signs, the hearer interprets them according to her own powers. Ordinarily this process is so common as to be unremarkable. However, when a scholar is reading a controverted text, perhaps from Aristotle or Kant, the task of determining the author's meaning becomes more difficult, and the logical procedure for determining it is instructive. Consider an example. Aristotle suggests that the intellectual part of the human soul may be "separable" and hence capable of survival after death. The interpreter must consider what the term "separable" (χωριστός) means in the ancient Greek[40] and whether this implies that it can have a separate existence "of its own" without the body. He may well consider Plato's conception of the soul as the separated mind and its afterlife, as well as St. Thomas's strong contention that Aristotle intended to say that each man's own agent intellect survives the death of the body. Having considered these things, he may relate

40 Aristotle, *De Anima*, Book III 430a18.

his understanding to what Aristotle says concerning the intellect in the *Ethics*. Eventually he forms his own hypothetical understanding of the Stagirite's meaning. This formation of the hypothesis is the critical step because the hypothesis—*this* is what Aristotle intended—is the creation of his own mind; it has arisen from his exercise of his own powers. If he is wise, he will compare and critique his own analysis with the interpretations of others. However, to the extent that he is confident in his own mind, he will affirm that his interpretation is true and right. He makes a judgment on the matter and proceeds with further aspects of his research and study. Proceeding with his reading, he expects to know ever more clearly the mind of Aristotle.

What we experience explicitly in the sophisticated processes of academic research occurs also in the everyday interactions with those around us. With one's friends, family, and neighbors it is possible to ask for clarifications and physical demonstrations. Nevertheless, the procedure is much the same. As we seek to interpret what another has said, we are attempting to enter the mind of the other, and by doing so, we allow the other to form our own thought. We can then become "of one mind." This is, of course, precisely what happens in education, where the teacher illuminates her students' minds not by pouring knowledge into it but by enabling the student to discover the truth through his own reasoning.[41] Thus it is that one intelligence enlightens the mind of another.

And so it is that dialogue, by which one person communicates his mind to another and simultaneously seeks to understand the other's mind, enables both partners mutually to deepen their understanding. Of course, not all human interactions are strictly verbal, as is the scholar's interaction with a deceased author. Most of our interactions include physical or sensual aspects. Indeed, some communications may be entirely physical. However, since the physical act arises from the mind and will of the person, expressing something of himself (often even more accurately than

41 See Plato, *Republic*, 518c.

words alone), actions also communicate the mind of the agent, and it remains for others to interpret that action, understanding this interpretation in the same way that a verbal communication is understood. This is how different persons come to know and understand each other. Of course, it may well be that a person's words may contradict or be contradicted by his deeds. With his words the cad may express the noble ideals that the woman holds in order to seduce her into believing that he loves her.

Because it forms the mind and thereby transforms the intellectual part of the soul, reason is far more than the collecting and categorization of data. Rather it is deeply personal. Therefore, by its nature dialogue is an act of love. As John Paul II notes, friendship is "one of the most appropriate contexts for sound philosophical inquiry." John Paul II proceeds, "it emerges that men and women are on a journey of discovery which is humanly unstoppable—a search for truth and a search for a person to whom they might entrust themselves."[42] In principle, the human intellect is infinite in its scope in that it yearns for and can receive all truth—not simply a vast array of facts—but truth according to its inmost structure, its causes. From this it follows that the human mind seeks and is capable of wisdom, which is the knowledge of the first causes of things.[43]

Communion and the image of God

The reality of dialogue between persons as rational beings points to the possibility of communion between persons, and in this the image of God is more fully realized.

> For every individual is made in the image of God, insofar as he or she is a rational and free creature capable of knowing God and loving him. Moreover, we read that man cannot exist "alone" (cf. Gen 2:18); he can exist

42 John Paul II, *Fides et Ratio*, §33.
43 *Gaudium et Spes*, §15.

> only as a "unity of the two" and therefore *in relation to another person.*[44]

Elsewhere he writes, "Man becomes the image of God not so much in the moment of solitude as in the moment of communion."[45] Let us consider the implications of this. The reader of Descartes, Kant, or certainly Hume finds himself implicitly in the lonely world of his own consciousness. Other persons can exist only as bodies to be encountered in the sensible world, as the sources of messages to be decoded and interpreted for the purpose of getting on with one's own activity. Love can consist only in emotion and desire. The other person is not one with whom one can enter any meaningful communion beyond these factors. John Paul II's position goes well beyond this, as he insists that love is defined by the sincere gift of self. As such, interpersonal communion founded on love is an essential mark of the image of God in the human being.

We do well to consider the logical structure of this intercommunion. Certainly, one aspect of this interaction between two person is the simple communication of information. Parents fill the minds of their children with all sorts of information about the world. Teachers, especially at the elementary school level, do the same. However, the process of communication never rests only at the level of mere facts. Communication is always about the shape of the word, about *how things are*. In other words, no statement of fact stands alone, representing the fact at issue by its own physical structure and properties. Rather the terms of any statement of fact all have a general character. Even the most specific statement of fact—"It is there," for instance—depends on general conceptions. Speaker and hearer both need to understand in the situation what "it" refers to (Does it refer to the cat or to the fur on the cat?) and what "there" indicates. The legend is that a French trader asked the name of the area he viewed from the hilltop. His Indian guide,

44 John Paul II, *Mulieris Dignitatem*, §7.

45 Theology of the Body, 163.

thinking that the Frenchman referred to the village immediately below, responded "Kanata," and so the entire country was named. It is universally true that in communicating facts, even the simplest of fact, there is also communicated a world in which those facts are situated and find their meaning. This is why we can say that communication is always implicitly about *how things are*.

The human mind is not like a computer, which electronically stores huge amounts of memory in the form of electrical charges. Rather, the human mind knows what it knows within an ordered *world* that has an intrinsic structure of its own. To be sure, the mind's world is incomplete in significant ways. One may know clearly where the local grocery store is and be ignorant of the location of Alice Springs. Each person lives in a life-world that is his and which he shares to a greater or lesser extent with others. This is perhaps most immediately evident in the rearing and education of children, who learn not only facts about the world they live in but also the principles governing that world from the parents and other grown-ups, the use of language, as well as traditions governing food and drink. Similarly, we live in worlds governed by culture in a way that our animal friends do not. The human world is not a nexus of bare facts that constitute different sorts of threats and opportunities for survival. The world where the person lives is formed not only by facts and events but by values. An infant animal needs to know how to identify food and to recognize danger. The human being needs to understand the values governing reality in all its aspects. In other words, the human person lives not only physically but spiritually in the world that is itself spiritually formed by its governing values.

This truth about the person's knowledge of the world profoundly forms the communications between persons. Except in the most trivial instances, communication is of more than one's assertion of facts. When two persons communicate, they are challenged to enter each other's world as it were, to understand one another's mind. To be sure, in a given conversation one party may well enter inauthentically by ignoring the other's mind, as when one insists that the other simply parrot what he has maintained. This is the strategy of the ideologue who demands that his subjects adhere to formulas proposed by the ideological regime. Similarly, one can refuse to accept what another intends to communicate by receiving only those things that cohere with his own preconceptions, which is to refuse to acknowledge the legitimacy of the other person's understanding. However, when two persons engage in a genuine dialogue on any real subject, important or trivial, they are to a greater or lesser extent sharing their minds with each other.

With this we can begin to understand John Paul II's claim, "Man becomes the image of God not so much in the moment of solitude as in the moment of communion." When two persons communicate, when they act together, a union that is far deeper than the physical forms between them. In *Person and Act* Karol Wojtyła shows that *participation* is essential to human activity together. When a person acts together with others, his action is more than a kind of parallel series of events alongside the motions of the others. Rather, when acting together with others, the subjectivity and therefore the transcendence proper to the human person is also engaged. The person's act together with others is properly his own act, even as he participates in his acting with others. *Participation* means that several persons are engaged, each and every one personally, in the common work. This participation is ordered by the common good for which the persons live and act.[46] Authentic participation—participation can be rendered *inauthentic* by personal attitudes of conformism or evasion—allows for the creation of a communion among those who participate in the common life, for the common participation offers the basis of a common responsibility and, indeed, love among those who are so joined.

Furthermore, man is a religious being. That is, the human being is by his nature ordered to God. "The root reason for human dignity lies in man's call to communion with God. From the very

46 Karol Wojtyła, *Person and Act*, 377–78.

circumstance of his origin man is already invited to converse with God."[47] Because of this call, whether expressly recognized or not, the human person seeks to know and understand the ultimate causes of things, especially the cause of his own being. As Aristotle wrote, "All men desire to know,"[48] and it is this desire, which is called *wonder*, which is the engine of scientific inquiry. Beyond the truths of science, however, what the human being seeks most fundamentally is the truth that gives meaning to his life, a truth on which he can depend. John Paul II writes, "It is the nature of the human being to seek the truth. [...] Their search looks toward an ulterior truth which would explain the meaning of life. And it is, therefore, a search which can reach its end only in reaching the absolute."[49] Implicitly, therefore all human beings are ordered to God as the ultimate end of their search for truth and meaning.

As the one who by his power of reason knows and understands, the human person is offered the gift by God to know him and enter into communion with him.[50] "The desire for knowledge is so great and it works in such a way that the human heart [...] yearns for the infinite riches which lie beyond, knowing that there is to be found the satisfying answer to every question as yet unanswered."[51] The yearning for God of which St. Augustine wrote so ardently—"You made us for yourself, and our heart is restless until it rests in you"—is implanted in every heart by the very fact that man is a rational being. Just as the desire for intimacy and communion with other human beings is a consequence of our rational nature, so too is our yearning to know the Creator and Ruler of the world. This is how God

47 *Gaudium et Spes*, §19.
48 Aristotle, *Metaphysics*, book I, ch. 1.
49 *Fides et Ratio*, §33.
50 Ibid., §15.
51 Ibid., §17.

> has created us to be as those who bear his image, an image that is realized not only in knowledge and understanding but also in love.

The rich young man

This conception of communion and the image of God is most fully developed in the first chapter of *Veritatis Splendor*. The rich young man's question is simple enough: "Teacher, what good must I do to have eternal life?" (Matt 19:16). For John Paul II the young man is Everyman.

> For the young man, the *question* is not so much about rules to be followed, but *about the full meaning of life.* This is in fact the aspiration at the heart of every human decision and action, the quiet searching and interior prompting which sets freedom in motion. This question is ultimately an appeal to the absolute Good which attracts us and beckons us; it is the echo of a call from God who is the origin and goal of man's life.[52]

With this, Pope John Paul II fundamentally changes the terms of the discussion and with that the underlying principles of his analysis going forward. Yes, the encyclical is about morality and ethical decision-making. He has already made clear that he intends to address errors arising from dissent in contemporary moral theology.[53] However, the fundamental issue at stake is not to decide between deontological and teleological ethics or to address emotivist and subjectivist theories. Instead, for John Paul II, "*The moral life presents itself as the response* due to the many gratuitous initiatives taken by God out of love for man. It is a response of love [...]. "[54]

52 *Veritatis Splendor*, §7.
53 Ibid., §5.
54 Ibid., §10.

If morality is about response to God, then one's knowledge of God and awareness of his love is morally relevant. There is no question here of a "morality without God." Every human being is, in fact, a religious being—perhaps unwittingly—ordered to God.[55] Indeed, the guiding theme, as it were, of John Paul II's encyclical on faith and reason is the universal quest for an ultimate meaning of life. Reflecting on the inscription over the portal at the ancient shrine at Delphi, "Know yourself," he writes,

> Moreover, a cursory glance at ancient history shows clearly how in different parts of the world with their different cultures, there arise at the same time the fundamental questions which pervade human life: *Who am I? Where have I come from and where am I going? Why is there evil? What is there after this life?* [...] These are questions which have their common source in the quest for meaning which has always compelled the human heart. In fact, the answer given to these questions decides the direction which people seek to give to their lives.[56]

John Paul II is deliberately far from the modern conception of philosophy understood as simply an esoteric academic specialty dealing with problems raised by professional philosophers themselves. Nicholas Rescher describes American philosophy as an "academic industry," and he asks, "Do American philosophers exert influence? Here the critical question is: Upon whom? Certainly as far as the wider society is concerned, it must be said that the answer is emphatically negative."[57] John Paul II's vision is of philosophy as classically conceived, a way to wisdom for life:

55 John Paul II, *Teachings for an Unbelieving World* (Notre Dame, Indiana: Ave Maria Press, 2020), 4–6, 11; *Crossing the Threshold of Hope* (New York: Alfred A Knopf, 1994), 31–32.

56 *Fides et Ratio*, §1.

57 Nicholas Rescher, "American Philosophy," in Ted Honderich (editor), *The Oxford Handbook of Philosophy* (Oxford, New York: Oxford University Press, 1995), 23–27.

"With its enduring appeal to the search for truth, philosophy has the great responsibility of forming thought and culture, and now it must strive resolutely to recover its original vocation."[58] Indeed, more is to be said, for philosophy as the search for ultimate meaning is the concern of every human person. Granting that professional philosophers study the works of their predecessors, developing and criticizing various philosophical systems, all men and women are in some sense philosophers.[59] Because the human heart is far deeper than it appears "on the surface," the human mind inevitably seeks those truths that lie below the surface of direct experience and emotion. Thus it is that Augustine's words about the "restless heart" resonate with the human mind. The thesis of the encyclical *Fides et Ratio* is that God's Revelation of himself is demanded by his own love by which he creates the human being for communion with him.

The fundamental ethical requirement for every human being, therefore, turns out to be the demand to live in accord with God's love. Implicitly, this amounts to the requirement that one live according to truth. John Paul II writes, "Although each individual has a right to be respected in his own journey in search of the truth, there exists a prior moral obligation, and a grave one at that, to seek the truth and to adhere to it once it is known."[60] Recognizing the truths about the good concerning God and other persons, which constitute the fundamental ethical norms, we are led to the two great commandments found in the Scriptures.

> You shall love the Lord your God with all your heart, and with all your soul, and with all your mind. This is the "great and first" commandment. And a second is like it. You shall love your neighbor as yourself. On these two commandments depend all the law and the prophets. (Matthew 22: 37–40)

58 *Fides et Ratio*, §6
59 Ibid., §30.
60 *Veritatis Splendor*, §32.

The love of God

In the writings of Karol Wojtyła/Pope John Paul II we find two central truths about the good—norms—from which we infer the two great commandments. In *Veritatis Splendor* John Paul II recalls how Christ tells the rich young man that God alone is good, that he is indeed the good from which all goods derive. God is the highest, the supreme good. From this we can infer the first great commandment, "You shall love the Lord your God with all your heart, with all your soul, with all your mind, and with all your strength" (Matt. 22:37). If the first principle of the natural law is to seek and do good and to shun and avoid evil,[61] then this commandment follows with logical necessity from the truth that God is the supreme good.

John Paul II develops the point.

> Only God can answer the question about what is good, because he is the Good itself. To ask about the good, in fact, ultimately means to turn towards God, the fullness of goodness. [...] He is the source of man's happiness. Jesus brings the question about morally good action back to its religious foundations, to the acknowledgment of God, who alone is goodness, fullness of life, the final end of human activity, and perfect happiness.[62]

This is a radical claim. John Paul II states that the questions about every moral action have a religious foundation which relates directly to the acknowledgement of God. Effectively, he affirms that one cannot come to a correct moral judgment—or even a coherent one—without acknowledging God. His is not a simplistic "divine command" theory, which would hold that since God (who is omniscient and almighty) punishes bad acts and rewards good ones, it is best to obey him. In such a case, the divine will is purportedly

61 *Summa Theologiae* Ia, IIae, q. 94, a.2.
62 *Veritatis Splendor*, §9.

added to and often superimposed on the relationships of power in the secular world. Rather, John Paul II is saying that the moral question itself—"Shall I terminate this pregnancy?," "Shall I claim an illicit deduction on my tax return?," "Shall I, as a student, turn in another's work, representing it to be my own?"—is a religious question. That is, lacking a highest good, an ultimate standard of good, then no moral good is adequately founded. We decent people who go to church and read books about morality are horrified by torture and rape, by the deliberate killing of children in war. However, at the time of this writing intelligent men in a highly cultured society find these practices morally acceptable for the sake of a perceived higher good.

Here we do well to turn to St. Thomas Aquinas and his treatise on happiness. Arguing very much along the same lines as does Aristotle in his *Nicomachean Ethics*, Thomas concludes that the human being's perfect happiness must so fill his will's desire that, having achieved happiness, he cannot lack any necessary good. There is nothing further for him to desire.[63] Having arrived at this conclusion, Aristotle acknowledges that such perfect happiness is beyond the reach of human beings.[64] Aided by Christian revelation, Aquinas argues that happiness can be attained, albeit outside the conditions of this life and only with God's help, and that this happiness is the direct vision of the divine essence.[65] It is important to understand that this vision of God is the end for all human beings, and not only Christians. This conclusion is reflected by the Second Vatican Council, which maintained, "The root reason for human dignity lies in man's call to communion with God. From the very circumstance of his origin man is already invited to converse with God."[66] Then, answering the question whether rectitude of will is required for happiness, Aquinas writes,

63 *Summa Theologiae*, Ia, IIaae q. 2, aa. 4, 7.

64 Aristotle, *Nicomachean Ethics*, I, 10 (1101a 20).

65 *Summa Theologiae*, Ia, IIae, q.3, a. 8.

66 *Gaudium et Spes*, §19.

> And therefore none can obtain happiness, without rectitude of the will. Concomitantly, because as stated above (I-II:3:8), final Happiness consists in the vision of the divine essence, which is the very essence of goodness. So that the will of him who sees the essence of God, of necessity, loves, whatever he loves, in subordination to God; just as the will of him who sees not God's essence, of necessity, loves whatever he loves, under the common notion of good which he knows.[67]

It will pay us well to look carefully at this text, especially its final clause which speaks formally of the will's relationship with its object, the good in general. The will of any human being, "of necessity, loves whatever he loves, under the common notion of good which he knows." This "common notion of good" may well be inchoate and even unconscious for some particular individual. Nevertheless, it is operative in the person's will simply because whatever one wants, he wants because it is in some sense good. Although the one who has attained his final and perfect happiness (who is, of course, one of the blessed in heaven) enjoys the vision of the divine essence, he does not cease to love those lesser things he has loved in his earthly life. Rather, "of necessity, [he] loves whatever he loves, in subordination to God." This is what rectitude of will consists in, that one loves the highest good and everything else in relation to that good. Doubtless, one can misidentify the highest good, choosing to live for wealth, pleasure, power or some other created good, and this misidentification will inevitably lead to a distorted conception of lesser goods (as, for instance, is the case with one whose highest good is power and who therefore misconstrues the nature of friendship). If one is to live a truly good life, to make moral decisions that are truly good, then it is necessary to choose them in relation to one's love for God. This is so, even if he does not yet know who or what the true god might be. A god, to be truly God, must be the perfection

67 *Summa Theologiae*, Ia, IIae, q. 4, aa. 4.

of goodness and the model for all goods. Therefore, whoever is truly seeking the perfect good, is seeking the one God. Ultimately, every human being, wittingly or not, is thus bound to the first great commandment, to love God above all things, to seek him out, and to live according to his goodness.

Love of neighbor

Simply to state the law of love of God is not sufficient. Joseph Ratzinger writes, "Someone who does not love God with all his heart does not love man either."[68] Expanding on his answer to the Pharisee, Jesus cited a second great commandment which is like the first: "You shall love your neighbor as yourself" (Matt. 22:39). This second great commandment, which underlies the commandments of the second table of the law, is inferred from the truth about the good of the human person. Indeed, most of the text in chapter two of *Veritatis Splendor* is concerned with morality in interpersonal relationships. Our author first lays this out as the personalist norm in *Love and Responsibility:*

> As a principle formulated negatively, this norm states that the person is a kind of good that is incompatible with using, which may not be treated as an object of use and, in this sense as a means to an end. Hand in hand with this goes the positive formulation of the personalistic norm: the person is a kind of good to which only love constitutes the proper and fully-mature relation.[69]

If we attend closely to it, the basis for this norm is found by reason reflecting on human experience. The human being is a person, that is, a rational being capable of self-determination on the basis

68 Joseph Ratzinger, *Western Culture: Today and Tomorrow*. Translated by Michael. J Miller, (San Francisco: Ignatius Press, 2019), 129.

69 Karol Wojtyła, *Love and Responsibility*, 25.

of its own understanding and free will.[70] Like Kant before him, Karol Wojtyła insists that the person cannot be reduced simply to the status of a tool, a thing, because whereas a tool is subject to the will of its user to achieve the tool-user's end, the person lives from his interior to attain the ends of his own choosing. To use a person is to violate his nature and in this his dignity.

Karol Wojtyła carries the analysis a step further than Kant.[71] After stating, like Kant, that the person is not to be treated as an object for use, he writes that "the person is a good towards which the only proper and adequate attitude is love." He argues this philosophically and not on theological or religious grounds. For one to access the services of another, to get the other to help him or to work with him, it is necessary for that person to agree to do so.[72] Because the person acts on the basis of his own will (rational appetite), he must make that act his own, as it were, by agreeing to perform it. This is to say that without agreeing to some good he will not act. The basis, therefore, for acting in common is the mutual embrace of some common good. This principle is clearly realized in marriage.[73] However, it also applies even in situations where a manifest inequality among persons is at work, such as in the military, where the unequal relationship between the commander and the soldier is not only manifest, but even essential for their mutual task. In such a case, a proper understanding of the relationship is that both parties act out of love for their country and fellow citizens. Likewise, in the realms of commerce and industry, the love for the common good governs proper human interactions. Workers and their supervisors foster the common

70 Ibid., 98.; Karol Wojtyła, "Człowiek jest osoba," in K. Wojtyła, *Osoba i czyn – oraz inne studia antropologiczne* (Lublin: Towarzystwo Naukowe KUL, 2000), 418.

71 Michael Waldstein, *Glory of the Logos in the Flesh* (Ave Maria, Florida: Sapientia Press, 2021), 375 ff.

72 *Love and Responsibility*, 12.

73 Ibid., 14; Karol Wojtyła, "Person: Subject and Community," in K. Wojtyła, *Person and Community: Selected Essays* (New York, London, Berlin: Peter Lang, 1993), 247.

good of the society by their ordered efforts to produce goods and services. Wojtyła argues that it is precisely the common good and common aim that joins two persons in love. Their love is constituted and, as it were, formed by the nature of the common good that joins them.

It goes without saying that the love that should exist between persons can be abused. The general may command his soldiers to act not for victory over the enemy, but for the commander's own advantage; consider King David's orders that Uriah the Hittite be exposed to death in battle to cover up David's adultery with Uriah's wife (2 Sam. 11:14–25). The production of cotton benefits the entire society, providing inexpensive, durable, and attractive fabric for clothing. In principle all those engaged in growing and harvesting cotton contribute to the common good of the society. However, the plantation owner uses slaves to plant and harvest his crop. The slaveholder seeks wealth, but he does not expect the slave to share this aim. Rather, he threatens the slave with pain to compel him to obey his orders. One could multiply examples, of course, but the principle is always the same. One person *uses* another and treats him as a *thing* by threatening evil or depriving his subject of some good. Uriah fought and died for king and country, but David commanded him to engage in a perilous sortie to hide his own sin with Uriah's wife. The slave wants not to pick cotton or mine salt, but to preserve himself from torture or death. He lives and acts for a good different from that proposed by his superior. In ordinary, less dramatic situations the same pattern is repeated as persons manipulate each other by means of seduction, emotional pressure, financial inducements, promises of future pleasure, and the like. Even two partners in sin, who support and cooperate with each other in wrongdoing, do not work for a common good. Violating the personalist norm, they work not for a common good but simply for simultaneous pleasures or benefits.

From this personalist norm we can validly infer the evangelical commandment of the love of neighbor.[74] Like Kant's "practical

74 *Love and Responsibility*, 25.

imperative," the personalistic norm is founded on the conception of human dignity, the dignity of a being that is free and capable of self-determination. Indeed, as *Gaudium et Spes* states, this being—the human person—is created in the image and likeness of God. Therefore, the commandment to love others finds its anthropological foundation in the dignity of the human person. Here we may turn to the text of *Veritatis Splendor.*

In his dialogue with the rich young man, Christ cites the commandments of the second table of the Law (Mt 19:18–19), which are summed up in the commandment of the love of neighbor. John Paul II continues,

> In this commandment we find a precise expression of *the singular dignity of the human person,* "the only creature that God has wanted for its own sake." The different commandments of the Decalogue are really only so many reflections of the one commandment about the good of the person, at the level of the many different goods which characterize his identity as a spiritual and bodily being in relationship with God, with his neighbor and with the material world.[75]

This text supports and complements the argument that Karol Wojtyła had developed in *Love and Responsibility*. Let us note especially his reference to the good of the person in the second sentence of this text. Because of the "singular dignity of the person" one is commanded to act for the good of the person. The continuation of this sentence makes it clear that fostering the good of the person amounts to more than simply providing material or sensual benefits, although these may be included; the Good Samaritan bound up the victim's wounds and took him to an inn for care. However, the good of this person involves many different goods related to his spiritual and bodily being. In every case, the one to be loved is a spiritual and bodily being with both

75 *Veritatis Splendor*, §13.

spiritual and bodily needs. If the hungry and homeless man turns out to be the prodigal son, then to love him may require one to encourage him to swallow his pride and return to his father. Implicit in the text too is the requirement that the agent also act in accordance with his own dignity as a person, whom "God has wanted for his own sake." John Paul II continues,

> *Jesus brings God's commandments to fulfillment,* particularly the commandment of love of neighbor, *by interiorizing their demands and by bringing out their fullest meaning.* [...] Jesus shows that the commandments must not be understood as a minimum limit not to be gone beyond, but rather as a path involving a moral and spiritual journey towards perfection, at the heart of which is love (cf. *Col* 3:14).[76]

Summary and conclusion

In *Veritatis Splendor* we find a distinctively personalistic and theocentric development of natural law, which obliges every rational creature to act according to truth, in particular, the truth about the good. Because God is the Supreme Being, the Creator and First Cause of everything, he is necessarily supremely lovable and admirable. His creative and providential will is ordered to his own perfect good. Therefore, God is to be sought as the supreme good and embraced as the source of all truth. God is the absolute behind all contingent truths and goods, from which it follows that one is to love him with all one's heart and souls and mind and strength.

Because the human being is a person, a *substantia individua rationalis naturae,* a free and self-determining being, he is not a fit object of use. His dignity demands respect; to use him for one's own end is an abuse. If the person is a good the only fitting attitude toward which is love, then it follows that one is obliged to love his

76 *Veritatis Splendor,* §15.

neighbor. *Love and Responsibility* implies that this is a truth which can be known philosophically, even without the aid of Revelation.

The import of this derivation of the two great commandments is that morality is not a purely this-worldly affair. Thomas Aquinas argues that the basis of morality is the destination of every man to God as his ultimate good. John Paul II carries this thought forward in a personalistic way, recognizing the incoherence of building morality on a purely immanent foundation.

ENLIGHTENMENT PERSPECTIVES

The modern turn

If contemporary Western civilization arguably has no longer any use for the concept of ultimate good, the concept plays no role in contemporary ethics. With the scientific revolution and philosophical reflection based on science, the ultimate good—indeed, good itself—has largely disappeared from scientifically formed Western thought. We can trace this disappearance to two principal events that have profoundly shaped the modern era.

The first of these was the Protestant Reformation. Although Pope John Paul II did not address himself significantly to the Reformation, it deserves our attention here for two reasons. The first is that the Reformation constituted a rupture of the spiritual unity of the West. No longer did the adage hold true, *Roma locuta est, causa finita est.*[1] The decisive authority of the Catholic Church to pronounce on faith and morals was no longer recognized in a religiously divided Europe. Furthermore, the split among Christians into Catholics and Protestants, effectively according to the principle *cuius regio eius religio* (the religion of the region is that of the ruler), led eventually to the religious wars of the 17th century. That Christians fought a bloody war against other Christians precisely over Christian identity constituted a grave scandal. (Of course, in all these wars political and dynastic considerations played a significant and indeed often primary role.) The second, and philosophically more important reason for our attention, is Martin Luther's own statement of principle at the Diet of Worms. Challenged to retract the theses he had presented and defended, Luther states,

1 Rome has spoken, the case is closed.

> Unless I am convinced by Scripture and plain reason—I do not accept the authority of the popes and councils, for they have contradicted each other–my conscience [*Gewissen*] is captive to the Word of God. I cannot and I will not recant anything for to go against conscience is neither right nor safe. God help me. Amen.[2]

Affirming the authority of his own *conscience* over that of "the popes and councils," Martin Luther accented the role of subjectivity in religious thought. Doubtless, Luther had no intention to subjectivize the truths of Christianity. He still held to the Commandments and the Creed, and he would have resisted the efforts to overturn the primacy of Christ on the basis of his own conscience, which he testified to be "captive to the word of God." He did not, however, clarify what conscience is, and the question of conscience has since become increasingly important in Christian thought.

The second major event forming the modern era was the scientific revolution. Science had been practiced since ancient times. Indeed, Aristotle's *Organon* constituted a veritable handbook for the acquisition of scientific knowledge. The rediscovery of Aristotle's writings in medieval Europe was a major scientific event.[3] Remarkable as was the discovery of Aristotle's work, the Aristotelian logic remained insufficient to address all the problems posed by nature. A new method was needed and developed: the mathematical-experimental method. Rather than to rely primarily on observation, this method was structured on the interplay between mathematics and controlled experimentation. If an object or a system within nature could be represented mathematically,

2 Martin Luther, "Luther at the Imperial Diet of Worms." downloaded 5 July 2023 from https://www.luther.de/en/worms.html.

3 Richard E Rubenstein, *Aristotle's Children: How Christians, Muslims, and Jews Rediscovered Ancient Wisdom and Illuminated the Middle Ages* (Orlando, Austin, New York: Harcourt, 2003).

in a mathematical model, then by manipulating that model, the scientist can determine how the reality can be tested. By testing the model, the theory that it represents can be corrected and refined. Indeed, this new scientific method enabled scientists to advance their researches at a previously unknown pace. Science was successful, and in its wake as a direct offshoot came remarkable technological advances.

The fruit of both these events was to discredit religion as a source of knowledge and to establish the supremacy of science. Increasingly, Western intellectuals turned to empirical science as the touchstone and standard of knowledge. If you want to know something, ask a scientist.

A key figure in the development of the new sciences was René Descartes, whose integration of algebra and geometry provided the tools to show that all physical reality can be represented mathematically. The mathematical representation of things in space and time, combined with Newton's laws of motion and gravitation (and a few others) suggested that the physical universe can, at least in principle, be described with mathematical precision. Even the overthrow of the neat Newtonian structure by relativity and quantum theory did not undermine the fundamental vision of a universe ruled by invariant mathematical laws. The Cartesian coordinate system with its analytic geometry is ideal for representing extended substances existing in space and time. But what of the man himself? The conscious self has no place in the physical universe. If this is so, then how can mind and body relate or interact? Indeed, from the publication of Descartes's work to this day, the mind-body problem and the related problem of the nature of consciousness have remained to bedevil philosophers.

Consciousness is a frequently discussed topic today in scientific circles. We regularly see articles with titles such as "What Is Consciousness?" (several articles and even a TED talk), "What Actually Is Consciousness?," "Consciousness Is a Big Problem for Science," as well as articles relating consciousness to quantum theory—and even one titled "There Is No Such Thing as

Conscious Thought."[4] What these scientists, and philosophers associated with their work, generally agree upon is that although we all know what consciousness is—we are all conscious—it is impossible to define consciousness itself.

Modern philosophy has readily and even unquestioningly accepted consciousness as the primordial cognition. Descartes could hold nothing as true until he determined that he is a conscious being.

> But what then am I? A thing that thinks. What is that? A thing that doubts, understands, affirms, denies, wills, refuses, and that also imagines and senses.[5]

Whatever he can know can arise only from his consciousness of clear and distinct ideas, such as the concepts of mathematics. Similarly, David Hume acknowledges no other truth than that which can be traced back to the phenomena given to his senses.[6] The task of reason then becomes that of interpreting and organizing the data and contents of consciousness. This foundationalism of consciousness leads to paradox and even confusion, most notably concerning the existence of the world outside consciousness. The premise underlying such conceptions is that in consciousness are the fundamental data, the "givens," on which all our cognition is founded, that the world in which each of us lives is contained in consciousness.

When the British Empiricists, especially Hume, picked up on this, good became disconnected from the physical world. Similarly, Kant found no room for morality in the realm of phenomena. In the mathematized universe good has no place. For this

4 Steve Ayan, "There Is No Such Thing as Conscious Thought," *Scientific American*, December 20, 2018.

5 René Descartes, *Meditations on First Philosophy* (Indianapolis: Hackett, 1963), 28.

6 David Hume, *An Inquiry Concerning Human Understanding* (Indianapolis: Bobbs-Merrill, 1955), 28, 30.

reason, Karol Wojtyła will argue that Kant has failed to address the truth about the good.[7] Indeed, the good—the notion of teleology—has disappeared even from biology. This has been an admittedly slow achievement, which came to fulfillment only in the 20th century. According to contemporary Neo-Darwinism, evolution is never toward the better nor higher; there is no better, only survival success.[8] And so, because of their ubiquity and the enormous range of sub-species, the most successful species on earth is not the human being, but the bacterium.

At the root of this loss of the teleology is Descartes' dualism of mind and body. In distinguishing sharply between himself as a "thinking thing" and his body as an "extended thing," Descartes removed his own body and, indeed, everything outside his mind from the realm of meaning. The world of bodies, if we may speak this way, is not a world of "things," much less of substances, that interact with other things according to their own laws. Rather they are bodies in the mathematical sense, three-dimensional solids occupying determined locations in space, from which every other body is excluded. Every body, occupying and moving within its spatial-temporal parameters, interacts with other such bodies according to the applicable physical laws. Comparably to the image consisting of pixels on the television screen, each of which has its own location and color-value, every physical point in space is a kind of three-dimensional pixel characterized by its gravitational mass, color, electromagnetic charge, "spin," and whatever else physicists may discover. Consequently, if the drama of good and evil on the television is found only in the minds of the viewers, it may well be—as Hume will eventually argue—that the evil we find in human acts is located only in the mind.[9] The world in which we live is thus conceived only as a

7 Karol Wojtyła, *The Lublin Lectures/Wykłady Lubelskie*, 381.

8 John R. Searle, *The Rediscovery of the Mind* (Cambridge, MA/ London: MIT Press, 1992), 51–52.

9 David Hume, *An Enquiry concerning the Principles of Morals*, in *Hume's Ethical Writings* (London: Collier Books, 1965), 109, 118.

four-dimensional space-time continuum in which individual points (pixels) have their changing physical values which are unrelated to any standard of good. Therefore, human morality is not a matter of attaining any properly human excellence or of meeting some preestablished moral standard (such as the moral law).

In his philosophical works, Karol Wojtyła turns repeatedly to the problem of the replacement of the *philosophy of being* with the *philosophy of consciousness,* a concern that ultimately appears in the Encyclical *Fides et Ratio*.[10] The philosophies of consciousness find their historical root, of course, in the thought of Descartes, who famously could accept no belief that was not clearly and distinctly present to his mind. His intellectual heirs—and here we must think especially of Edmund Husserl and the phenomenological school, most notably Max Scheler—located the distinctively human in consciousness. The person, we may say, becomes reduced to his subjectivity. If this is done, then the person disappears. So, at the very outset of his study on human love and its sexual expression, Wojtyła insists that the person must be an objective being, that if regarded as pure subjectivity, he disappears.[11] The project of his study was to give a philosophical account of sexual morality, of love and responsibility, and this "appealing to the most elementary and undeniable moral truths and [...] to the most fundamental values or goods."[12] The author intended his work to be based on human experience. On the one hand, the experience of human love involves such powerful emotions and desires that love appears as a subjective reality. Indeed, our common human experience is that persons who feel themselves in love may become deluded and therefore guided by their emotions. On the other hand, the sexual love between a man and a woman has an objective physical basis in the attraction of the sexes for the

10 John Paul II, Encyclical *Fides et Ratio* (Vatican City: Libreria Editrice Vaticana, 1998), §§83–85.

11 Karol Wojtyła, *Love and Responsibility* (Boston: Pauline Books & Media, 2013), 3.

12 Ibid., xxii.

purpose of reproduction. As it is with all mammals, men and women are drawn to sexual union, the fruit of which is the reproduction of their kind. Wojtyła addresses both aspects in his book precisely because no adequate account of the relationship between man and woman can be given without integrating the understanding of both the subjective and the objective aspects of the being of those involved. Thus, in his work Wojtyła avoids both the romanticism that reduces all discourse about love to the nature and intensity of the feelings involved, and a materialist account that reduces human love to a nexus of purely biological events. This same insight that underlies his work on human love is developed further in *Person and Act*, where Karol Wojtyła seeks to account for the human person through a phenomenological analysis of the act.[13] Just as the act cannot be reduced either to subjectivity or to its objective structure, so is it impossible to reduce the person to either the subjective or to the material objectivity. Wojtyła further develops this theme of the primacy of the philosophy of being over that of consciousness in several other writings.[14]

Karol Wojtyła shows that neither science nor human subjectivity can found an objectively knowable conception of good. The most we can hope for is a widely accepted consensus of what a given population regards as good. So, most decent Americans think that education is good and child pornography is evil. *The good* as such, however, cannot be discovered. In our contemporary philosophical climate, formed as it is by the heritage of the Enlightenment, *moral realism* is almost impossible to justify. It seems impossible to defend "universal, objective moral values which we humans are capable

13 Karol Wojtyła, *Person and Act* (Washington, D.C.: Catholic University of America Press, 2021), 101.

14 See, for example, Karol Wojtyła, "Thomistic Personalism," in K. Wojtyła, *Person and Community: Selected Essays*, 165–75; "Subjectivity and the Irreducible in the Human Being", 209–17; "Person: Subject and Community," 219–61.

of grasping—contra the many cultural influences that seem to have put us out to sea, morally speaking."[15] Consequently, the conception of an ultimate or highest good has become impossible.

Modern perspectives on choosing between good and evil

The case of Hume

It is well to examine closely David Hume's position, who famously wrote:

> Reason is, and ought only to be the slave of the passions, and can never pretend to any other office than to serve and obey them. A passion is an original existence, [...] and contains not any representative quality, which renders it a copy of any other existence or modification.[16]

Passions according to this account are given in experience—Karol Wojtyła would say they "happen in a man"—and as such they cannot be controlled by reason, whose function is to compare and calculate relations among things. For its part, a passion is an experiential urge to which the agent is subject and which evokes some response. Further on Hume argues,

> Since a passion can never, in any sense, be call'd unreasonable, but when founded on a false supposition, or when it chuses means insufficient for the design'd end, 'tis impossible that reason and passion can ever oppose

15 Erica Lucast Stonestreet, Review of Markus Gabriel *Moral Progress in Dark Times, Notre Dame Philosophical Reviews*, 7 April 2023, downloaded 7 July 2023 from https://ndpr.nd.edu/reviews/moral-progress-in-dark-times-universal-values-for-the-twenty-first-century/.

16 David Hume. *A Treatise of Human Nature* (Digireads.com Publishing, 2019), 296.

> each other, or dispute for the government of the will and actions.[17]

What we call reasonable actions of will are simply our responses to the calmer or milder passions. These are often attributed, wrongly according to Hume, to reason. In fact, however, all that we are able to do is to follow the dictates of desire. A passion is, for Hume, an "original existence," that is, a non-rational interior impulse that arises in the mind (or the breast) and over which the agent has little or no control. We can recognize our passions and identify them, but we cannot control them or overcome them with reason. From these premises it follows that moral evil (or good) cannot be found by reason, which is capable only of comparing mental impressions.

These premises have serious implications for morality. Most important is that morality is not subject to reason. As we gaze upon the world and consider the sensations that arise from things, nowhere do we perceive moral good or evil. Of course, certain events give rise to feelings of approbation or disapproval which may be strong. These feelings are not justified or warranted by the events that give rise to them. Hume writes,

> In every system of morality, which I have hitherto met with, I have always remark'd, that the author proceeds for some time in the ordinary way of reasoning and establishes the being of a God, or makes some observations concerning human affairs; when of a sudden I am surpris'd to find that instead of the usual copulations of propositions, *is* and *is not*, I meet with no proposition that is not connected with an *ought* or an *ought not*. This change is imperceptible; but it is, however, of the last consequence.[18]

17 Ibid., 297.
18 Ibid., 333.

In this famous text, Hume discovers the principle, which has since bedeviled undergraduate students and not a few professional scholars, that "is" cannot imply "ought." In education, we may ask why it is permissible for a teacher to forbid cheating on texts. If she says that cheating is *wrong*, she is imposing a personal value judgment that her students may not accept. On the other hand, if she maintains that this is her class and that she strongly values honesty and therefore forbids cheating, is she not simply using her power to give grades to impose her own values? In our day, moral theologians have insisted on this same principle, insisting that it is illegitimate to confuse statements of fact (*Tatsachenbegriffe*) with those of value (*Wertbegriffe*).[19]

At the root of Hume's analysis and logical critique is his sensationalism, his insistence that all our knowledge is founded on sensations. According to this conception, all that we can know are our sensations and the patterns we discover among them, patterns of "*Resemblance, Contiguity* in time or place, and *Cause or Effect*."[20] Effectively, Hume denies causality in the world—he insists on this denial—because we cannot perceive causation in things. The world of David Hume is a realm of sense impressions, behind which the mind cannot legitimately go. It was this vision that gave rise to Kant's *Critique of Pure Reason*.

Where morality is concerned, all that we can know are our interior emotional responses to different things. Indeed, these reactions are not to *kinds* or *classes* of things, but to individual experiences.[21] As one engages in the world, no moral principles or laws are to be found there. The experience of willing is no more than a sensation of wanting some outcome and of moving toward that outcome. We certainly have no consciousness of a will

19 Richard A. McCormick, S.J., *The Critical Calling: Reflections on Moral Dilemmas since Vatican II* (Washington D.C.: Georgetown University Press, 1989), 58.

20 David Hume, *An Inquiry concerning Human Understanding* (Indianapolis: Bobbs-Merrill, 1955), 32.

21 David Hume, *A Treatise of Human Nature*, 334.

moving our limbs.[22] All that we have is the consciousness of wanting and then of some event following. It is a following of one's passions. Concerning the objects of those passions, we find in them no unmistakable signs of good or evil. Hume gives his famous example of the parricide tree. An elm or an oak tree drops its seed, which germinates and grows, eventually overtopping the parent tree, leading to its death. We are not dismayed by this, as we are when a man kills his father. In the latter case we attribute the action to the will (presumably ill) of the killing son, but in both cases (regardless of a will that we cannot perceive) the facts are the same: the offspring has killed its parent.

> There is no other matter of fact in the case. The vice entirely escapes you, as long as you consider the object. You never can find it, till you turn your reflection into your own breast, and find a sentiment of disapprobation, which arises in you, towards this action. Here is a matter of fact; but 'tis the object of feeling, not of reason.[23]

David Hume's philosophy is important, not so much for his *ipsissima verba*—nobody today regards his system as completely adequate and accurate—as for his inspiration. His intellectual heirs continue his fundamental insights concerning the relativity of good and evil in the natural world and of human acts, the foundational importance of sensation, the loss of the concept of causality, and the obscurity of the acts of the will. Consider this quote from James Wolcoll Sperry, a 20th-century philosopher.

> The common, naïve impression that we use the mind to initiate and control our physical actions has long been rejected almost universally in science, following the doctrine of scientific materialism, which predicates

22 *An Inquiry concerning Human Understanding*, 78.
23 *A Treatise of Human Nature*, 332.

> that a full account of brain behavior and reality is possible in terms purely physical.[24]

Both Hume and Sperry, as well as most who implicitly follow Hume, confuse the will with mental events, arguing against a position that, as it were, holds that a conscious act is accompanied by a mental act or decision that is alleged to cause the action. Such a view is, on its face, untenable, as the intelligent behavior of good drivers and championship athletes shows. They do not stop and think before acting, but, in a sense, the thought *is* the action. The Humean analysis foreshortens human experience, reducing it to only that which is felt or perceived. Karol Wojtyła argues that such phenomenalism (as he calls it) loses the unity of experience. He writes, "The phenomenalist position seems to exclude this unity of many experiences, seeing in the individual's experience only a group of impressions or emotional stirrings that are in turn ordered by the mind."[25] The reduction of experience to mere sensation implicitly denies that experience itself is intellectually formed. To maintain that experience reduces to sense data or Humean "ideas" is itself an abstraction. Every experience, even sense experience itself, is meaningful and therefore constitutes an interpretation. The great mistake here is that the human mind receives raw data which it must then somehow sort into categories and make use of. But this is not how the mind works at all. It is contrary to human experience.

Immanuel Kant

Kantian moral theory proceeds from a stance of subjectivist rationalism—"subjectivist" because the criteria of right and wrong are interior to the person. Kant writes,

24 James Wolcoll Sperry, "Consciousness and Causality" in R. L. Gregory (editor) *Oxford Companion to the Mind* (Oxford, New York: Oxford University Press, 1987), 164.

25 *Person and Act*, 95.

> There is no possibility of thinking of anything at all in the world, or even out of it, which can be regarded as good without qualification, except a *good will*.[26]

Wealth, virtues, intelligence, happiness do not make one good unless one has also a good will. Desiring and striving for some great and worthy goal does not of itself constitute goodness. Only the good will is of moral value. What makes a will good is not what it performs or even intends to achieve. Only the *volition*—the very act of willing—regardless of any other factor, makes the will good. Even if it should achieve nothing, the good will must, "like a jewel, still shine by its own light."[27]

The first and fundamental principle of a good will is duty. To be morally good, the act must not merely be *according to* duty, but *from or for the sake of* duty, simply because duty requires it. Kant gives the example of the shopkeeper who is honest because it is good for business. Although he should be honest in any case, his honesty is praiseworthy only if his behavior is for the sake of honesty itself. Similarly, we have a duty to preserve our lives. But because one is inclined to do this anyway, unreflective self-preservation has no moral content. However, if life has been too hard and he preserves his life for the sake of duty, then refusing suicide does have moral content.[28] Only actions for the sake of duty have moral worth. And because duty is founded on the conception of law, "The preeminent good which we call moral can therefore consist in nothing else than the conception of law in itself, which is certainly possible only in a rational being."[29]

The moral law is based first on the categorical imperative: "Act only according to that maxim whereby you can at the same time will that it should become a universal law." And this imperative leads necessarily to the practical imperative: "Act in such a way

26 Immanuel Kant, *Grounding of the Metaphysics of Morals*, 393.
27 Ibid., 394.
28 Ibid., 398.
29 Ibid., 401.

that you treat humanity, whether in your own person or in the person of another, always at the same time as an end and never simply as a means."[30] This principle is the supreme limiting condition on everyone's freedom of action. Particularly important to Kant is that this is not based on experience but upon reason itself, on what belongs to a rational being as rational. It arises from pure reason.[31] In short, the ground or basis of all practical lawgiving lies rationally in the form of universality, which makes the rule capable of being a law. However, it is the rationality of the individual moral subject who derives the law for himself. From this follows the principle that the will of every rational being legislates universal law, even if subjectively that law applies only to himself.

> The will is thus not merely subject to the law but is subject in such a way that it must be regarded also as legislating for itself and only on this account as being subject to the law."[32]

Such a law must be founded not on self-interest but only on reason. The worthiness of morality arises from the fact that the rational being legislates universal laws.

> For nothing can have any worth other than what the law determines. [...] Hence autonomy is the ground of the dignity of human nature and of every rational nature.[33]

> That will whose maxims are necessarily in accord with the laws of autonomy is a holy, or absolutely good, will.[34]

30 Ibid., 429.
31 Ibid., 431.
32 Ibid.
33 Ibid., 436.
34 Ibid., 439.

In sum, Kant gives us a conception of the individual will as a law unto itself, governed, of course, by the rules of reason but not by any appeal to an objectively existing good. From this follows the conception of conscience as independent and autonomous, bound by its own understanding of the rules of reason.

Because in many respects it accords with our common moral sense, Kant's ethics has much to recommend it. It is true, for instance, that even the best qualities of intelligence and charm do not make a person good. Indeed, these can make wicked person positively dangerous. We can appreciate T. S. Eliot's insight in *Murder in the Cathedral*, "The last act is the greatest treason. To do the right deed for the wrong reason."[35] Furthermore, we recognize that a person can be good if his efforts prove futile and even go awry. The goodness or evil of a human act does have to depend on the goodness or evil of the will. One can be a failure in his project and nevertheless be a good person. Most important, especially for Karol Wojtyła, is insistence on the importance of binding moral obligation. Some things are simply wrong to do regardless of any benefit. According to Wojtyła, Kant's theory fails because it absolutely disconnects the will from the objective order. Reason is incapable of knowing the *truth about the good*.[36] Later, in his account of the personalistic norm which, in its negative formulation closely resembles Kant's "practical imperative" ("Act in such a way that you treat humanity, whether in your own person or in the person of another, always at the same time as an end and never simply as a means"),[37] he completes that norm with the judgment—missing in and impossible for Kant—that the only proper and mature relation toward the person is love.[38]

35 T. S. Eliot. *Murder in the Cathedral* (New York: Harcourt, Brace, and Co, 1935).

36 Karol Wojtyła, *The Lublin Lectures/ Wykłady Lubelski*, 307, 322–30.

37 Immanuel Kant, *Grounding for the Metaphysics of Morals* (Indianapolis: Hackett, 1993), 429.

38 Karol Wojtyła, *Love and Responsibility*, 25.

J. S. Mill

If there is a morality for the modern industrial, consumerist, democratic culture, it is utilitarianism. In real life, nobody is or can be a true Kantian. However, utilitarianism is the implicit moral philosophy that most of our contemporaries in the West have adopted and live by. Its governing principle is simple, practical, and compelling.

> The creed which accepts as the foundation of morals "utility" or the "greatest happiness principle" holds that actions are right in proportion as they tend to promote happiness: wrong as they tend to produce the reverse of happiness. By happiness is intended pleasure and the absence of pain; by unhappiness, pain and the privation of pleasure.[39]

Mill continues:

> Pleasure and freedom from pain are the only things desirable as ends, and [...] all desirable things [...] are desirable either for the pleasure inherent in themselves, or as a means to the promotion of pleasure and the prevention of pain.[40]

Mill qualifies this doctrine with some important nuances. First, the greatest happiness principle does not call for crass selfishness. It does not mean "greatest happiness for *the agent*," but instead the "greatest amount of happiness altogether."[41] It is a public-spirited philosophy whose focus is as much social as it is individual.

> In an improving state of the human mind, the influences are constantly on the increase which will tend to

39 John Stuart Mill, *Utilitarianism* (Indianapolis: Hackett, 2001), 7.
40 Ibid., 7.
41 Ibid., 11.

> generate in each individual a feeling of unity with all the rest; which, if perfect, would make him never think of, or desire, any beneficial condition for himself in the benefits of which they were not included.[42]

The ultimate end is "an existence exempt as far as possible from pain, and as rich as possible in enjoyments, both in point of quantity and quality." [43] And the criteria for these is determined by those who "in their opportunities of experience, to which must be added their habits of self-consciousness and self-observation, are best furnished with the means of comparison." This means that the educated and cultured classes know best what happiness really is. They need to lead the way in establishing customs, values, and laws.

Mill summarizes his vision of the good life:

> [...] not a life of rapture, but moments of such, in an existence made up of few and transitory pains, many and various pleasures, with a decided predominance of the active over the passive, and having as the foundation of the whole not to expect more from life than it is capable of bestowing.[44]

In a wisely governed and progressive society, poverty can be almost completely eliminated, and, thanks to modern scientific developments, the principal sources of human suffering can be greatly reduced.[45] Further, through the agencies of education and propaganda, public authorities "should use that power to establish in the mind of every individual an indissoluble association between his own happiness" and universal happiness.[46] This project

42 Ibid., 35.
43 Ibid., 12.
44 Ibid., 13.
45 Ibid., 15.
46 Ibid., 17.

of establishing such an association between one's own happiness and that of everyone else is precisely the project of forming conscience, which is "a feeling in our own mind; a pain more or less intense, attendant on violation of duty. This feeling, when disinterested and connecting itself with the pure idea of duty [...] is the essence of conscience."[47]

If conscience is a pained feeling we get when we feel we have done something wrong, the challenge is to bring this into line with the principle of utility, the greatest happiness principle. It may be that a sense of moral obligation arising from "things in themselves" as a transcendent reality—that is, a belief in God—will be especially compelling for many people, but this is not necessary. What is important is the feeling that arises from a guilty or a satisfied conscience. Note, however, that a person's conscience can change, often under the impulse of external pressure.

> "Unhappily it is also susceptible, by sufficient use of the external sanctions and of the force of early impressions, of being cultivated in almost any direction, so that there is hardly anything so absurd or so mischievous that it may not, by means of these influences, be made to act on the human mind with all the authority of conscience."

A chilling admission. Mill acknowledges that conscience is malleable, that it can be deformed in almost any direction, as indeed we have so often seen in the 20th century. His hope and proposal is that enlightened social leadership will form consciences according to his principle of utility, the greatest happiness principle. By this they will foster a progressive and enlightened society in which all will live happy lives.

The basis for the philosophy of utilitarianism is the "greatest happiness principle." Of the philosophies and philosophers that he examined Karol Wojtyła had perhaps the least regard for

47 Ibid., 29.

utilitarianism. He notes that Jeremy Bentham firmly and sternly repudiated all metaphysical claims relevant to morality.

> Bentham's condemnation of all "the great words full of conceit" such as *ratio, ratio vera (recta) natura, ius naturae, iustitia naturalis, aequitas naturalis, bonus ordo, veritas* is much stronger, for all these serve as "dogmas" to veil commands imposed upon other people. [...] Bentham wishes to say that metaphysical phraseology has contributed to an eclipse of the proper truth about good and evil.[48]

That truth is that good and evil come down simply to pleasure and pain respectively. As far as religion is concerned, Bentham holds that because God is benevolent, he wants his people to enjoy pleasure. The calculus of pleasure is the only standard by which morality and religion can be judged.[49] The core of Wojtyła's critique of Bentham is that "pleasure, by its essence a purely subjective good, cannot be a constituent element of the objective norm."[50]

Karol Wojtyła carried his critique forward in *Love and Responsibility,* where he reiterated that pleasure cannot be the proper objective of a human act.

> But pleasure itself is not the only good; it is also not the proper end of man's action [...]. Pleasure in its essence is something collateral, accidental, something that may occur when acting. Thus, undertaking to act for the sake of pleasure itself as the exclusive or highest end naturally clashes with the natural structure of human acts.[51]

48 *Lublin Lectures*, 529.
49 Ibid., 532.
50 Ibid., 546.
51 *Love and Responsibility*, 20.

The key point here is that pleasure is something collateral to an act. Wojtyła here accepts St. Thomas's analysis of pleasure as a proper accident of attaining some appropriate good.[52] To adopt a utilitarian ethic is effectively to treat oneself as "a subject that wants to have as many sensations and lived-experiences possessing positive emotional-affective charge as possible, and at the same time as an object that may be used in order to evoke these sensations and lived-experiences."[53]

Bentham's utilitarian successor, John Stuart Mill, carries forward, albeit less abrasively, Bentham's anti-metaphysical perspective. Mill repeatedly affirms that metaphysical and theological truth claims are irrelevant to his arguments, which are founded ultimately on the experiences of pleasure broadly understood. Mill presents not so much a hedonistic philosophy as a philosophy for the contemporary free-market economy under enlightened democratic institutions. The basis of a well-ordered society is not mere survival but happy or pleasant survival. Mill's utilitarianism envisions no transcendence, but rather a progressive civilization with (effectively) a compelling "civil religion" to instill public-spiritedness manifest in a concern for the well-being of all.[54] Mill's social concerns notwithstanding, however, the bases of utilitarianism are inherently and irredeemably subjective. Happiness is a *feeling* of pleasure. For Mill, utilitarianism is divinely sanctioned because God wants his creatures to be happy.[55] In fact, the bases of his utilitarianism are totally immanentist and hence subjective. As such, even Mill's variant of utilitarianism is inadequate for a proper, realistic understanding not only of morality but of the exigencies of life itself.

Max Scheler

Max Scheler was the "anti-Kant." Reacting to the perceived rigidity of Kant's system, specifically to the notion of obligation,

52 Thomas Aquinas, *Summa Theologiae*, Ia, IIae q. 2, a. 6; q. 4, a. 1.
53 Ibid., 21.
54 John Stuart Mill, *Utilitarianism* (Cambridge, Indianapolis: Hackett, 2001), 33.
55 Ibid., 22.

Scheler appeals to the person's lived experience of values and the response to these. Values, including moral values, are realities that can be *felt* or *intuited*, and do not constitute objects of reason.[56] As such, values are not understood or analyzed but appreciated. One responds to the value emotionally. Scheler's account of morality is formed around the concept of value response. Morality concerns this response to moral values.

Particularly important is Scheler's rejection of the concept of obligation or duty (*Pflicht*) that might arise from the intuition of a value. Rather,

> We have [...] a consciousness of the rightness or wrongness of an act to which we feel an inclination *without* its being the case that a judgment is made about it. [...] With a fine ear for these facts of consciousness, in the skill and practice of observing them consists primarily what we call "conscience"—*not*, however, in the acts of judgment or assessment.[57]

Because values are felt, perceived by feelings, the perception of the moral value of an act can only be the work of the feelings. Conscience is therefore a kind of emotional response to an act relating to a value. For Scheler, *conscience* is simply the practiced observation of the facts of one's consciousness as it encounters moral values. For example, having observed and experienced the value of honesty, the person "interiorizes" this virtue. Reflecting on St. Francis' embrace of the dirty and disgusting leper, whose contagion he had good reason to fear, one is filled with admiration and can become sensitive to the sufferings of others in a way new to him. His emotional sensitivity to love and generosity is enhanced, and this sensitivity can flow into his actions. The

56 Max Scheler, *Der Formalismus in der Ethik, und die materiale Wertethik: Neuer Versuch der Grundlegung eines ethischen Personalismus* (Bern und Munich: Franke Verlag, 1966), 38.

57 Ibid., 203.

experience of moral value leads to an "ideal should" (*ideales Sollen*), which does not and cannot constitute a norm or obligation. Neither norm nor duty can provide a standard for moral behavior or a basis for ethics.[58]

For Max Scheler, duty has "essentially a negative and restrictive character."[59] In the final analysis, Scheler sees the person as the unity of his experiences, especially those experiences of values.[60] Hence, his goodness lies not in his acts or intentions, but in his interiorized values. A good person is one whose sentiments are appropriate to the values he encounters. Conscience does not "guide" (as the saying goes), nor is it a standard to form one's acts. It is, at best, a state of inner peace or complacency in one whose life responds appropriately to the higher values.

Max Scheler adopts an emotionalist ethics, according to which moral values are felt and not necessarily acted upon. Compared with Kant, Bentham, and Mill, Scheler is least able to provide specific guidance to the conscience of the acting person. On the other hand, the notion of conscience implicit in his thought—that one must follow his heart—is particularly congenial to the contemporary mentality.

Contemporary discussions of morality therefore tend to waver between the utilitarian and the emotionalist. On the one hand, it is urged that the person "follow her heart," but on the other hand, it is necessary to weigh the foreseeable consequences of the act. We might add, however, that the individualism and, indeed, libertarianism of Mill, who celebrates the principle of the "free development of individuality,"[61] is amenable to Scheler's reliance on interior feelings. Mill writes,

> It is not by wearing down into uniformity all that is individual in themselves, but by cultivating it and calling

58 Ibid., 211.
59 Ibid., 202.
60 Ibid., 371.
61 J. S. Mill, *On Liberty* (Indianapolis: Hackett, 1978), 58.

> it forth [...] that humans become a noble and beautiful object of contemplation. [...] In proportion to the development of his individuality, each person becomes more valuable to himself, and is therefore capable of being more valuable to others. There is a greater fullness of life about his own existence [...].[62]

Arguably, we of the modern industrial, democratic West are emotionalist utilitarians. Such is the ethics that Karol Wojtyła addresses in his writings. These approaches, as well as the dualism of Descartes and the Empiricism we find in Hume, form the substructure of the contemporary accounts of morality that *Veritatis Splendor* critiques and corrects.

62 *On Liberty*, 60.

THE HUMAN ACT

St. Thomas writes:

> Since [...] man is said to be made to God's image, in so far as the image implies an intelligent being endowed with free-will and self-movement [...]; it remains for us to treat of His image, i.e., man, inasmuch as he too is the principle of his actions, as having free-will and control of his actions.[1]

As the image of God, man acts similarly to God, determining by his intelligence what he shall do and then by his will, which is free, choosing to act and then acting. Just as every divine act is ascribed to the intelligence, will, and power of the Creator, so too every human act is ascribed to the intelligence, free will, and power of this human agent.

Most important—indeed, of paramount importance—is that he direct himself to his last end. St. Thomas is clear that one can know something of what this ultimate end is, even if divine help is needed to attain it. One can know fairly easily and clearly that a life dedicated to the pursuit of wealth or fame is badly directed, that such things cannot constitute the true good of the human being.[2] Even if he cannot fully recognize that this ultimate end can be only the vision of the essence of God, he can know that it transcends all that he does know in his experience, that it can only be the perfect good. For Thomas, a person's life is a serious matter that must be shaped according to reason. Indeed, living well demands that one live intelligently.

1 *Summa Theologiae,* Ia, IIae Prologue.
2 *Summa Theologiae,* Ia, IIae q. 2, aa. 1, 3.

Because the human being is intelligent, he can participate in the divine intelligence. He too makes his world, forming things as the craftsman and directing them as the governor. Just as no thought, which can be expressed symbolically in sentences, stands alone but within a meaningful and logical nexus of thoughts, so too does no act stand alone. It results from a plan relating to other acts and situations that it proposes to address. The action affects something in the world and can be expected to have some effect in the world or in oneself (as a cardiac workout strengthens the heart). One act may fall within a nexus of acts directed toward an end; to serve the ball is one action in the totality of acts involved in playing a game of tennis. In short, no act is accomplished as an isolated event or in a vacuum. An intelligent being coordinates his acts. And every act expresses the intellect of the person performing it.

Karol Wojtyła on the human act

Essential to every human act, as Karol Wojtyła analyzes it, are consciousness and efficacy. A human act is subjectively experienced in the agent's consciousness and is intended objectively to result in some change.

The problem of consciousness

Following the foundationalism of Descartes and Hume, modern philosophy has readily and even unquestioningly accepted consciousness as the primordial human cognition from which or upon which reason and knowledge are founded. Commonly, discussions of the possibility of intelligent life elsewhere in the universe will refer not to intelligence but to "conscious life," as though what makes human beings (and presumably Klingons, Wookies, and Daleks[3]) distinct is consciousness. Hence, Descartes could hold nothing as true until he determined that he was a conscious being.

3 Referring to intelligent life-forms in *Star Trek, Star Wars,* and *Doctor Who,* respectively.

Only within his consciousness could he find the certainty upon which the rest of his cognitions can be founded.

> But what then am I? A thing that thinks. What is that? A thing that doubts, understands, affirms, denies, wills, refuses, and that also imagines and senses.[4]

Whatever he can know can arise only from his consciousness and from clear and distinct ideas, such as the concepts of mathematics. Similarly, David Hume acknowledges no other truth than that which can be traced back to the phenomena given to his senses.[5] The task of reason then becomes that of interpreting and organizing the data and contents of consciousness. This foundationalism of consciousness leads to paradox and even confusion, most notably concerning the existence of the world outside consciousness. The premise underlying such conceptions is that in consciousness are the fundamental data, the "givens," on which all our cognition is founded, that the world in which each of us lives is contained and even constituted in consciousness.

A central distinction running through Karol Wojtyła's work is that between "man acts" and "what happens in man." This is found both in *Love and Responsibility*[6] and *Person and Act*.[7] This distinction is experienced as the difference between *agere* (to act) and *pati* (to suffer), which are two basic aspects of the dynamization of the human person. The human being is a complex being that experiences events over which he has no control—the beating of his heart, hearing a clap of thunder, fear when faced with a bear—as well as actions that he himself initiates and completes. The latter are *acts*, strictly speaking, and the former are *happenings*.

4 René Descartes. *Meditations on First Philosophy* (Indianapolis: Hackett, 1963), 28.

5 David Hume. *An Inquiry concerning Human Understanding* (Indianapolis: Bobbs-Merrill, 1955), 28, 30.

6 *Love and Responsibility*, 47.

7 *Person and Act*, 24 ff. See also *Love and Responsibility*, 30–31; Karol Wojtyła, *Person and Community*, 182, 189.

Of course, one is not always conscious of everything that happens in him; think of digestion and heartbeat or even of the pressure of the seat back against one's spine. The act, however, is always and intimately related to consciousness, and this itself indicates what consciousness is.

Consciousness and the will

Early in *Person and Act*, Karol Wojtyła states, "The act is conscious action" [Czyn jest działaniem świadomym.][8] and by this he relates consciousness to the will, the *voluntarium*. His point is quite simple; we say that what one has done voluntarily he has done consciously. Consciousness arises not from cognition but from willed activity.[9]

The mistake that we philosophers (as well as many in the scientific community) make is to confuse consciousness with sense data, the responses of our various sense organs to their stimuli. However, consciousness does not consist simply of sense data, even if these do provide a kind of source for our knowledge of the physical world. Rather, the intellect interprets sensations and integrates them into the understanding. The person, an individual substance of a rational nature, relates to the world rationally, through his power to reason, and not mechanically or instinctively. Interpreting the environment and understanding its structure, the person transcends the biological mechanisms of stimulus and response. Of course, he *can* try to act simply in response to stimuli, but even to do this amounts to an implicit decision to "let things take their course." Hence, Wojtyła writes, *"The principal function of consciousness is the fact that it forms lived-experience* [kształtuje ona przeżycie] which allows man to experience his own subjectivity in a particular way."[10] Therefore, consciousness accompanies

8 Karol Wojtyła, *Person and Act*, 124, 201–03, 216; *Osoba i czyn* (Lublin: Towarzystwo KUL, 2000), 76.

9 Adrian J. Reimers, *The Soul of the Person* (Washington, D.C.: Catholic University of America Press, 2006), 153–222.

10 *Person and Act*, 140-141; *Osoba i czyn*, 91.

willed acts, acts that are performed *deliberately*. It is the application of the person's knowledge to the act but is not that knowledge itself. The sleepwalker, who knows the layout of his bedroom and who has become so accustomed to his movements about the room as to perform them habitually (consider how little thought or attention one ordinarily gives to daily tasks of walking about or driving a well-known route), is not conscious because he is not implementing a plan that he has made but is responding to stimuli of a dream or some such thing. In consciousness the person interiorizes his act and makes it his own. Furthermore, consciousness has a reflexive function by which the acting person interiorizes the truth that he is the agent, that he recognizes the acts as his own.[11]

By contrast, we may consider the materialist position of philosopher John Searle who proposes a thought experiment involving a highly sophisticated "silicon brain" which can perform all the operations of an organic brain by which it governs the movements of the body. If you have such a silicon brain, proposes Searle, "it is perfectly conceivable for you to imagine that your external behavior remains the same, but that your internal conscious thought processes gradually shrink to zero." Searle goes on to assert, "Ontologically speaking, behavior, functional role, and causal relations are irrelevant to the existence of conscious mental phenomena." This illustrates the "principle of the independence of consciousness and behavior."[12] Consciousness plays no role in the causing of behavior or of any form of behavior. In one way, of course, Searle is right. Consciousness does not fire the neurons in the brain or trigger the muscles by which motion is carried out. It is not a factor that intervenes somewhere in the physical, biological processes by which a human being perceives and acts. But this is not Wojtyła's point.

Karol Wojtyła does not propose that mental events—data of consciousness or even thoughts—cause physical events. On the

11 *Person and Act*, 142–44.

12 John R. Searle, *The Rediscovery of the Mind* (Cambridge: MIT Press, 1992), 67, 69.

other hand, he certainly rejects Searles's materialism, as well as any other materialist account, as an inadequate account of causality in the world. The problem with materialism is that it implicitly posits that only determinate laws of nature, those that admit of mathematical description,[13] can govern the behavior of physical things. But this simply excludes the possibility that some beings—rational beings—can form the principles of their own behavior spiritually, that is, by reason and decision of the will. Wojtyła's appeal to the spiritual nature of the person is not an appeal to some mysterious non-physical motive power but to a *power of forming its own principles or habits*. This is why the person is capable of self-governance, not because he can merely by thinking put inanimate matter into motion, but because he can change his habits, putting away vices and acquiring virtues in order to act according to reason. Materialism is not justified by reason or evidence. Based on the premise that only mechanical, mathematical accounts of change are legitimate, materialism excludes the spiritual, the intellectual, or ideal; this is irrational, because human acts of symbolic expression, such as speech, writing, and signage, are governed by the laws of reasoning. Logic provides spiritual, not physical, norms of behavior, and we conform our acts to them. There is no warrant for the fundamental premises of materialism.

Wojtyła's conception of consciousness enables us to understand the uncanny richness of conscious experience. The brute animal responds to objects in his environment according to his needs and wants which are dictated by nature, by instincts and sense appetites. Human beings respond to desires formed by reason according to reason's standards. To be sure, the hungry human subject craves food, but it is intellectually formed perception that recognizes food

13 Keep in mind that topology and statistics are also branches of mathematics. So, the biological account of heredity is based on the reactions of DNA molecules, made possible by the double-helix topology of the molecule. The circulation of blood is based on a topological analogy. And quantum mechanics is inextricably probabilistic.

and identifies it as good. A tomcat will mate with any female in heat, but a man must find the woman attractive in some way. (Rape is very seldom driven by sexual desire alone.) If consciousness is the application of knowledge to the act, then the awareness of the satisfaction permeates the consciousness. One who has long desired to see Paris will become fondly conscious of his first glimpse of the Eiffel Tower, far more so than of another ironwork structure. It was said that Louis Armstrong's trumpet was simply an extension of his voice. The sound of the oboe is haunting and even melancholy because of its likeness to a singing human voice. Blues and greens are calming colors, largely because they are the colors of the natural environment. Red is exciting because it stands out against the sky and the green plants. Blue sugar water will not attract hummingbirds; it must be red.

But further, human desires are integrated in a way that animal desires are not. Every animal needs food, but human eating requires a setting that integrates human desires. The family meal, the romantic dinner by candlelight, the Thanksgiving feast are all to occur in appropriate settings to integrate the several values that transcend the mere intake of nourishment. A meal can be enhanced or ruined by values unrelated to the food. If the woman sitting in the restaurant rejects the ring and the proposal, the man may well neglect the rest of the food on his plate. Human consciousness is formed by values and knowledge that far transcend the immediate environment. This is why one may speak of the patriotic or proletarian consciousness. Consciousness is not a condition for human cognition but a consequence of cognition and will.

Consciousness and the self

Wojtyła further identifies a reflexive function of consciousness, that by which the subject is aware of his own "I" as subject of the experience and act. Reflexivity means the subject's natural turning toward himself so that he lives interiorly as subject.[14]

14 *Person and Act*, 142.

> We can say, thanks to this function of consciousness, that man exists "inwardly," as it were, and at the same time exists in the full dimension of his intellectual (rational!) being. [...] [I]t constitutes *the proper form of the human subject's actualization, which man owes precisely to consciousness.*[15]

By his reflexive consciousness the person identifies his acts and experiences as his own. We might say that they become part of his life story. For Searle's "silicon brain" this kind of consciousness is impossible—indeed, inconceivable. To be sure, a robot with artificial intelligence might well be programmed to maintain in its internal memory a record of its various encounters and responses to other things, but it does not preserve these as part of itself as a human does. It is unable to achieve an overview of any segment of its activity to determine its meaning or attend to its experience as such, because this would require a separate metaprocess to oversee the ongoing processes or operations. The machine can monitor its functioning, but it cannot supervene to interpret that functioning for itself, because this would amount to a reprogramming of itself.[16] After its first loss to Garry Kasparov in 1996 the IBM computer Deep Blue was not crushed and driven to self-examination to improve its game. (Its human managers, however, did reexamine the computer's program and further adapt it.) The human person, by contrast, recognizes certain experiences as important or even definitive for his own personal history. In the film *Gone with the Wind*, Scarlett O'Hara vows after the devastation of the Civil War never to be hungry again and structures her future according to that vow. She becomes aware of her recent past, reflects on her sufferings and values, and decides concerning her future.[17] By his reflexive consciousness the

15 Ibid., 146.

16 Adrian J. Reimers, "Truth and the Open-Endedness of the Natural Order," *Studies in Science and Theology*, (no. 1: 1995): 195.

17 Film *Gone with the Wind*. Director, Victor Flemin, 1939.

person experiences and makes his life his own. Consciousness does not govern one's life. Rather it reflects the willed governance of his life. Furthermore—and this is of especial importance today—the *self* cannot be discovered in consciousness. A person can survey his memories, but he cannot find his *self* as an element within consciousness.

Consciousness and freedom

We are conscious because we are free. The free act is one which arises from the person's intellect and will. Freedom is the capacity to love the good as known and to choose to act according to the good. The good may be some one thing strictly limited to the here and now—"I want *that* diamond"—but it will necessarily be related to a transcendent good, known according to truth. (The diamond is beautiful and manifests one's wealth and status to others.) Karol Wojtyła identifies this as "vertical transcendence," which "is connected with self-governance and self-possession as a specific structural property of the person."[18] Self-governance implies that one has a plan, a vision of reality and a system of values, by which he governs his life and himself. These are not given to him by consciousness but rather are known by reason as this is directed by the will. Confronted with the world before him and finding himself needing to act, the person is necessarily conscious of the world as the field in which he must act and of himself as the one to realize the plan or vision. This world—one might even say "life-world"—is defined or formed by one's values; it is not a realm of bare, value-free facts. And indeed, these values are not simply given in experience but are accepted or rejected by the person through his intellectual understanding. The principle that every human interaction constitutes a kind of economic exchange and that one does best to maximize his own profit from such an exchange may serve unconsciously as one's guiding value, but this principle itself can be discovered and either accepted or replaced.

18 *Person and Act*, 234.

With this the person is aware of his own moral responsibility. Even if he evades or tries to deny responsibility, it remains before him. Inevitably, he becomes ethically responsible for his life, confronted with moral norms which arise precisely because of his awareness of the truth about the good—or rather because he realizes that there is (or at least may be) a truth about the good. Wojtyła writes,

> The ethical norm [...] is nothing other than the objectification (and at the same time the concretization) of the truth about the good, of the good linked to a given action of the person, willed in it and realized in it. For precisely this reason the norm is something transcendent with respect to the action and its tension toward that which it contains, toward the objective value.[19]

The very fact that he is aware of the good, concerning which he can know the truth, creates for him a moral consciousness for which he is responsible.[20] The entirety of his consciousness is formed by this moral awareness. The person is conscious because he is free.

Efficacy

By his deliberate conscious act, the person attempts to make something happen, to change something real by exercising his own efficient causality. This is called *efficacy*. The moment of efficacy constitutes the decisive difference between "man acts" and

19 Karol Wojtyła, *L'uomo nel campo della responsabilità* [Man in the realm of responsibility] in K. Wojtyła, *Metafisica della persons* (Rome: Bompiani, 2003), 1269–70. Author's translation.

20 See William F. Murphy, "Reflections on Fundamental Morality, Conscience, Norms, and Discernment," in V. Paglia (editor), *Etica Teologica della Vita* (Vatican City: Libreria Editrice Vaticana, 2022), 217–43. We find in his article ambiguities about the notion of norm, which give rise to further ambiguities of moral judgments.

"what happens in man."[21] The experience of efficacy enables us to differentiate the human act from other forms of actuation or dynamization. In virtue of his efficacy the person cannot be conceived as pure subjectivity or consciousness. We may say that both consciousness and efficacy are the distinct experiential aspects of the human act. By his efficacy, the person not only creates something in the world, but in a way, creates himself.

> Man is not only the agent of his action but *also its creator*. The task of evoking the coming to existing and the existence of the effect belongs to the essence of efficacy. However, the task of forming a work belongs to the essence of creativity.[22]

It is in virtue of his efficacy that the act, and by it the agent himself, is morally determined as good or evil.

In *Person and Act*, Karol Wojtyła analyzes that perspective in terms of its subjectivity and its objectivity. The subjectivity of the act lies in consciousness. However, the act of the person is more than an event in consciousness. It is marked also by efficacy [*sprawczość*]. The acting person behaves—chooses his act and its execution—in order to effect something. As a datum to be analyzed phenomenologically, the human act is both conscious and efficacious. Hume, and implicitly materialists such as Sperry, find a great mystery in the notion of an interior act that gives rise to an exterior result, because there is no clear causal connection between a mental event—the thought "I will put water into the pan"—and the physical movement. A thought frequently does not issue in action. We may think of the skydiver's first jump as he tries to convince himself to leap. The only way he resolves the inner debate is by jumping. Wojtyła's point directly evades (and by doing so, addresses) this issue. The act is not an event in consciousness followed by a motion. It is simply a conscious act for some end.

21 *Person and Act*, 162.
22 Ibid., 171–72.

Materialist philosophy has a limited concept of causality. Contemporary materialists find the Aristotelian notion of *cause* puzzling, if not downright incoherent. For instance, Peter van Inwagen finds agent causality incomprehensible: "To me, the suggestion that an individual thing, as opposed to a *change* in an individual thing, could be the cause of a change is a mystery."[23] This is because in the mechanical system a cause is simply an interaction that precedes and influences another interaction. The cue ball colliding with the 7-ball transfers its momentum and moves it. At the heart of materialism lies a mechanistic conception of human nature, by which the human organism is conceived as a highly complex organic mechanism that interacts with other things according to invariant laws which in principle admit of precise formulation. Such a conception of causality simply eliminates the notion of *cause*. If every event is simply a phase in the operation of a machine nothing causes anything.

The efficacy of the person in act is his exercise of efficient causality. Wojtyła writes, "To be a cause means to evoke the coming into existence and the existence of an effect, its *fieri* and *esse*."[24] This is exactly what the acting person does; desiring some good, whether this be some new thing or some change in the world, he engages himself in the exterior order—that order exterior to his own mind—and sets himself to bring about that good. He is the agent and experiences himself as such. Therefore, he is a creator, and his creativity redounds upon himself.

> The task of evoking the coming to existing and the existence of the effect belongs to the essence of efficacy. However, the task of forming a work belongs to the essence of creativity.
>
> Human efficacy seems to be some creativity. *This is the*

23 Peter van Inwagen, *Metaphysics* (Boulder, San Francisco: Westview Press, 1993), 194.

24 *Person and Act*, 169.

> *creativity for which man himself is the first material. Man first of all shapes himself by action.*[25]

He is creator because the existence of the effect originates from himself and is realized by him.

> Creating as derived from thinking is so characteristic of a person that it is always an infallible sign of a person, a proof of a person's existence or presence: we create something either outside ourselves in the surrounding world or within ourselves—or outside and within ourselves at the same time.[26]

Therefore, by his act he also creates himself insofar as he determines himself. Rotating within the gearbox, the cog will slowly wear down, but it is not creating itself to be a worn cog. The human person's engagement in the act is only superficially like this. By his physical activity he may strengthen his muscles, but this is merely incidental. As the intelligent author of the act, he has become a creator in the fuller sense. He has determined how the world—"his" part of the world—is different and in conformity with his vision of a good world. He intends his act to realize the good. It is in virtue of this creativity that the person is a moral agent. He is not simply the agent whose acts result in good effects. Indeed, his factual ignorance or his lack of dexterity may even spoil the goodness of the act (or blunt the evil of a wrong act, as when a clumsy burglar sets off an alarm).

Wojtyła writes that the man shapes himself by his action. This can be understood in two ways, both of them true. By his actions the person shapes his character because repeated acts form or change habits. Aristotle taught this as a foundation of his account of virtue.[27] Performing virtuous acts reinforces one's virtue, and

25 Ibid., 172, 173.
26 Karol Wojtyła, "Thomistic Personalism" in *Person and Community* (New York, San Francisco: Peter Lang, 1993), 171.
27 Aristotle, *Nicomachean Ethics*, Book II.

the same holds for vicious acts. In this sense one can gradually become a better or a worse person. The second sense cuts deeper into the reality of the person. "Through his acts, through conscious action, man becomes good or evil, good or evil in the moral sense." Wojtyła continues:

> This becoming, the *fieri* of man in the moral sense, the *fieri* most closely connected with the person, *determines the realistic character of good and evil, of the moral values themselves.* By no means are they contents of consciousness alone; they are contents of human, personal *fieri*. Morality is the reality that belongs to the reality of human acts as a specific *fieri* of the subject—the deepest *fieri*, most essentially connected with both his nature, that is, his humanity, and the fact that he is a person.[28]

Wojtyła does not simply say that through his act the person sets himself on the path toward good or evil or predisposes himself to virtue or vice. Rather he *becomes* ["*fieri*" means "becoming"] good or evil. The root of this becoming (*fieri*) is his freedom. On April 14, 1865, John Wilkes Booth became a murderer. The following day he woke up different than he was the morning before. Although the assassination of Lincoln had been in his mind as he planned the shooting, by his own will he deliberately fired the pistol on that fateful evening. The killing of Abraham Lincoln was not something outside him. By his freedom he has dynamized himself, empowered and directed his being toward the values realized in his chosen act.

> However, the act—in relation to the causation of the person—contains the transcendence that passes into the immanence of the action itself, for action also consists in the dynamization of the subject. The dynamic transcendence

28 *Person and Act*, 202.

> of the person is based on freedom, which is absent in the causation of nature.[29]

The act—every human act—bears within it the seeds of the transcendent, and therefore the act has an eternal effect. The act stands in relation to the truth about the good and especially the perfect Good. This is the insight that theorists of the fundamental freedom, such as Karl Rahner, were doubtless looking for. To be sure, a person can change himself and the direction of his life. At some point, Judas turned away from Christ and hence from God. Ignatius of Loyola repudiated his nobility and soldiering to follow Christ. Conversion *is* possible, but it is hard because such radical conversion amounts to a fundamental change of the person himself.

The act bears the seeds of the transcendent because the act engages the eternal. This is evident from the simple fact that the intellect can grasp the eternal. Even if we cannot imagine eternity, we can understand the concept itself. We can define it and work with it. We know and argue on the basis that some principles are unchanging and eternal. One such notion is the principle of noncontradiction. Furthermore, we desire the eternal and unchanging good, even if we do not know what it is.[30] The "divine discontent" characteristic of human life arises from the fact that any created good—however wonderfully good it might be—turns out to be not quite good enough. We can always at least imagine how it might be better or what kind of good might be even higher. Because of this openness to the eternal (and to the infinite), no human act is merely a temporal, earthly event.

This is the reason that every act, every conscious action by which the person engages effectively with the world, is morally qualified. It is not merely one event among many. Rather it is the act of one who is a "partner of the Absolute."[31] By his acts,

29 Ibid., 204.
30 *Summa Theologiae,* Ia, IIae, q. 2, a. 8.
31 Theology of the Body, 151 (6:1).

therefore, the human person is engaged, however indirectly, with the Absolute who is Goodness itself. John Paul II writes,

> In order to be able to grasp the object of an act which specifies that act morally, it is therefore necessary to place oneself *in the perspective of the acting person.*[32]

This perspective is defined in *Person and Act* as Karol Wojtyła traces the interrelationship between the immediate consciousness and deliberate efficacy of the person as he dynamizes himself for an act.

Good and bad acts

The most controversial and hotly argued position in Pope John Paul II's *Veritatis Splendor* is that human persons can perform acts that are of themselves intrinsically evil. We will address this issue more fully in a subsequent chapter. Here we do well to consider the goodness and evil of human acts in general, starting with St. Thomas's account. Thomas begins by asking whether a human act can even be evil. Perhaps all human acts are fundamentally good simply in virtue of their being human acts. In one sense, simply to accomplish an act *is* a good thing. This is why wise parents let their children make mistakes. Thomas agrees with this, albeit cautiously. He relies on the basic principle that a thing produces the kind of action according to the kind of thing it is.

> We must therefore say that every action has goodness, in so far as it has being; whereas it is lacking in goodness, in so far as it is lacking in something that is due to its fullness of being; and thus it is said to be evil: for instance if it lacks the quantity determined by reason, or its due place, or something of the kind.[33]

32 *Veritatis Splendor*, §78.
33 *Summa Theologiae*, Ia, IIae q. 18, a. 1.

So, an act is bad insofar as it lacks something that it should have. There are various ways in which an act can lack its fullness of being, and not all of these constitute a moral evil, and St. Thomas summarizes these as follows:

> Accordingly a fourfold goodness may be considered in a human action. First, that which, as an action, it derives from its genus; because as much as it has of action and being so much has it of goodness, as stated above. Secondly, it has goodness according to its species; which is derived from its suitable object. Thirdly, it has goodness from its circumstances, in respect, as it were, of its accidents. Fourthly, it has goodness from its end, to which it is compared as to the cause of its goodness.[34]

An action derives goodness from its genus "as much as it has of action and being." We might say that an action is good generically to the extent that it is well executed. This means, in the first instance, that the agent be able to perform the act sufficiently well. The sniper is trained to perform the act of firing his rifle well, that is, in such a way that the bullet strikes the intended target. In this respect a shot is bad if the aim is poor, the handling of the rifle clumsy, or something similar. If someone wants to build, he must become proficient in (say) carpentry. Implicit here is the requirement that the acting person develop the proficiencies to accomplish his work.

That evil which is moral is derived from the object of the act, which does not refer to a physical object as such. The object of the act of stealing is not the money nor that of adultery the lover. Rather, the "object of the action" is its intended term. For instance, it is generally a good act to make use of what is one's own, but to take what belongs to another, without that person's consent, is the act of stealing. Therefore, stealing is a *kind* of act different than simply putting one's own money into his pocket.

34 Ibid., a. 4.

We can name several such categories: lying, adultery, murder, extortion. The object of the act is what the agent is attempting to do. A simple description of the physical action may well not suffice to account for the object of the act. On July 11, 1804, Aaron Burr and Alexander Hamilton met at dawn in an isolated place for a duel. Both men performed the act of firing their pistols. Burr aimed and shot well, wounding Hamilton mortally. As attested by his statements to others and the physical evidence, Hamilton deliberately fired badly and missed his opponent. Both men performed the same physical action—firing a pistol—but the objects of their respective acts were quite different. Burr attempted to kill his rival; that was the object of his act. To save his honor Hamilton performed the actions appropriate to participating in a duel, which included firing a pistol. His action was criminal under the law, which forbade dueling, and foolish, as it exposed him to unnecessary danger, but it was not an act of assault or intended murder. Similarly, a married couple engaging in sexual relations performs the same action as a prostitute and her customer, but the object is quite different. Husband and wife express and physically realize their conjugal union, while the prostitute engages in commercial exchange with a customer seeking venereal pleasure. This act is one of fornication or adultery. The object of the act is that which the agent is attempting to do by the act. The object of the act determines the species, the kind of act that it is: murder (Burr), upholding one's honor (Hamilton), conjugal intercourse, prostitution, or adultery.

Further light on this is shed by Thomas' analysis of the interior act of the will, what the acting person has decided upon interiorly prior to his act. One may have decided to kill his rival (perhaps by shooting him), not realizing that his intended victim is a dangerous enemy to his country. By his action he may be hailed as a hero who has saved the community from serious harm. Nevertheless, because his object was to kill a rival and not to disable an enemy, the object of his act remains as murder and not national defense. Thomas writes,

> Good and evil are essential differences of the act of the will. Because good and evil of themselves regard the will; just as truth and falsehood regard reason; the act of which is divided essentially by the difference of truth and falsehood, for as much as an opinion is said to be true or false. Consequently good and evil will are acts differing in species. Now the specific difference in acts is according to objects, as stated above (I-II:18:5). Therefore good and evil in the acts of the will is derived properly from the objects.[35]

The object of the will is the good in general,[36] and it is because of this that the act of the will is good or evil. When directed to what is not the good which is known by reason, then the will is evil. In the example of Aaron Burr's duel, to kill one's rival is murder, which reason identifies as an evil act.

It follows that an evil act derives no goodness from circumstances, although these circumstances can make an act bad. The Scriptures tell us, "He who blesses his neighbor with a loud voice, rising early in the morning, will be counted as cursing" (Proverbs 27:14). To bless someone is a good act, but the circumstances of the loud voice and the time of day make it bad. However, the circumstance that a personal rival is also an enemy to the nation does not redeem the murderous act from its wickedness.

Neither does an act whose object is evil become good because of its effects. To have sexual relations with one other than one's spouse is adultery; this is the object of that act. Thomas points out that this act may even result in a great good, namely the generation of a human being. However, this generation is a result of the natural goodness inherent to the act of sexual union, not of the reason by which this particular action was chosen and guided.

The fourth point is particularly tricky: "Whether a human act is good or evil from its end."[37] We ask whether the end justifies

35 *Summa Theologiae* Ia, IIae q.19, a.1.

36 *Summa Theologiae* Ia, IIae, q. 1, a. 2 ad 3.

37 *Summa Theologiae* Ia, IIae q. 18, a. 4.

the means. St. Thomas puts the issue sharply in the third objection.

> Further, a good action may happen to be ordained to an evil end, as when a man gives an alms from vainglory; and conversely, an evil action may happen to be ordained to a good end, as a theft committed in order to give something to the poor. Therefore an action is not good or evil from its end.[38]

On the one hand, Aquinas maintains that the goodness of an act depends on the end. If the end is bad, such as exalting oneself in vainglory, then the act, even if it be good in its species, is bad, as the example of giving alms illustrates. This is consonant with St. Thomas' fundamental premise, that the moral life is ordered by its ultimate end.[39] An end or purpose contrary to the ultimate end is in that respect bad. However, as Thomas' own example indicates, the specific goodness of an act is not lost if the end is evil. To give alms to the poor *is* good. The poor are benefitted and by the example of one person others may be inspired also to give alms. However, the actor himself has not done well; he has not acted well, because he has acted for vainglory. The problem is not with what he did but rather with the end for which he did it.

The more difficult and controversial question is whether a good end justifies an act that in its species is evil, that is, whose object is evil. Thomas gives the example of theft committed in order to alleviate the lot of the poor. This might be called the "Robin Hood" justification of theft.[40] Even if the poor do benefit and a more just distribution of wealth be established in Nottingham, the agent has performed an act of theft. He has no warrant

38 Ibid., a. 4 obj. 3.

39 *Summa Theologiae*, Ia, Iae qq. 4, 6.

40 I put the name in quotes in order not to refer to the historical character, who may, according to some of my friends, have had legal warrant to usurp the authority of the Sheriff of Nottingham.

to appropriate the possessions of others. We may also consider the example of the spy who, to serve her country and save the lives of many soldiers, seduces an enemy operative to get information from him.[41] If it is justifiable to kill an enemy soldier in war, might it not be all the more justifiable to sleep with one?

Let us dwell briefly on this issue. In support of this principle, one may be tempted to appeal to a Kantian or even utilitarian argument (paradoxically, the two become very close here), maintaining that success of a "Robin Hood" undermines economic justice in the long run or that the seducing spy may well harden herself against truly loving another. These may be valid points, but Thomas' argument rests not on these but on the fact that these acts, which are wrong according to their species, are contrary to reason and therefore violate the natural law. And for its part the natural law is a participation in the eternal law, which is God's plan for the government of his creation.[42] In other words, such an act is contrary to God's providence, as we shall see subsequently.

A further and rather subtle point that we must address is Thomas' distinction of the interior and the exterior act of the will.

> Now, in a voluntary action, there is a twofold action, viz. the interior action of the will, and the external action: and each of these actions has its object. The end is properly the object of the interior act of the will: while the object of the external action, is that on which the action is brought to bear. Therefore just as the external action takes its species from the object on which it bears; so the interior act of the will takes its species from the end, as from its own proper object.[43]

41 Thinking of Mata Hari, I use the feminine pronoun here, but male spies have also cynically used seduction.

42 Martin Rhonheimer, *The Perspective of the Acting Person: Essays is the Renewal of Thomistic Moral Philosophy* (Washington, DC: 2008), 208.

43 *Summa Theologiae*, Ia, IIae, q. 18, a. 6.

To illustrate he quotes Aristotle's comment from the *Ethics*: "He who steals that he may commit adultery, is strictly speaking, more adulterer than thief."[44] Formally, the act is considered in terms of the end, but materially in terms of the object of the external act. The interior act of the will is what the agent hopes to realize: in Aristotle's example the seduction of another's wife, in the "Robin Hood" case the alleviation of the lot of the poor. Theft in the service of adultery remains evil, because both the end and the physical act are evil. In the "Robin Hood" case, however, the end is good, but the object of the act is an evil, theft. The good end does not suffice to justify the theft, because stealing is not intrinsically ordered to giving alms. The agent in such a case cannot even be said to give alms. Rather he is transferring money to which he holds no title to those in need of it. Should he sell something of his own or do some paid work, then he would have something of his own to give. In short, the will, whose object is universal good, cannot realize that good by choosing specifically evil acts to attain it.

Evil

After all this, the question of evil remains. Even if we acknowledge that the acts of the seductive spy constitute adultery or that the Robin Hood character commits robbery (indeed, armed robbery), we are inclined to excuse their acts precisely because of the good purposes that they serve. If moral evil falls under the judgment of the Almighty such that one who performs such a deed and dies unrepentant will be cast into the everlasting fire prepared for the devil and his angels (Matt 25:41), then how can such acts that are performed clearly for the good of others be evil? Can we not acknowledge the good in such a person whose acts, though technically evil, have been done with good intent and for good results? Let us consider two related literary examples concerning the same person: Shakespeare's *Julius Caesar*, and Dante's *Divine Comedy*.

44 Aristotle, *Nicomachean Ethics*, V, 2 1130a24.

In Shakespeare's play, Brutus, who planned the assassination of Julius Caesar and delivered the final thrust with his dagger, is called the "noblest Roman of them all."

> All the conspirators save only he
> Did that they did. In envy of great Caesar;
> he only in general honest thought
> and common good to all, made one of them.[45]

Brutus acted to save Rome from tyranny, and for this even his enemy, Antony, praises his nobility. But Dante places Brutus at the lowest place in hell. As the penalty for his betrayal not only of a friend but of the ruler of the realm, he is condemned to be gnawed forever in Satan's maw.[46] The difference between these two great works[47] illustrates the issue at hand.

One might argue that Shakespeare's Brutus, an "honorable man," can be faulted for his misjudgment that plunged Rome into civil war, but this error hardly warrants endless punishment in the teeth of Satan. After all, his intention was to save the Roman republic from dictatorship. Dante looks at something beyond the political and social effects of the assassination. He sees Brutus' killing as a betrayal of a personal friend and rightful ruler of the realm, a grievously wicked act deserving of condemnation. Because God gave life to Caesar, it is the responsibility of every other human being to love him. The natural law that is written on every human heart makes clear that murder is wrong. Caesar was ambitious and conducted wars against other peoples, wars that were arguably unjust. A Gallic ruler would indeed be justified in fighting to repel Rome's attempt to conquer his lands. Caesar may

45 William Shakespeare, *Julius Caesar* Act V, scene V, 68–72.

46 Dante Alighieri, *Inferno*, trans. Allen Mandelbaum (New York: Bantam Books, 1980), Canto XXXIV, 64–66.

47 Of course, both *Julius Caesar* and *Inferno* are artistic creations, not treatises, and as such reflect the artistic aims of their respective authors.

have had ambitions to become dictator in Rome. However, Brutus chose to be the cause of Caesar's death. Even if he conceived the murder as an act of patriotism to Rome, it was not an act of love for Caesar. Rather, Brutus determined that Caesar must lose his life and at Brutus' hand in the Senate on the Ides of March. Because Brutus has deprived his victim of his own life, which God had given to *him*, Dante identifies his act as damnable. We may talk about Caesar's transformational role in history, the wars he fought and the booty he won at the expense of other peoples. We may recognize his ambition and (if Shakespeare's portrayal is accurate) his bombastic vanity. We may even speculate on the unfolding of Roman history had Caesar lived. But these are irrelevant to the moral issue, which is that by directly killing Caesar Brutus performed an act that cannot be conformed to the will and love of God. This is why his act was wicked, damnable. Concerning Brutus we must agree with Dante.

CONSCIENCE

The relationship between truth and law, on the one hand, and human freedom, on the other, is a tortured one, especially in the period after Vatican II. Law, together with an insistence on absolute or certain truth, seems to constitute a restraint on freedom. To insist on law and its prerogatives is to constrain others and to limit their freedom. At the center of this debate is the issue of conscience as the touchstone of moral reflection. Is not conformity to one's conscience, rather than conformity to external law, the authentic standard of morality?

Tradition and the Council

St. Thomas Aquinas on conscience

> For the name "conscience" [*conscientia*] means the application of knowledge to something. Hence to be conscious [*conscire*] means to know together. [...] Hence conscience cannot denote a special habit or power, but designates the act itself, which is the application of any habit or of any act to some particular act.[1]

In general, *conscientia* is the application of knowledge to an act. When thinking of the application of practical knowledge to an act, we use the English term *consciousness*.[2] Moral conscience is

1 Thomas Aquinas, *Disputed Questions on Truth* (Chicago: Henry Regnery, 1951), henceforth *De Veritate*, q. 17, a. 1. See also *Summa Theologiae*, Ia q. 79, a. 13.

2 Adrian J. Reimers, *The Soul of the Person* (Washington, DC: The Catholic University of America Press, 2006), 172.

the application of one's knowledge of the truth about the good. Prior to the act, conscience can advise for or against performing the act, and afterward stands as either rebuke or approval of the act.

Particularly important is that St. Thomas denies that conscience is a special power (or faculty) that can be counterpoised to the faculty of reason. Although often represented as a *voice*, conscience is nothing more than the person's knowledge of the truth in relation to a proposed or accomplished act. Therefore, the "pangs of conscience" are the feelings of guilt that arise from the awareness (consciousness) that one has acted against the good that he knows. An examination of conscience prior to the act is an intellectual inquiry into the end of the act and the act's consonance with the authentic or honest good.

This becomes clearer if we consider cases where one might appropriately advise, "Let your conscience be your guide." Generally, Christians are called to be merciful to those who are suffering and to alleviate their lot by contributing money to their cause. However, the question arises how much one ought to contribute and through what channels (whether directly to specific poor persons, some charitable institution, or a church's outreach ministry). The "conscience" in this case is a prudential judgment based on a rational analysis of the various factors involved—the wealth of the giver, the situation of the recipients, the effectiveness of the charitable agencies, and so on. The obligation to show mercy to the poor is not in question, but only the variety of ways in which that obligation can be discharged. The guidance that conscience is encouraged to give is to be based on a judgment of prudence.

A juridical notion of conscience is the application of law to a particular case. Before me lies property that belongs to another. Recognizing this fact, I remember the seventh commandment and apply this law. In conscience, therefore, I am bound not to take it for my own. The traveler comes across a man bloodied and beaten by robbers. Recalling that Jesus commands us to love our neighbor, he stops, bandages the victim's wounds, and takes him to an appropriate care facility. He is bound in conscience to show mercy to this victim.

As the application of knowledge to the act, conscience is far more than simply a mental reflection by which an imperative is mentally compared with a course of action, as though having seen a victim of robbers beaten and bloodied by the side of the road, the Samaritan (or the priest or the Levite) surveys his memory of what God commands concerning love of neighbor and recognizes that he is bound to act. The situation of the victim is not a bare fact, to which one might ascribe a value, but is encountered as laden with value. The act does not stand alone, in a vacuum, as it were, but in relation to higher goods. The decision to act is more than a response to a good desired here and now. Rather, because the person is ordered to the good as such—the good known in truth—the decision to act "is like the threshold through which the person as such goes out toward the good."[3] The behavior of the acting person is governed by his conception of the good as such, by the universal good.

Concerning the good as such, St. Thomas writes,

> Now, that man is capable of the Perfect Good, is proved both because his intellect can apprehend universal and perfect good [*apprehendere potest universale et perfectum bonum*], and because his will can desire it.[4]

In this text, St. Thomas does not argue that the person knows precisely what the perfect good is. Rather one apprehends "universal and perfect good"; he can make sense of the *ratio* or the notion of good. Furthermore, he is capable of desiring and acting for the universal and perfect good, whatever that may be. This is clear from the simple fact that concerning *any* good he can question first, whether there might be a higher good, and second, what is the objective basis for this good—what the principle of its goodness is.

3 *Person and Act*, 225, 230.

4 *Summa Theologiae* Ia, IIae q. 5, a. 1.

His task, therefore, is to determine as best he can—and for this Divine Revelation is a decisive help—what that universal and perfect good is. His conception of that good, even if vague and indefinite, determines his conception of the various finite goods that he may encounter and choose among. Saint Augustine testifies to this in his own life. Immersed in the life of pleasures, he grew dissatisfied and sought his happiness in pursuit of wisdom, first in Manicheism and then in pagan philosophy. By an immense mental effort and by the grace of God, he found the highest good in God himself.[5] Or as Plato puts it,

> Every soul pursues the good and does whatever it does for its sake. It divines that the good is something but it is perplexed and cannot grasp what it is or acquire the sort of stable beliefs it has about other things [...].[6]

It is against this background and within the context of one's own understanding of the good and its demands, that one acts and is conscious of the moral value of his acts.

Vatican II and subsequent controversies

> In the depths of his conscience, man detects a law which he does not impose upon himself, but which holds him to obedience. Always summoning him to love good and avoid evil, the voice of conscience when necessary speaks to his heart: do this, shun that. For man has in his heart a law written by God; to obey it is the very dignity of man; according to it he will be judged. Conscience is the most secret core and sanctuary of a man. There he is alone with God, Whose voice echoes in his depths. In a wonderful manner conscience reveals that law which is fulfilled by love of God and neighbor.[7]

5 Augustine of Hippo, *Confessions* (New York: Image Books, 1960).

6 Plato, *Republic*, VII 505e.

7 *Gaudium et Spes*, §16.

Following the Council, however, the notion of conscience became problematic. How can conscience, which is the *proximate* norm for morality and as such necessarily subjective, be subject to law exterior to the person? Charles Curran writes,

> The dilemma of conscience recognizes that I must follow my sincere conscience, but my conscience can be wrong. How can I be sure that my conscience is not wrong? There are no criteria that can give an infallible answer. [...] Many different criteria have been proposed down through the years, but the most adequate criterion in my judgment is the peace and joy of a good conscience. [...] In the approach developed here, the primary emphasis is on the knowing subject. [...] Such primacy does not reject the importance of the objective, but the ultimate criterion for judgment comes from the subjective.[8]

If "conscience is the most secret core and sanctuary of a man" where he is alone with God, then how can an "external" authority determine its obligations? Curran clearly believes that ultimately it cannot. He writes elsewhere:

> For moral maturity one must be one's own person. It is not enough to follow what one has been told. The morally mature person must be able to perceive, choose, and identify oneself with what one does. In short, we create our character and give our lives meaning by committing our freedom, not by submitting it to someone in authority [...]. As long as we do not direct our own activity, we are not yet free, morally mature persons.[9]

8 Charles Curran, "Conscience in the Light of Catholic Moral Tradition" in C. Curran, *Conscience: Readings in Moral Theology No. 14* (New York: Paulist Press, 2004), 18, 58.

9 Charles Curran, *Conscience: Readings in Moral Theology No. 14*, 58.

Noteworthy here are Curran's personalist criteria. He speaks of being one's own person and morally mature, indeed, of creating our character and giving our lives meaning. The touchstone of the rightness of one's moral decision is not conformity with some external standard but rather the agent's interior "peace and joy." If one is not autonomously directing his own activity, then he is not truly free and morally mature. So, according to Richard P. McBrien, "Conscience is the *radical experience of ourselves as moral agents*."[10] Particularly important here is that obedience to external authority is contrasted with the authentic exercise of conscience, by which the person gives his life meaning by his commitment of his freedom.

Under such a conception, the teaching authority of the Church can be only advisory. Advocates of this position acknowledge that the Church, which has existed for two thousand years and whose scope is international and trans-cultural, has resources of memory and experience far beyond those of any individual person or group. As such, the Church's pronouncements should be taken seriously by the Christian. Nevertheless, they cannot be binding. The individual Christian believer, relying on what he takes to be the voice of conscience, is the ultimate judge of how he should behave, of the right course of action.

The problem is that in conscience both the objective and the subjective are at stake in conceivably contradictory ways. Some actions seem to be clearly and objectively wrong; consider the torture and murder of children. On the other hand, one sometimes seems to be obliged to perform acts that his conscience tells him are wrong. As Curran writes, "The dilemma of conscience recognizes that I must follow my sincere conscience but my conscience can be wrong." For instance, we cannot rightly condemn the terrorist for obeying the will of Allah by bombing a crowd of civilians in a restaurant. Or to move to the realm of sexual morality, the adulterous couple feel almost compelled by the power of their

10 Richard P. McBrien, *Catholicism*, New Edition (New York: HarperCollins, 1994), 969.

desire to move beyond convention and rules to the full expression of their love. The old cliché has it: "How could anything so wrong be so right?" As Curran suggests, we seem unable to determine when our own conscience is ill-formed and when not.

Here we do well to consider the elements of the characterization of conscience from *Gaudium et Spes*. According to the Council, in conscience one "detects a law which he does not impose upon himself, but which holds him to obedience." That is, conscience is different from the will or one's interior sentiments and desires. Conscience detects a law that is separate from himself but to which he is subject. Furthermore, "Conscience summons him to love good and avoid evil; when necessary it speaks to his heart: do this, shun that." This requirement presupposes that one can recognize good and evil and further that he is free to choose one over the other.

"For man has in his heart a law written by God; to obey it is the very dignity of man; according to it he will be judged." Here is the most serious issue. The next sentence explains: "Conscience is the most secret core and sanctuary of a man. There he is alone with God, Whose voice echoes in his depths." We may—indeed, must—ask how this law is written on the person's heart. In what way is one alone with God? The Council does not mean that every moral decision is accompanied by a mystical encounter with the Almighty, that to decide aright one needs supernatural revelation. Writing after the Council, Karol Wojtyła clarifies this by relating conscience to personal responsibility, which is always "responsibility 'to somebody,' thus to a person."[11] Wojtyła goes on to argue that within the religious context, "the responsibility 'to somebody' acquires the meaning of religious responsibility to God."[12] In this case, "human conscience [...] acquires a particular authority. This authority permits us to think and speak of conscience as the voice of God himself." The point is precisely that confronted with the issue of doing good

11 *Person and Act*, 274.
12 Ibid.

or evil, one is confronted, even if only obscurely, with God, to whom he is personally responsible.[13]

We read that conscience is the most secret core and sanctuary of a person. The person's behavior, his choice of acts is his alone, arising from within himself and not from some other source. In this secret core, the person is alone with God. As he considers his acts, he must rely ultimately on his own grasp of the truth about the good. To be sure, he may surrender to inner desires, but he does so in the (at least implicit) awareness that he has chosen to do so. That which one holds to be the definitive source of truth and the standard of goodness is what he takes to be God. Within this "core and sanctuary" one wrestles with himself to discern the law of God.

We must be careful here to avoid a simplistic interpretation that can lead to a kind of mystical infallibilism of conscience, as though if one listens hard enough or approaches moral matters is just the right way, he can determine what exactly God wants. In all innocence one can fail to recognize the good. The point is that in conscience he is engaged in dialogue with God as he knows him. We can see this in the case of Socrates when he relates his conviction that he must obey the god (possibly Apollo) and not abandon his vocation.[14]

What then is this law that he finds written on his heart? If it is the law based on the requirement to seek and do good and avoid evil, then it is the natural law. According to St. Thomas, the natural law is the human being's participation in the eternal law of God.

> But the rational creature is subject to God's providence in a more excellent way than other things, since such a creature also shares in God's providence in providing for itself and others. And so it shares in the eternal plan

13 See John Henry Newman, *An Essay in Aid of a Grammar of Assent* (Garden City, NY: Image Books, 1955), 97.

14 Plato, *Apology*, 28e–29b.

> whereby it has its natural inclination to its requisite activity and end. And we call such participation in the eternal law by rational creatures the natural law.[15]

John Paul II: Conscience and the heart

The person is a spiritual being, one whose life "focuses on truth and the good. It also deals with a multitude of problems: it seems that the most central of these are the following two: what is the final cause of everything, and how to be good and possess the fullness of the good."[16] This means that the life of the human being is formed by spiritual, and not only material, factors. This is not to deny that the body's reactivity to environmental factors can be disregarded. Reactivity is a property of the body as a body.[17] However, contrary to the materialist position, reactivity does not of itself determine human behavior, much less human life. Rather, ethics is central to the study of man. The special sciences—biology, psychology, sociology, etc.—fail to suffice for an adequate anthropology, because the factors upon which these sciences depend are physical, material. Man is a person—an individual substance of a rational nature—and as such he lives from his interiority, which is constituted by intellect and will. We identify this interiority with the heart.

Conscience, truth, and duty

By his free acts the person exteriorizes himself. Karol Wojtyła writes:

> To be free means not only to *will*, but also to *choose* and to *decide*, and this already suggests a transcendent subordination of the good to the true in action. Conscience, however, is the proper place for this subordination. The

15 *Summa Theologiae* Ia, IIae q.91, a. 2.
16 *Love and Responsibility*, 5.
17 *Person and Act*, 316–317.

> person's authentic transcendence in action is realized in conscience, and the *actus humanus* takes shape as the willing and choosing of a "true good" thanks to conscience.[18]

By his acts the person exteriorizes himself. In this rich text. the point is that the human person is not compelled by his *wants* or *desires*. In *Person and Act,* Wojtyła argues at length that the human act transcends what "happens in a man," that which is beyond the control of the will. The person's freedom means that he is capable of self-determination. The experience, "I can, but I do not have to," marks the characteristic discovery of freedom.[19] Wants and desires occur as events that may happen in a person, and one might respond to them by acting. Because decision is for one known or cognized good among several alternatives, Karol Wojtyła argues that it is the dependence on truth that makes the will independent from its objects.

A person acts when he engages his efficacy by his will. Efficacy refers to the person's engagement with the world by exercising his own efficient causality. It is the experience of being the agent.[20] As such, he is responsible for the act and is therefore morally responsible. The act is therefore different from anything that merely *happens* in the man. The experience, "I can, but I do not have to," is the moment of freedom, the characteristic discovery of freedom.[21] The person may want or desire, but to act he must also choose and decide. For an animal, action follows directly upon desire, but the person acts upon decision. Because decision is for one recognized alternative among several, Karol Wojtyła argues that this "already suggests a transcendent subordination of the good to the true in action."[22]

18 Karol Wojtyła, "Person: Subject and Community" in K. Wojtyła, *Person and Community: Selected Essays*, 234.

19 Ibid., 203.

20 *Person and Act*, 168.

21 Ibid., 203.

22 Ibid.

With Thomas Aquinas, Karol Wojtyła accepts the Boethian definition of the person as an individual substance of a rational nature. We note that the authors of the Pontifical Academy for Life text *Etica teologica della vita* find this definition to be inadequate, preferring instead the notion of person as relational. They write, "A hermeneutic of the person in terms of freedom-in-relation represents a definitive surpassing of the traditional notion of the person as *rationalis naturae individua substantia*."[23] This rejection of Boethius' definition is tendentious, because the capacity of the human person for relations with other is founded precisely on her interiority by which she can enter into relation with others. Wojtyła argues that because of his rational nature the person necessarily lives from the interior, from reason.[24] By the power of reason, the person can know truth and form his acts and himself in truth. Although the object of a desire is a good of some sort, desire is of itself incapable of determining the truth of the good. Reason—and only reason—can recognize truth. Wojtyła writes, "Truth is in man a function and a task of reason."[25] And further on:

> Man possesses reason not first and foremost so that he can calculate the maximum of pleasure in his life, but above all so that he can know the objective truth, ground the principles possessing the absolute meaning (norms) in that truth, and in turn live by them.[26]

Therefore, to know the truth about the good, it is necessary to transcend the realm of sense experience to that governed by reason and understanding. The normative power of truth is rooted

23 Vincenzo Paglia, (ed) *Etica teologica della vita: Scrittura, tradizione, sfide pratiche* (Vatican City: Librería Editrice Vaticana, 2022), 183.

24 Karol Wojtyla, *Love and Responsibility* (Boston: Pauline books & Media, 2013), 4.

25 Ibid., 61.

26 Ibid., 225.

in the intellect. By his intellect, the human person can think and understand over an infinite range. *Intellectus est quodammodo omnia.*[27]

The intellect is subordinate to truth, which is the end or purpose of intellect, standing beyond subjectivity. If as St. Thomas Aquinas argues, truth is the adequation of intellect to thing (*adequaetio res et intellectus*),[28] then truth cannot be created by the mind. To be sure, the mind must attain to truth and possess it, and one's ability to attain to and perceive truth may be conditioned by his experiences. Furthermore, the attainment of understanding changes or—more accurately—forms the intellect. Truth is in this respect is possessed subjectively.

In our age, the most serious question is whether there is a truth about *good*. Ever since David Hume raised the sharp challenge that from a fact one cannot infer a value— "is" cannot imply "ought"—philosophers and undergraduates alike have been stymied by the apparently inexorable logic of this principle. Indeed, many contemporary moral theologians continue to insist on a sharp distinction between fact-concepts (*Tatsachenbegriffe*) and value-concepts (*Wertbegriffe*).[29] Karol Wojtyła addresses this issue.

> It is in conscience that the particular *linking of truthfulness with duty takes place, linking that is manifested as the normative power of truth.* The human person in his every act is an eyewitness of the transition from "is" to "should": from "*x* is truly good" to "I should perform x."[30]

27 *De Veritate,* q. 1, a. 1; Aristotle and Aquinas, *Commentary on De Anima* (New Haven: Yale University Press, 1951), 431b21; §787; *Person and Act,* 260.

28 *De Veritate,* q.1, a. 1.

29 Richard A. McCormick, S.J., *The Critical Calling: Reflections on Moral Dilemmas Since Vatican II* , 58.

30 *Person and Act,* 264.

His point here is the simple but inevitable consequence of the nature of human acting. Underlying Hume's argument is a conception of the person as a mere observer of facts and not an efficacious agent. However, whenever a person acts, he acts for some good.[31] One cannot act without intending some end, which he takes to be a good according to some standard that preexists his choice. This standard (principle) is called a *norm*. A norm is a truth about the good, which conscience can recognize. And further:

> Duty—that is, the normative power of truth in the person, most closely connected with conscience—attests to the fact that the person in action is free.[32]

Through his acts, the human person realizes himself as a specific someone. Certainly, this is evident on the horizontal plane, as by his acts one makes oneself into an accountant, a pianist, a farmer. More significantly, by his acts the person realizes in himself the values to which he is drawn, from which there arises a certain imperative: To realize this value, do this. This demonstrates his transcendence and the responsibility for his own self-realization and self-fulfillment. Faced with Scarpio's lustful advances, Puccini's Tosca sings: "I have lived for art; I have lived for love. Never have I done evil to a living soul." The beauty of art and love for others formed Tosca's life and behavior. She tried to relieve the unfortunate. She made beautiful music for heaven. She decorated the altar of the Virgin. In this plea to God, which the aria purports to be, she presents to God the person she has become. She argues, in effect, that her life deserves better than that she be raped by the villain.[33] Conscience is the awareness of

31 Thomas Aquinas, *Summa Theologiae* Ia, IIae q. 1, a.1; *Commentary on the Nicomachean Ethics* (Chicago: Henry Regnery Company, 1964), 5, 8.

32 Ibid., 268.

33 Giacomo Puccini, Aria "Vissi d'arte" in opera *Tosca*. Downloaded January 19, 2023 from https://www.opera-arias.com/puccini/tosca/vissi-

one's obligation not only to perform or to avoid a particular act, but to realize certain goods in one's self. Since self-determination is the sign and basis of freedom, the person makes herself to be good or evil in her acts.

> The point here is not only the objective truthfulness of the norms *in abstracto* but also *the lived experience of this truthfulness, which is expressed by the conviction, that is, by a subjective certitude*, that this or that norm indicates a true good.[34]

We must note Wojtyła's understanding of the concept of norm. In both his philosophical writings and in his pastoral works as pope he understands *norm* as some *truth about the good* and not as a rule or law. From a moral norm, a truth, one can infer an imperative or law. For instance, from the personalistic norm that a person is not an object for use but rather a good to be loved, we can infer the Gospel commandment to love.[35] Wojtyła writes, "norm, in the most general sense of the term, is the name we give to a principle of moral good and evil."[36] The norm is a truth about some good. Therefore, although an imperative may admit of exceptions—killing is prohibited but may be allowable in self-defense—the norm, which is a truth—a person is possessed of inherent dignity as a child of God—is always and everywhere true. The fundamental moral obligation or duty is therefore to live in and act according to truth. This distinction is notably important when we consider the question of divorce and remarriage. The ground for

d%27arte-vissi-d%27amore/. We may acknowledge, however, that the Puccini heroine's impetuous jealousy brought her and her beloved to their tragic end.

34 *Person and Act*, 266.

35 *Love and Responsibility*, 25.

36 Karol Wojtyła. "The Problem of the Theory of Morality," in K. Wojtyła *Person and Community*, 139; *L'uomo nel campo della responsibilit* in *Metafisica della persona*, 1272; A. J. Reimers, *The Truth about the Good*, 148.

the prohibition of remarriage after divorce is the truth that a valid marriage is indissoluble, not simply according to law, but according to the very nature of marriage itself.[37]

Experience of guilty conscience

The problem of the guilty conscience, which is particularly relevant to our concerns here—are feelings of guilt a pathology to be remedied or manifestations of some neurosis? Karol Wojtyła writes:

> The experience of guilt is in its essential core an experience of moral evil. This evil is contained in a human act, in a conscious and free action whose author is a human being—or, one could say, a concrete human self.[38]

In his apostolic letter on suffering John Paul II illuminates and verifies this: "It can be said that man suffers whenever *he experiences any kind of evil.*"[39] Arising precisely as an effect of the efficacy of the person, guilt is the experience of the evil of one's own acts. Efficacy is far more than the ability effectively to change things in the world beyond one's subjectivity. Through his act, the human being creates himself.[40] Therefore the pangs of guilt reflect the harm one has done to his own self by violating a norm of morality.[41]

Unlike other evils that may afflict a person—pain resulting from injury to the body, bitterness from failure to accomplish a goal, or even despair of finding some meaning in one's life[42]—moral evil affects the entire person *as person,* because moral evil

37 John Paul II, Theology of the Body, 112–13.

38 Karol Wojtyła, "The Problem of the Theory of Morality," 137.

39 John Paul II, Apostolic Letter *Salvifici Doloris* (Vatican City: Libreria Editrice Vaticana, 1984), §7.

40 *Person and Act,* 173.

41 Karol Wojtyła, *Sign of Contradiction* (New York, The Seabury Press, 1979), 168.

42 Adrian J. Reimers, "Human Suffering and John Paul II's Theology of the Body," *Nova et Vetera,* (2: 2: 2004): 447–48.

entails the disintegration of the person in his self-determination.[43] To be sure, the victim of severe burns or the recently widowed wife who finds herself alone feels an immediate pain that cannot be easily alleviated, whereas the grave sinner (think of Macbeth or Michael Corleone[44] after committing their respective murders) may not immediately be consciously aware of the harm they have done to themselves. However, both Shakespeare's play and Coppola's movies illustrate artistically the spiritual disintegration of the respective killers. It is also worth noting at this point that one may feel unnecessary pangs of conscience for violating some expectation not based on an authentic good. This could be as trivial as failing adequately to support the sports team of one's alma mater or more substantially by changing one's political allegiance. Such pangs are real but not justified, because no genuine good is at stake but only a social, familial, or personal expectation. Conscience cannot ultimately rest on emotional feelings but only on the truth about the good.

Ethos and the "heart"

With these considerations we arrive at John Paul II's concept of the *heart*, which develops his teaching on conscience. Here we return to St. Thomas' definition of conscience as the application of knowledge to the law. Knowledge is not simply a collection of facts and rules that one may access as a computer accesses its memory files. Rather, knowledge is held in the intellect through understanding and memory. Here we consider a pertinent objection to Aquinas' definition of conscience, specifically that conscience is a kind of power or faculty. The objection reads,

> [Conscience] is not an act; for thus it would not always exist in man. Nor is it a habit; for conscience is not one thing but many, since we are directed in our actions by many habits of knowledge.

43 *Person and Act*, 298–302.

44 In Francis Ford Coppola's *Godfather* film trilogy.

Therefore conscience is a power.

To which St. Thomas replies:

> Although an act does not always remain in itself, yet it always remains in its cause, which is power and habit. Now all the habits by which conscience is formed, although many, nevertheless have their efficacy from one first habit, the habit of first principles, which is called "synderesis." *And for this special reason, this habit is sometimes called conscience.*[45]

The objection is that conscience seems to abide in a person as a kind of power. In his reply, St. Thomas observes that the act is always present in its cause, which abides in the agent as power and habit. The person's habits form the conscience. One who, as Aristotle observes, is well brought-up by his parents will be virtuous and have a well-formed conscience. However, defects in his upbringing will affect the knowledge and habits on which the conscience is based. Therefore, the scion of a slaveholder in the antebellum American South, a faithful son reared to respect his father and his values, will likely accept as true and good the values that underlie the slaveholding society. The habits formed in youth or in response to teaching and social conditioning constitute the "voice" of conscience, the experience of conscience urging one to this or that course of action. Therefore, although Aquinas identifies conscience with the act and not as a faculty, he provides an account by which the experience of conscience as an inner power is explained. The result of the habits one has formed, conscience can be said to abide within the person as a voice judging his acts.

The term "heart" does not often appear in Karol Wojtyła's writings. It is in his papal writings that we find him regularly using the concept of heart. Pope John Paul II frequently cites St.

45 *Summa Theologiae*, Ia q.79, a. 13 obj 3, and reply ad 3. Emphasis added.

Augustine's dichotomy between love of God to the contempt of self and, by contrast, love of self to the contempt of God.[46] The person who is formed by the love of God has necessarily adopted a different system of values from one who is formed for love of self. We may call this system of interiorized values an *ethos*,[47] and one's *ethos* is what forms his heart.

The importance of these concepts of *ethos* and heart lies in the fact that one's acts arise from a common source. Consider Plato's "democratic man":

> And so he lives on, yielding day by day to the desire at hand. Sometimes he drinks heavily while listening to the flute; at other times, he drinks only water and is on a diet; sometimes he goes in for physical training; at other times, he's idle and neglects everything; and sometimes he even occupies himself with what he takes to be philosophy. [...] There's neither order nor necessity in his life, but he calls it pleasant, free, and blessedly happy, and he follows it for as long as he lives.[48]

Plato argues that no one can live such a life for long, because, lacking an inner principle of order, eventually one overweening, tyrannical desire will take over his life. The notion that a free person is one who today drinks and plays the flute and tomorrow works as a philosophical humanitarian is pure fiction. Every person's values must fall into some kind of order or nexus, which constitute an *ethos*. Even if a man be a hero and martyr for justice but is unfaithful to his wife, he has a fairly consistent *ethos* by

46 Augustine of Hippo, *City of God*. In *Great Books of the Western World* (Chicago, London: Encyclopedia Britannica, Inc. 1952), Book XIV, ch. 28; Karol Wojtyła, *Sign of Contradiction*, 83; John Paul II (K. Wojtyła), *Teachings for an Unbelieving World*, 53.

47 Karol Wojtyła. *Valutazione sulla possibilità di costruire l'etica cristiana sulle base del sistema di Max Scheler*, in K. Wojtyła. *Metafisica della persona* (Milano: Bompiani, 2003), 284–86, 305.

48 Plato, *Republic*. In *The Collected Dialogues of Plato*, VIII, 561c–d.

which he habitually lives. If his *ethos* is internally inconsistent in some respect, he may eventually realize that he should bring his values into harmony. Here we discover an important element of the moral life, which cannot be reduced to a serious of discrete moral decisions but is in fact *a life* flowing from its living source. We call this source the *heart*.

This heart is, in fact, identical with the conscience. In his encyclical on the Holy Spirit John Paul II writes,

> By becoming "the light of hearts," that is to say the light of consciences, the Holy Spirit "convinces concerning sin," which is to say, *he makes man realize his own evil* and at the same time *directs him toward what is good*.[49]

Elsewhere he writes, "The sacredness of life gives rise to its inviolability, written from the beginning in man's heart, in his conscience."[50] And in *Veritatis Splendor*, he identifies the heart with the conscience.[51] As the site of the person's beliefs about and understanding of the truth concerning the good, the heart can then rightly be called the person's *inner core*. If conscience is application of knowledge to the act, and if the knowledge cannot be reduced simply to one's belief concerning particular facts, then conscience addresses the facts, not only in their existential singularity but in relationship with other truths. An Austrian Catholic, Franz Jägerstätter, made fidelity to Jesus Christ his fundamental moral obligation to govern his life. Faced with the requirement that he swear a soldier's oath to obey the country's leader (*Führer* in his native German), Jägerstätter refused to swear an oath to *this* leader, whose claims rivalled those of Christ. Others may have seen the issue differently, but for Jägerstätter to swear the oath

49 Encyclical *Dominum et Vivificantem* (Vatican City: Libreria Editrice Vaticana, 1984), §42.

50 John Paul II, Encyclical *Evangelium Vitae* (Vatican City: Libreria Editrice Vaticana, 1995), §40.

51 *Veritatis Splendor*, §54.

would be to deny the core of his relationship with God, who is the supreme good.

Conscience and the moral law

The Second Vatican Council teaches, "Always summoning him to love good and avoid evil, the voice of his conscience when necessary speaks to his heart: do this, shun that."[52] The judgment of conscience thereby acquires an imperative character.[53] Responding to (or ignoring) the voice of conscience, the person chooses and acts, and in this choice of act the encounter between conscience and freedom comes to the fore.[54]

The human act is free. The freedom to act is a fundamental prerogative of the person.[55] If the agent is not free, then it is not a moral agent; its acts lack moral value. From this it follows that to perform a free act is of itself a value. Realizing this, wise parents will allow—indeed, encourage—their children to make decisions appropriate for their age or stage of development. This is good for the child, and indeed many an adult has had occasion to recognize that it must be a priority that he choose to exercise his own freedom, to act on the basis of his own judgment and choice. Freely to perform an act is itself a kind of good, a personalistic good. Nevertheless, that an act is one's own, freely chosen, does not make that act good of itself. Here we are reminded of Charles Curran's confused and confusing contention, cited above that "For moral maturity one must be one's own person. It is not enough to follow what one has been told."[56] Curran speaks of moral maturity as being one's own person, that is, of being morally adult, no longer a child who lives according to the directions of others. This is reminiscent of Kant's insistence that

52 *Gaudium et Spes*, §16.

53 *Veritatis Splendor*, §60; see also *Person and Act*, 266.

54 See William F. Murphy, "Reflections on Fundamental Morality, Conscience, Norms, and Discernment," in V. Paglia (editor), *Etica Teologica della Vita*, 217–43.

55 *Person and Act*, 222.

56 Charles Curran, *Conscience: Readings in Moral Theology No. 14*, 58.

the person is to be autonomous, indeed a law unto himself.[57] The autonomous agent may follow another's instructions, but only insofar as he personally validates them as his own choice. But this is not sufficient to qualify an act as good. Curran goes on to characterize the morally mature person as the one who can "perceive, choose, and identify oneself with what one does." Here we see much more than Kant's autonomous self-legislating subject. Curran's conception of conscience implies a strong assertion of self. What is decisive, then, is not that I have *decided for the good,* but that *I* have decided, and by that personal decision it is good. Here we are reminded of the saying (falsely) attributed to Martin Luther at the Diet of Worms: "Hier stehe ich: ich kann nicht anders." ("Here I stand; I can do no other.")[58] Implicit in such a statement is the claim that the speaker is so identified "in conscience" with his judgment that to speak or act otherwise would be a betrayal of his own self. St. John Henry Newman characterizes this conception of conscience.

> When men advocate the rights of conscience, they in no sense mean the rights of the Creator, nor the duty to Him, in thought and deed, of the creature; but the right of thinking, speaking, writing, and acting, according to their judgment or their humour, without any thought of God at all. They do not even pretend to go by any moral rule, but they demand, what they think is an Englishman's prerogative, for each to be his own master in all things, and to profess what he pleases, asking no one's leave, and accounting priest or preacher, speaker or writer, unutterably impertinent, who dares to say a word against his going to perdition, if he like it, in his own way. [...] Conscience is a stern monitor,

57 Immanuel Kant, *Grounding of the Metaphysics of Morals,* 434–36.

58 Despite the traditional attribution, which became the basis for the title of a popular biography, it is doubtful that Luther actually spoke these words at the Diet.

> but in this century it has been superseded by a counterfeit, which the eighteen centuries prior to it never heard of, and could not have mistaken for it, if they had. It is the right of self-will.[59]

The last sentence of this text captures the point. Conscience is to be identified with self-will, to which the person has a fundamental right. As such, the conscience becomes essential to the person's own identity. To violate it is to betray one's deepest self and most fundamental values. It is this sense of conscience that appears to dominate many contemporary discussions of freedom of conscience. According to this conception, conscience can claim its rights and insist on its inviolability vis-a-vis heteronomous authority. This is a false understanding of conscience.

If conscience is the application of knowledge to the act, then the proper concern of conscience is truth about the good, not the will's decision. John Paul II writes:

> In their desire to emphasize the "creative" character of conscience, certain authors no longer call its actions "judgments" but "decisions": only by making these decisions "autonomously" would man be able to attain moral maturity.[60]

The knowledge at stake is the person's knowledge of the moral law, and herein lies the rub. Every human act occurs within a rich nexus of circumstances and may potentially issue in a wide variety of results, some desirable and some not. To plant a garden may mean especially flavorful meals in the fall at the cost of a mild sunburn on the neck. It may also mean that the gardener missed seeing an unexpectedly exciting sports event on televi-

59 John Henry Newman, *Newman Reader:* "Letter to the Duke of Norfolk," downloaded July 20, 2023, from https://www.newmanreader.org/works/anglicans/volume2/gladstone/index.html, 250.

60 *Veritatis Splendor*, §55.

sion. The young woman with an unexpected pregnancy, for which she is not prepared, knows the prohibition in the moral law against taking human life.[61] She also knows with reasonable accuracy what the birth of a child will mean for her and what hardships the child will face. One could multiply examples, but the point is that any choice can and ordinarily will issue in a variety of conflicting values and disvalues. The *creative conscience* sees its task as balancing these values in such a way that the core values embraced by the subject are realized.

Here it is helpful to consider John Stuart Mill's conception of freedom and the free man.

> A person whose desires and impulses are his own—are the expression of his own nature, as has been developed and modified by his own culture—is said to have character.

And further,

> It is not by wearing down into uniformity all that is individual in themselves, but by cultivating it and calling it forth [...] that humans become a noble and beautiful object of contemplation; and as the works partake the character of those who do them, by the same process human life also becomes rich, diversified, and animating, furnishing more abundant aliment to high thoughts and elevating feelings, and strengthening the tie that binds every individual to the race, by making the race infinitely better worth belonging to. In proportion to the development of his individuality, each person becomes more valuable to himself, and is therefore capable of being more valu-

61 Andrzej Szostek, *Natur-Vernunft-Freiheit: Philosophische Analyse der Konzeption "schöpferischer Vernunft" in der zeitgenössischen Moraltheologie* (Frankfurt am Main: Peter Lang, 1992), 269.

> able to others.[62]

Mill's ideal is the person become a "noble and beautiful object of contemplation" by his diverse thoughts and feeling arising from the genius of his own individuality. He is one who has made his desires and impulses his own. He can choose what he shall do, not on the basis of some law, but *on the basis of who he is*. He does not live merely according to custom but by his own individual genius. This is precisely the conception of individuality that Newman criticized in his reflection on conscience. Granting that Mill greatly overestimated the richness of individuality he had hoped to find in free individuals, his vision is echoed in the modern mind as an ideal. Charles Taylor summarizes this conception of the modern individual self.

> Everyone has a right to develop their own form of life, grounded on their own sense of what is really important or of value. People are called upon to be true to themselves and to seek their own fulfillment. What this consists of, each must, in the last instance, determine for him- or herself. No one else can or should try to dictate its content.[63]

The Supreme Court of the United States, ruling for the constitutional right to abortion, argued effectively that a person's liberty is prior and superior to any ethical judgment, no matter how grave the matter of that judgment might be and no matter how fundamental the values at stake. Speaking for the majority Justice Anthony Kennedy wrote, "At the heart of liberty is the right to define one's own concept of existence, of meaning, of the universe, and of the mystery of human life."[64]

62 J. S. Mill, *On Liberty*, 57, 60.

63 Cited in Rod Dreher, *The Benedict Option: A Strategy for Christians in a Post-Christian Nation* (New York: Sentinel, 2017), 44.

To be sure, an Associate Justice of the Supreme Court is not a moral theologian. However, he is intelligent and intellectually accomplished. The views expressed in his Opinion do represent those of the educated classes of American society (and indeed Western culture in general). The individual's claim to liberty is absolutely prior to any ethical principles and the contemporary conception of the human person. It is the free individual's rightful prerogative to "define one's own concept of existence, of meaning, of the universe, and of the mystery of human life." Therefore, in the face of the claims of the natural law or moral law, it falls to the person in his or her own individuality to judge the standing of any moral judgment. This liberty is ultimately a decision of the *will*, as Newman had warned.

The essence of conscience

Hence John Paul II comes to the definition of conscience:

> But whereas the natural law discloses the objective and universal demands of the moral good, conscience is the application of the law to a particular case; this application of the law thus becomes an inner dictate for the individual, a summons to do what is good in this particular situation. [...] The judgment of conscience states "in an ultimate way" whether a certain particular kind of behavior is in conformity with the law; it formulates the proximate norm of the morality of a voluntary act, "applying the objective law to a particular case."[65]

64 Supreme Court of the United State, *Planned Parenthood of Southeastern Pennsylvania v. Casey*, 505 US 833, June 29, 1992.

65 *Veritatis Splendor*, §59.

As the final subjective judge of what is the good to be done, conscience is infallible. That is, one is always obliged to follow an upright moral conscience.[66] This implies that to follow one's conscience is always right—provided that the conscience is "upright" or well formed. The question must inevitably arise concerning the characteristics of a well-formed conscience. How does the individual know whether his conscience is upright? By what sort of self-examination can one determine that his conscience is well-formed?

In truth, this is the wrong question. Strictly speaking, the conscience is not a kind of personal attribute or mental state that might have the property "well-formed." As we saw earlier, St. Thomas Aquinas denies that conscience is some sort of property. St. John Paul II characterizes conscience,

> in its primordial reality as an act of a person's intelligence, the function of which is to apply the universal knowledge of the good in a specific situation and thus to express a judgment about the right conduct to be chosen here and now.[67]

As an act of intelligence, conscience is to be governed by the rules of thought, the logical principles by which one attains to truth. When confronted with a significant or important decision, the challenge to conscience is to apply one's general ("universal") knowledge about the good to the situation. In virtue of that knowledge, one is able then to judge what is the right course of action.

John Paul II's characterization presupposes that the agent does have a "universal knowledge of the good." In some cases, might it not be the case that an agent lacks that universal knowledge of good, that he is unsure of this knowledge? In such cases, might it not fall to him to determine for himself what that knowledge of

66 *Catechism of the Catholic Church*, 1778–82.

67 *Veritatis Splendor*, §32.

the good is? Here we can turn to St. Thomas. In response to the question whether the human being can attain happiness, which he has already shown to be the vision of the Divine Essence, he argues:

> Whoever, therefore, is capable of the perfect good can attain happiness. Now, that man is capable of the perfect good, is proved both because his intellect can apprehend the universal and perfect good [*quia et eius intellectus apprehendere potest universal et perfectum bonum*], and because his will can desire it.[68]

Aquinas here asserts the evident fact that the human intellect—any and every human intellect—can apprehend "universal and perfect good." This is not, of course, to affirm that every person actually does apprehend what this good is, but only that each one can understand the terms, the concept of universal and perfect good. This is not merely the notional grasp of an abstract definition but is rather an existentially important concept in one's life. It is one's ultimate standard of life and behavior. This conception of the perfect good may, to be sure, implicitly be one's own comfort and survival. It may be explicit—perhaps the realization of the workers' paradise in history. One person may live for pleasure and another for wealth. In every case, though, one's conception of the perfect good, even if vague and undefined, serves as the standard of his choices. Therefore, in *Veritatis Splendor* John Paul II writes,

> Although each individual has a right to be respected in his own journey in search of the truth, there exists a prior moral obligation, and a grave one at that, to seek the truth and to adhere to it once it is known.[69]

68 *Summa Theologiae* Ia, IIae q. 5, a. 1.
69 *Veritatis Splendor*, §34

This is why John Paul II insists in his Encyclical on faith and reason that it is vital for humans to seek out the meaning of life.[70]

In the years following the Council—and particularly in the wake of *Humanae Vitae*—the nature and prerogatives of conscience have been controverted. In that encyclical, Pope Paul VI had solemnly presented the moral requirement that in their conjugal relations, married couples refrain from using contraceptives. In many parts of the world this was not well received, and some churchmen sought ways to "soften the blow" of the encyclical by appealing to conscience. The bishops of Canada, addressing the moral requirements of *Humanae Vitae* for married couples, wrote,

> In accord with the accepted principles of moral theology, if these persons have tried sincerely but without success to pursue a line of conduct in keeping with the given directives, [pastoral counsellors] may be safely assured that, whoever honestly chooses that course which seems right to him does so *in good conscience*.[71]

This implies that the Pope Paul VI's teaching in the encyclical constitutes a kind of *directive* for married couples, which they should try to follow. However, they can or even must counterbalance this papal teaching with their own experience ("tried sincerely but without success") and reflection on their own situation. Having tried and reflected seriously, they can act according to their own lights "in good conscience." Indeed, religious educators in the years following *Humanae Vitae* regularly presented the Church's teaching about contraception as wisdom to be considered seriously, but not as moral law to be obeyed. This conception, of course, represents a significantly different notion of conscience than that which preceded the Council.

When we consider the elements of a crisis of conscience, such as that proposed in the "Winnipeg Statement," we find that ultimately a *choice of the will* is decisive. In *Humanae Vitae*, Pope Paul

70 John Paul II, Encyclical *Fides et Ratio*, §4 et passim.

71 Bishops of Canada, "Canadian Bishops' Statement on the Encyclical *Humanae Vitae*," (Winnipeg, Manitoba, 1968), henceforth "Winnipeg Statement." Emphasis added.

VI had solemnly presented the moral requirement that in their marital union couples refrain from using contraceptives. However, the Canadian bishops allowed that the married couple who find this requirement to be unduly burdensome can disobey the teaching "in good conscience."[72] If the conscience is a judgment of reason, then the couple experiencing undue burden is called to examine the truth concerning contraception. In the first instance, this *should* entail consideration of the moral instruction received from Pope Paul VI. *Humanae Vitae* makes clear that this is without exception a moral evil. To reject this judgment is effectively to reject Paul VI's authority to teach this as a moral truth. It is to claim that there is some higher authority than the Pope or that they are themselves capable of correctly arriving at a contrary moral evaluation. Most revisionist moral theologians (and possibly the Canadian bishops[73]) will allow that it is this second alternative which applies in such cases of dilemma of conscience,[74] that is, that the ordinary Catholic lay persons are able to judge whether they may use contraceptives without sin in their conjugal relations. It follows, therefore, that the Catholic who will not accept the teaching of *Humanae Vitae* effectively denies the authority of the Pope to teach definitively about sexual morality.

We generally presume that in most instances human persons are qualified to recognize moral goods and evils. However, many do not; Aristotle attributes much moral blindness to poor upbringing.[75] Children at play may repeat "finders keepers, losers weepers" as an ethical principle, but we expect that as adults they recognize a moral obligation to restore lost property when possible. Of course, many do not advance to moral maturity. As we examine human behavior more closely, we find that many people

72 Ibid.

73 We may also mention those of Austria and Germany as well. We should note that as Archbishop of Vienna, Cardinal Schönborn subsequently apologized for this Statement.

74 See also Charles Curran and 87 others, "Text of the Statement by Theologians," *New York Times*, July 31, 1968, p. 16.

75 Aristotle, *Nicomachean Ethics*, Book II, ch. 1, 1103b23–25.

do not actually have a well-developed sense for right and wrong, that they often continue to apply playground rules. So it is that we find it necessary for professional associations and government legislatures to define and proscribe "insider trading" as a form of theft and an evil to be avoided. It is not uncommon that young men at universities simply do not recognize that the sexual exploitation of young women is wrong. Despite clear evidence that the entity within a pregnant woman's belly is a baby, many people in Western societies refuse to acknowledge that abortion is a grave evil. The point of these examples is simply that we have little reason to believe that most human beings have well-developed powers of moral reasoning. And because readily available and reliable contraceptives obviate many difficulties and make life easier, the sentiments that once opposed contraceptives as somehow obscene have largely disappeared. Save for the Catholic Church, no contemporary moral authority opposes contraception. If our hypothetical Canadian couple is to make a conscientious choice independently of the Pope, then their resources reduce only to their own moral evaluation.

As good, moral persons, the hypothetical Canadian couple recognize that they are obliged to behave with love toward each other and their neighbors. Certainly, they want to cause no harm. Kindness is not only a moral fact; it is written into their bones, as it were. They do not live simply according to a set of rules—indeed, they seldom think of their decisions in terms of rules, but rather in terms of values and practices. They live according to an *ethos*, a world of values, that is to a great extent received from the surrounding culture and often uncritically so. The question of *ethos* sheds light on the consciences of our hypothetical Canadian couple who have chosen in conscience to reject the teaching of *Humanae Vitae*. As good Canadians, they are peaceful and considerate of their neighbors. They adhere to the values by which decent Canadians and (to a great extent, at least) their southern neighbors live. However, remarks John Paul II, "Man's growth in this life is hindered by the conditioning and pressures exerted upon him by dominating structures and mechanisms in the various spheres of society."[76] According to these values, by the shape of this *ethos*, sexual pleasure is *prima facie* a good; as philosopher Thomas Nagel writes, "bad sex is generally better than none at all."[77] We may characterize this *ethos* as bourgeois, middle-class morality. Those who behave according to it, are generally seen to be good, and their consciences accord with that morality.

Of course, this is not foolproof. One's inner standard on the law may be defective. Ingrained social or political loyalties can acquire the force of conscience. The scion of a slave-holding plantation owner in antebellum United States had difficulty seeing the evil of slavery. Or we may consider psychopathic criminals who, lacking a sense of empathy, experience no remorse after harming others. Even if a psychopath can recognize the fact that his behavior is wrong, he cannot (apparently) feel remorse or sympathy. Such a one must learn to behave well on the basis of "cold facts" and not from an emotional sympathy. Or we may consider the ordinary young person in contemporary society, whose sexual desires are growing stronger and whose surrounding culture presents images and ideas that encourage unrestricted sexual experimentation. We may seriously ask whether such a person can have a "well-formed conscience."

Here we encounter the critical issue. Can our hypothetical couple rely on this *ethos* to guide them in their consideration of contraception? As the example of the scion of the slaveholder shows, one cannot safely rely on the socially received *ethos* to form one's own grasp of moral values. This is precisely what Socrates warned his fellow Athenians about in his trial. It does not suffice, therefore, simply for this couple to consider their own situation, whether they can afford another child, whether they can forgo sexual intimacy for a time, and so on. Having called

76 *Dominum et Vivificantem*, §62.

77 Thomas Nagel, "Sexual Perversion" in J. Rachels (editor) *Moral Problems: A Collection of Philosophical Essays* (New York: Harper & Row, 1975), 15.

into question the moral teaching authority of the Pope, they must examine the roots and structure of the *ethos* by which they form their choices.

This examination of the *ethos* returns us to the question of the ultimate good. Proposing as the highest good the maximization of happiness, understood as pleasure and the absence of pain, John Stuart Mill proposed an ethic based on his "greatest happiness principle." By proper management of education and formation of public opinion, this principle can be fostered in the minds of the citizenry almost in the manner of a civic religion. What Mill has in mind is an enlightened civic elite that can establish institutions to form the consciences of the people. In fact, even without an express intent to form consciences as Mill proposes, Western societies have, in the main, accepted his utilitarian moral norms. However, Mill is well aware of the power of external forces to form one's conscience. In a chilling text he remarks:

> Unhappily it [conscience] is also susceptible, by sufficient use of the external sanctions and of the force of early impressions, of being cultivated in almost any direction, so that there is hardly anything so absurd or so mischievous that it may not, by means of these influences, be made to act on the human mind with all the authority of conscience.[78]

A man of this age of democratic governance, industrialized manufacture, and consumer markets, John Stuart Mill regards it as the responsibility of government and the organs of public opinion formation to foster the utilitarian conscience in the populace. To a great extent, Mill's project is being realized as contemporary moral approaches—"woke" ideologies—come increasingly to dominate public policy, academic teachings, and the opinion columns of the press. Diversity, equity, and inclusion (DEI) constitute the touchstone of contemporary moral behavior.

78 J. S. Mill, *Utilitarianism*.

Catholic teaching does indeed emphasize the primacy of conscience, that one is always obliged to act according to the dictates of conscience. However, he is equally obliged to inform his conscience and enlighten his judgment.[79] What this means is that the human person must critique the morality received from the culture according to criteria from a higher authority. Charles Curran and Immanuel Kant are wrong about human autonomy.

Fundamental to all this is that conscience is not a decision, that is, an act of the will. Good and evil are not determined by the acting person in his decision. After the publication of *Humanae Vitae,* several moral theologians argued that its judgment on artificial contraception constitutes a violation of the principles laid out in the Second Vatican Council's Declaration on Religious Freedom *Dignitatis Humanae,* in particular that "all men are to be immune from coercion [...] in such a wise that no one is to be forced to act in a manner contrary to his own beliefs, whether privately or publicly."[80] This objection reflects a fundamental confusion about freedom of conscience. In *Humanae Vitae* Paul VI presents no command as such, but a moral truth. The freedom of conscience arises precisely from the fact that the person can form his own acts according to the truth. The authors of *Dignitatis Humanae* were concerned that certain political regimes required, under threat of serious sanctions, that those under their command perform or refrain from certain acts as dictated by the regime. "Prisoners of conscience" were precisely those required to deny what they do know and affirm or act according to what they believe to be false. But the dignity of conscience is the capacity to decide to live according to truth. One who acts according to his conscience, according to the truth that he knows about the moral good, is most free. John Paul II writes, "The relationship between man's

79 *Catechism of the Catholic Church,* 1783.

80 Vatican Council II, Declaration on Religious Freedom *Dignitatis Humanae,* in *Documents of Vatican II* (Vatican City: St Paul Publications, 2009), §2.

freedom and God's law is most deeply lived out in the 'heart' of the person, in his moral conscience."[81]

From this becomes clear the error underlying the Winnipeg Statement, an error that also appears in a book recently published by the Pontifical Council for Life.[82] What is proposed is that the Catholic can appeal to a higher principle of authority than the Catholic Church. However, the Christian *ethos* is formed by the recognition that the highest good is union with God through the encounter with Christ. Furthermore, "In order to make this 'encounter' with Christ possible, God willed his Church."[83] Therefore, a conscience based on an *ethos* other than that proposed by the Church is inevitably ill-formed. To follow Jesus is to embrace a new way of life, a different *ethos*, which will form the person's moral values and decisions. In this way he will rightly form his conscience. Therefore, our hypothetical Canadian couple is not challenged to find a source of argumentation or valuation besides that of the Church. Rather, because the Church has so consistently insisted that the use of contraceptives is morally illicit, the couple is called to the *obedience of faith* (Rom 1:5). That the Church teaches on specific kinds of behavior does not violate consciences. One who acts according to his conscience, according to the truth about the moral good, is most free. John Paul II writes, "The relationship between man's freedom and God's law is most deeply lived out in the 'heart' of the person, in his moral conscience."[84]

It is often argued against the Church's Magisterium that since natural law is accessible to every human being and since the secular thinker is as competent intellectually as the Christian, the Church has no special competence to judge the morality of human acts, save perhaps those pertaining directly to religion and

81 *Veritatis Splendor*, §54.

82 Sigrid Müller, "Moral Responsibility as an Answer to God's Call," in V. Paglia (ed.) *Etica teologica della vita: Scrittura, tradizione, sfide pratiche*, 208.

83 *Veritatis Splendor*, §7.

84 Ibid., §54.

religious practice (one thinks here of the Sunday Mass obligation). Such an argument might be pertinent to favorite ethical puzzles concerning trolleys and crowded lifeboats,[85] but it seriously misses the deeper meaning of conscience. Implicit in the argument of *Veritatis Splendor* is that conscience cannot be divorced from *ethos*. This is why Pope John Paul II's theology of the body refers repeatedly and insistently on the *ethos* of Christian marriage.[86] The norms of *Humanae Vitae*, as well as others presented in the Magisterium, are founded on a different conception of the ultimate good than those of most secular moralities. Christ invites his followers to live by a different *ethos* than that of the world.

And hence ...

Conscience is the final court of decision, but the conscience must be well formed, which means that conscience is formed according to truth. To be formed by truth means that conscience must be guided by reason, which is the person's power to know truth. Conscience is not, therefore, a kind of inner sense or feeling, however deep or intense, that some act is right, permissible, or wrong. The discernment of conscience is not an examination of one's inner self, of his most persistent feelings or even convictions. Moral good and evil can be given to reason and known by human intelligence.

In his encyclical on the Holy Spirit, Pope John Paul II reflects on the Lord's words at John 16:7–11:

> And when [the Holy Spirit] has come, he will convict the world of sin, and of righteousness, and of judgment: of sin, because they do not believe in me; of righteousness, because I go to the Father and you see me no more; of judgment, because the ruler of this world is judged.

85 Lest I appear to concede too much, I happily admit that such dilemmas are only marginally about ethical decision-making.
86 *Theology of the Body*, 524, 541.

Dependent as it is on human reasoning and on the social ethos in which one lives, the conscience is indeed susceptible to error. Furthermore, it is very easy to minimize the seriousness of one's personal missteps. Because conversion requires the "convicting concerning sin" the Holy Spirit confers a "*double gift*: the gift of the truth of conscience and the gift of the certainty of redemption."[87] In practical terms what this means is that the Christian needs an active engagement with the Lord in prayer, Scripture reading, and reception of the sacraments, which if practiced daily will open one to the Holy Spirit's illumination of the conscience. This illumination is a matter not so much of resolving conflicts of conscience by seeking specific answers to particular issues, but of opening one's mind and heart generally to the Lord and his will. As one practices his faith, with special attention to Christ's sacrifice on the cross, the Holy Spirit can gradually shed light on the truth, one's personal responsibility, and the requirements of the moral law.

87 *Dominum et Vivificantem*, §31.

NATURAL LAW

In his encyclical *Humanae Vitae* Pope Paul VI expressed a critical moral judgment,

> Nonetheless the Church, calling men back to the observance of the *norms of the natural law,* [...] teaches that each and every marriage act (*quilibet matrimonii usus*) must remain open to the transmission of life.[1]

The day after the encyclical appeared, the *New York Times* carried a statement by Fr. Charles Curran, professor of theology at the Catholic University of America, and eighty-seven other Catholic theologians, criticizing and effectively rejecting the encyclical's conclusion. Of particular concern to the signers was the conception of natural law, on which Pope Paul had based his determination.

> Likewise, we take exception to some of the specific ethical conclusions in the encyclical [*Humanae Vitae*]. They are based on an inadequate concept of natural law: The multiple forms of natural law theory are ignored and the fact that competent philosophers come to different conclusions on this very question is disregarded.[2]

1 Paul VI, Encyclical *Humanae Vitae* (Libreria Editrice Vaticana, 1968), §11 (emphasis added).
2 Charles Curran and 87 others, "Text of the Statement by Theologians."

The term, "natural law"

One source of confusion is that the term "natural law" is often confused with "law of nature." Newton's law of gravity, Boyle's law of gasses, and Mendel's laws of heredity are laws of nature, which are quantifiable regularities in the behavior of natural things. Although we can learn and make technological use of such laws, we cannot violate them. Understanding the laws of aerodynamics enables us to make flying machines (which only *appear* to violate the laws of gravity). Disregarding nature's laws—say, by overexposing one's bare skin to sunlight—can lead to harm. The theologians' dissent cited above refers to such a confusion when it criticizes "overemphasis on biological aspects of conjugal relations as ethically normative [and] undue stress on [...] the faculty of sex viewed in itself apart from the person and couple." However, the term "natural law" is not correctly understood as "law of nature." St. Thomas Aquinas explains:

> Wherefore, since all things subject to Divine providence are ruled and measured by the eternal law, as was stated above (Article 1); it is evident that all things partake somewhat of the eternal law, in so far as, namely, from its being imprinted on them, they derive their respective inclinations to their proper acts and ends.[3]

This imprinting of divine providence on things lacking reason is what we call *laws of nature*. Concerning human beings, however, he continues,

> [...] the rational creature is subject to Divine providence in the most excellent way, in so far as it partakes of a share of providence, by being provident both for itself and for others. Wherefore it has a share of the Eternal Reason,

3 *Summa Theologiae*, Ia, IIae q. 91, a. 2.

> whereby it has a natural inclination to its proper act and end: and this participation of the eternal law in the rational creature is called the natural law.[4]

We shall return to this subsequently. First, however, we consider some alternative conceptions of natural law.

Euthyphro's problem

In *Euthyphro,* Plato raises the question of piety and what the gods want. Socrates is in the law courts of Athens, having just been formally charged with impiety, when he encounters the priest Euthyphro, who for his part is bringing murder charges against his own father—an act which his family and friends regard as impious. Since a priest, of all persons, should surely know what piety is, Socrates engages Euthyphro in conversation to define *piety*. After trying to define piety (or the holy) by means of examples, the priest accedes to Socrates's demand for a definition: "Well then, what is pleasing to the gods is holy and what is not pleasing to them is unholy."[5] At this point, however, he falls into a trap. First, not all the gods like the same things.[6] The more serious challenge, however, is to determine the one quality that all holy or pious things have by which one can determine that they are holy. Socrates asks, "Is what is holy holy because the gods approve it, or do the gods approve it because it is holy?"[7] In other words, what are the characteristics of piety, of the holy, by which it can be known? Euthyphro, full of confidence, indeed braggadocio at the start, becomes badly befuddled, and at the dialogue's end the reader can almost see him looking at his watch to make his escape.

What is at stake is the possibility that the moral law is knowable to the human mind. If piety is a virtue for which a person

4 Ibid.
5 Plato, *Euthyphro* in *The Collected Dialogues of Plato,* 6e.
6 Ibid., 5e–6a.
7 Ibid., 10a.

can be held morally responsible (Socrates is executed because the court judges him to be impious), then human reason can formulate a definition of this virtue. As a priest who knows the arcanum of sacrifices and ceremonies to please the gods, Euthyphro looks to what the gods want. Subsequent philosophy might call him a voluntarist. The gods want what the gods want. The human petitioner must accept this, and he seeks a priest to help him get what he wants from the gods. But piety is a virtue expected from every human being, and the human mind should be able to grasp it. Contrary to some popular interpretations, Plato did not intend *Euthyphro* to deliver the death knell to every sort of "divine command" theory of ethics. Socrates' issue is more complex than that. If there is a transcendent reality beyond the visible, tangible realities of this earth—think here of Plato's Cave, the Form of the Good, and the qualifications of the Philosopher king—then how can we know its demands? *Euthyphro* does require a certain rationality of the divine, but Plato also recognizes that the gods, whatever they may be, do impose certain obligations on us.[8] He does not refute, nor does he intend to refute the notion of ethical responsibility to the divine.

At this point we can consider the situation of the Christian, who has received definite Revelation from God, disclosing what God offers his creatures and what he expects of them. Having also inherited from the ancient Greeks and the Stoics a substantial account of the virtues and vices that are known by reason, Christian thinkers developed a rich account of natural law. By the late Middle Ages, however, Euthyphro's problem reappeared and with it the question of voluntarism.

> Voluntarism proposes to highlight the transcendence of the free subject in relation to all conditioning. Against naturalism that tended to subject God to the laws of nature, it emphasizes, in a unilateral way, the absolute freedom of God, with the risk of compromising his

8 Plato, *Phaedo*, 62b–e.

> wisdom and rendering his decisions arbitrary. In the same manner, against intellectualism, suspected of subjecting the human person to the order of the world, it exalts a freedom of indifference, understood as a pure capacity to choose contraries, which runs the risk of disconnecting the person from his natural inclinations and from the objective good.[9]

In his address at the University of Regensburg, Pope Benedict XVI commented,

> In all honesty, one must observe that in the late Middle Ages we find trends in theology which would sunder this synthesis between the Greek spirit and the Christian spirit. In contrast with the so-called intellectualism of Augustine and Thomas, there arose with Duns Scotus a voluntarism which, in its later developments, led to the claim that we can only know God's *voluntas ordinata*. Beyond this is the realm of God's freedom, in virtue of which he could have done the opposite of everything he has actually done.[10]

The problem with voluntarism, of course, is that it makes natural law—understood as law knowable by reason—relative and even

9 International Theological Commission, *In Search of a Universal Ethics: A New Look at the Natural Law*, 2009 §29. Downloaded June 2, 2021 from https://www.vatican.va/roman_curia/congregations/cfaith/cti_documents/rc_con_cfaith_doc_20090520_legge-naturale_en.html#2.2._Moral_experience:_%E2%80%9Cone_must_do_good%E2%80%9D. See also Servais-Th. Pinckaers, *The Sources of Christian Ethics* (trans. from the 3d edition by Sr. Mary Thomas Noble, O.P.) (Washington, DC: CUA Press 1995), 330–42.

10 Benedict XVI, "Faith, Reason, and the University" Lecture delivered September 12, 2006. Downloaded June 6, 2021 from https://www.vatican.va/content/benedict-xvi/en/speeches/2006/september/documents/hf_ben-xvi_spe_20060912_university-regensburg.html.

variable. At the beginning of the modern age, when the acceptance of papal authority was shattered by the Protestant Reformation and when the prestige of the new sciences was growing, Revelation increasingly was rejected as a reliable source of truth, even regarding moral questions.

Locke's natural law and Mill's utilitarianism

> We hold these truths to be self-evident, that all men are created equal, that they are endowed by their Creator with certain unalienable Rights, that among these are Life, Liberty and the pursuit of Happiness.[11]

To the minds of most Americans, this text sums up the heart of the natural law, affirming as it does the equality of all human beings and their fundamental rights, all of which are derived from their Creator. Jefferson's words in the Declaration do indeed present legitimate conclusions from natural law, conclusions that can accord with the classical presentations of that law. However, as its subsequent assertions concerning government make clear, the statement in the Declaration derives most directly from the writings of John Locke.

In his *Second Treatise of Government*, John Locke writes that the governing law of human beings is the law of nature,

> which obliges every one, and reason, which is that law, teaches all mankind who will but consult it, that being all equal and independent, no one ought to harm another in his life, health, liberty or possessions. [...] And, being furnished with like faculties, sharing all in one community of Nature, there cannot be supposed any such subordination among us that may authorise us to destroy one another, as if we were made for one

11 Declaration of Independence of the United States of America, July 4, 1776.

> another's uses, as the inferior ranks of creatures are for ours.[12]

The key to this law is the principle that each human being is *equal* to every other and therefore *free*. There is no natural hierarchy, no native ranking of superiority among men; rather, all are born equal. Most pointedly, the king of England is superior to no one *by nature*. That England has a hereditary monarch may well be good for peace and order in the realm. Nevertheless, King Charles II, under whose reign Locke lived, was by nature superior to no other man. Because all are equal and free, no human being is naturally superior to any other. The only authority one man can have over another (minor children excepted) is that to which the other consents. Therefore, as Locke maintains and the Declaration of Independence reaffirms, *consent* of the governed provides the only legitimate warrant for civil authority.[13]

In our own time, Peter Singer follows Locke, characterizing the basic principle of equality as "the principle of equal consideration of interests."[14] Therefore, no one may unwillingly be deprived of what is most personal to himself—"his life, health, liberty or possessions." As a moral law, Locke's concept of natural law reduces to the principle of personal autonomy. If the issues at stake are interpersonal, such as are encountered in sex, family life, and friendships, the only moral guidance that Locke's natural law can give us concerns non-compulsion, transparency in communication, and honesty regarding previous commitments. Thus, adultery is not wrong in itself, but only insofar as it involves deception of one's spouse or the possible emotional manipulation or deception of the partner.[15]

12 John Locke, *Second Treatise of Government* (Indianapolis: Hackett, 1980), §6.

13 Ibid., §15.

14 Peter Singer, *Practical Ethics* (Cambridge: Cambridge University Press, 1979), 19.

15 Ibid., 2.

Locke's position is amplified and, as it were, completed by moral utilitarianism, the touchstone of this is "that actions are right in proportion as they tend to promote happiness: wrong as they tend to produce the reverse of happiness. By happiness is intended pleasure and the absence of pain; by unhappiness, pain and the privation of pleasure."[16]

Therefore,

> The utilitarian doctrine is that happiness is desirable, and the only thing desirable, as an end; all other things being only desirable as a means to that end.[17]

Of central importance here is that happiness as pleasure is and can only be something perceptible, a matter of conscious experience situated in space and time. The good as such is recognized only by experience, and not by reason alone. According to this conception there can be no ultimate good, no perfect happiness such as that proposed by Aristotle. Indeed, pleasures are incommensurable. Which pleasure is greater: to enjoy sexual relations with a generous and attractive partner or to triumph in competition against a worthy opponent? Given such a conception of the human good, the notion of a highest, governing good for one's life is incomprehensible. The good life can be only one made up of many pleasant experiences and few pains.

Utilitarianism and consequentialism

Two important principles emerge from a close study of utilitarianism. First, from the utilitarian perspective, the morality of an act—the determination of whether it is good or bad—depends on the actual, anticipated, or intended *result*. Secondly, the goodness of this result rests ultimately upon the *subjective evaluation* of those it affects. A good result is one that makes those affected by it to

16 J. S. Mill, *Utilitarianism*, 7.

17 Ibid., 35.

experience it physically or emotionally as pleasant or somehow conducive to well-being.

Both of these principles are remarkably imprecise and can easily give rise to different variants of utilitarianism (or consequentialism). Indeed, ordinary experience shows that an act intended to produce some good results in an effect that others find undesirable. Therefore, the implications and manifestations of utilitarianism can take many forms according to the intended results, and subjective perspectives of both agents and those affected by the acts. Let us consider more closely the principles of utilitarianism.

The result

Even if the intent of the person performing the act is morally relevant, Mill holds the result to be the most important factor in the moral evaluation of an act. He argues that,

> [...] the motive has nothing to do with the morality of the action, though much with the worth of the agent. He who saves a fellow creature from drowning does what is morally right, whether his motive be duty, or the hope of being paid for his trouble.[18]

The utilitarian requirement is that the act be measured by pleasure and the avoidance of pain. However, despite Bentham's assertions, neither pleasure nor pain reduces to simple animal responsiveness. As Mill's example indicates, survival is good. The desired pleasures need not be those of sense but must include the higher pleasures of the mind. Furthermore, no one should be concerned only for his own good but rather for the pleasure of all those affected by his act. The greatest happiness principle embraces the happiness of all. From this, Mill concludes that the society itself must be structured in such a way that the cultural elites, who best appreciate the higher pleasures, such as literature

18 *Utilitarianism*, 18.

and history, determine and set up institutions to promote their conception of happiness by means of public education, propaganda, and the establishment of institutions.[19] By these measures they can introduce to the less educated and cultured sectors of society an appreciation for the best pleasures.

Although Mill insists that the most enlightened members of society are those best qualified to judge the relative merits of different kinds of pleasure, the variations among kinds of pleasures and the interests of different human persons make such determinations impossible. A dedicated professor of philosophy can find his life incomplete without nearby mountains to climb. The stage performer does not envy "the butcher, the baker, the grocer, the clerk," who "are secretly unhappy men because [they] get paid for what they do but no applause."[20] (Of course, the butcher or baker who gladly meet their customers might well break into a cold sweat if required to stand before a crowd and sing.) We know well know that scholars and cultural leaders can be remarkably profligate sensualists.

More significant is Václav Havel's devastating critique of the comforts of "normalization" in Communist Czechoslovakia in the 1970s, a period in which the Communist regime provided for all the needs and ordinary pleasures of the populace.

> In our offices and factories work goes on, discipline prevails. The efforts of our citizens are yielding visible results in a slowly rising standard of living: people build houses, buy cars, have children, amuse themselves, live their lives.[21]

Czechoslovak society in the 1970s may well have been reasonably comfortable, mildly prosperous, and secure, enabling cooperative

19 Ibid., 14–15.

20 Irving Berlin, "There's No Business Like Show Business."

21 Václav Havel, "Dear Dr. Husak," in V. Havel, *Open Letters: Selected Prose* (London: Faber & Faber, 1991), 50.

citizens to live their lives in peace. By the criteria of Mill's *Utilitarianism* Dr. Husák's regime of soft totalitarianism did deliver the results that Mill requires. Utilitarianism, by its very essence, must lead to good results that constitute happiness. However, Václav Havel found its requirement of mental submission to the regnant ideology dehumanizing.

A further consideration is that a well-intended and successful action may yield further consequences that are not good. History shows that an act can serve an immediate good but cause future results that may be bad; the invention of the airplane enabled rapid travel but also the bombing of cities. This forces the question of the extent to which one is responsible to foresee future effects of his acts. Mill dismisses this objection.

> [...] [D]efenders of utility often find themselves called upon to reply to such objections as this—that there is not time, previous to action, for calculating and weighing the effects of any line of conduct on the general happiness. [...] The answer to the objection is that there has been ample time, namely the whole past duration of the human species. During all that time mankind have been learning by experience the tendencies of actions; on which experience all the prudence as well as all the morality of life are dependent.[22]

As we see new technological developments (contraceptives, technological weapons, among others), we may well doubt Mill's optimism. An invention, a product, an activity may appear to be good and even be good in some respect, but also have unanticipated negative results. One plausible response to this objection—a response implicit in Mill's text—is rule-utilitarianism. The moral qualification is not dependent so much on the performance of *this* action but on the general rule or pattern of facts that similar acts address.

22 *Utilitarianism*, 23.

An important contemporary manifestation of the utilitarian theory is found in the writings of Peter Knauer. Recognizing that any particular act may have both desirable and undesirable effects, Knauer proposes that all moral judgments amount to an application of "double effect" reasoning.[23] By "harm" (*Schaden*) is meant some pre-ethical state that is not desirable, such as a broken leg or financial poverty. Because any act directed toward some good end may well also entail some harm, the criterion for moral evaluation must lie in whether there is an appropriate basis (*entsprechender Grund*) for choosing the act. Knauer writes:

> The question of the principle of double effect reads, "under which conditions can the permitting or causing of a loss or harm be ethically permissible?" This question assumes that an act allows or causes actual or at least supposed *harm* (whether for someone whoever or for the agent himself). In any case, this obtains: Not every allowing or causing of harm makes the act bad in itself.[24]

Two pages later, Knauer affirms that the allowing or causing of harm is ethically evil (*schlecht*) when the agent lacks an appropriate basis for it. What this comes down to is that the goodness or evil of the act has little to do with the agent (providing he has an "appropriate basis for his choice"); it is simply a choice between outcomes. By taking a walk one risks developing a blister on the foot or wearing away the soles of his shoes. This evil is warranted by the health benefits of his exercise. The surgeon is warranted in mutilating a donor's body by removing his kidney, if this is part of the act of performing a kidney transplant. Indeed, Knauer describes the whole context of acts by (presumably) decision is two surgeons and their respective teams as one act, to be morally

23 Peter Knauer. *Handlungsnetze: Über das Grundprinzip der Ethik* (Frankfurt am Main: Books on Demand, 2002), 37.

24 Ibid., 37.

evaluated as such.[25] Every moral essentially an appeal to the principle of double effect, a choice between two possible outcomes. As Mill indicates, the moral value of an act depends on its result. This is why so many philosophers treat "trolley and lifeboat problems" as moral issues.

Martin Rhonheimer offers a particularly dramatic but apt example of such moral reasoning. He tells of the French collaborator, Paul Touvier, who complied with an order to shoot seven Jews on June 28, 1944.

> On trial fifty years later Touvier argued that both he and the chief commander of the militia of Lyon knew that the Gestapo chief Werner Knab was planning to execute a hundred Jews [...]. By convincing Knab to execute only thirty, and then in fact executing only seven Jews, Touvier argued that they had in fact prevented the execution of one hundred desired by the Gestapo commander. The key point here is their argument that *what they did in reality (the morally relevant "object" of their doing) was not kill seven Jews, but save the lives of ninety-three of them.*[26]

Rhonheimer proceeds to observe that what was chosen here is not the action itself but the *consequences* of whatever action is chosen, wryly noting that he is happy (of course) if only seven are killed when an airplane with one hundred passengers are killed. But this is not a moral issue, just a happy result.

The principle of the result is well illustrated and, indeed, applied in the so-called "Majority Report" of Pope Paul VI's Papal Commission on Birth Control. After noting humanity's immense progress in controlling natural processes, including reproductive biology, progress that accords with the Creator's intention that

25 Peter Knauer, "Teleologische als deontologische Normenbegründung," *Theologie und Philosophie*, (55: 3: 2008): 344.

26 Martin Rhonheimer, *The Perspective of the Acting Person*, 78.

human beings use their intelligence to better their lives, the Commission concludes,

> [...] every method of preventing conception—not excluding either periodic or absolute abstinence—*carries with it some negative element or physical evil* which the couple more or less seriously feels. This negative element or physical evil can arise under different aspects: account must be taken of the biological, hygienic, and psychological aspects, the personal dignity of the spouses, and the possibility of expressing sufficiently and aptly the interpersonal relation or conjugal love. The means to be chosen, where several are possible, is *that which carries with it the least possible negative element,* according to the concrete situation of the couple.[27]

We note immediately the similarities between the language used in this evaluation and that of Knauer in his ethical analysis. The married couple confronting the moral decision concerning contraception has, according to this analysis, three possible outcomes: a possible pregnancy, a period (possibly extended) of sexual abstinence, or use of the birth-control pill. Each of these can result in some degree of harm. The moral choice, as understood by the Commission, is the best result among these three outcomes. The couple must decide which one they prefer. We may note that the judgment of their consciences will come down to their respective evaluations of these three results. Therefore, so argues this Majority Report, it is ultimately for them to determine whether it will be acceptable and good to them to conceive

27 Papal Commission for the Study of Problems of the Family, Population, and Birth Rate. "Majority Report of the Papal Commission for the Study of Problems of the Family, Population, and Birth Rate," 1966. Downloaded 18 September 2014 from http://www.bostonleadershipbuilders.com/0church/birth-control-majority.htm. Emphasis added.

another child, periodically to refrain from intimacy (even then with the risk of conceiving a child), or to use the Pill.

The same reasoning applies to warfare and the bombing of civilian areas with incendiary or nuclear weapons. If the war continues, both sides will suffer huge loss of lives, both civilian and military. If such weapons of mass destruction are used, then the enemy will sue for peace. This was precisely the argument used to justify the United States' nuclear attack on Hiroshima and Nagasaki in August 1945, as well as air attacks on London, Dresden, and Tokyo in that war, and subsequent air attacks on Hanoi, North Vietnam, and Serbia. The justification of such attacks is that the suffering and loss of life from such attacks can be expected to be less than if the war were protracted. Therefore, the use of such weapons is morally justified. In a utilitarian ethical system, technique comes to replace virtue. For example, it is said that the Japanese Samurai disdained the use of firearms, because a courageous warrior must face his enemy with a sword and not shoot him from afar. Modern war has arguably become more dependent of technology than upon fearless warrior classes.

Mill praises virtue, but not in the same way as Aristotle. Virtue may make a person attractive to others and an agreeable companion, but it does not make him morally good.

> Utilitarians are quite aware that there are other desirable possessions and qualities besides virtue, and are perfectly willing to allow to all of them their full worth. They are also aware that a right action does not indicate a virtuous character, and that actions which are blamable often arise from qualities entitled to praise.[28]

Plato or Aristotle will insist on the importance of the virtues of wisdom (or prudence), justice, temperance, and courage as the defining marks of a good character. By contrast, the utilitarian

28 *Utilitarianism*, 20.

looks for the capacity to make the most effective decision for the case at hand, availing oneself of available resources. For Aristotle it was of supreme importance to become a person of good character, formed by virtue, because only then was one ordered to the true good. The utilitarian morality requires rather that one become competent at life's challenges in the setting where one finds himself. We see this clearly in contemporary educational philosophy according to which students are to develop professional or vocational expertise, by which they can not only support themselves but also "make a contribution" to society. In a very real sense, the utilitarian life is constituted by a series or nexus of cost-benefit calculations.

The subjectivism of utilitarianism

Subjectivism is a dangerous characteristic of utilitarianism. Ultimately the greatest happiness principle rests not on some objective good but on feelings, on subjective responsiveness. Doubtless Jeremy Bentham and John Stuart Mill regarded the issue in terms of the "respectable" pleasures that a decent British gentleman would value. Even granting that some persons may be sadomasochists, enjoying pain and inflicting it, most people understand this to be a perversion. However, one may question whether the notion of sexual perversion has any meaning.[29] As long as those engaged in sadomasochism do so of their own accord and do not inflict pain on others, then there is no serious problem with their pleasures. Mill's point was that everyone wants to feel good, and we do our best to promote good feelings. For the most part, we agree on the kinds of activities that constitute pleasures.

Such a perspective fails to take seriously the facts of history and even of life around us. According to Genghis Khan:

> The greatest happiness is to vanquish your enemies, to chase them before you, to rob them of their wealth, to

29 Thomas Nagel, Op. cit., 3, 11–12.

> see those dear to them bathed in tears, to clasp to your bosom their wives and daughters.[30]

On what grounds can one disagree? Certainly, Khan violates the greatest happiness principle if we consider the happiness of his victims. But why should he (or we) care? Khan writes of his own joys, which he gladly shared with members of the Golden Horde. If others disagree, that was no concern of his. We may ask seriously on what grounds Mill or a contemporary utilitarian may disagree. A prominent utilitarian of our time, Peter Singer, acknowledges that there are no such grounds, because if an individual fails or refuses to value an ethical life, then there is no argument to show that he is wrong.[31] Let us note further that Khan's perspective was shared by prominent voices of the 20th century. To gain *Lebensraum* for the German people, Poles and Russians must be enslaved or die. To realize the triumph of Communism in an industrialized Russia, Ukrainian *kulaks* must starve. If some suffer now, so the argument goes, many more will live well in the future.

The greatest happiness principle stands ultimately on the subjective feelings and inclinations of the individual. *My* pleasure has no connection with *your* good. Every populist demagogue knows that the people can be deluded by pleasure, by *panem et circenses.* Strictly speaking, pleasures cannot be shared. This is one of Havel's complaints against the normalization of Czechoslovakia after 1968. Everyone could have consumer goods. Entertainment was available to everyone. Therefore, everyone had a pleasant life—or so maintained the government propaganda.[32] On the personal level this is equally true. Even when engaging in common activities, not all those in the circle of friends agree on what counts as "great fun." Some friends may simply go along

30 Henry H. Howorth, *History of the Mongols from the 9th to the 19th Century* (New York: Cosimo, 2008), I: 110.

31 Peter Singer, op. cit. 216–18.

32 Vaclav Havel, *Open Letters*, 50–51.

for the sake of the others and their pleasure. Indeed, two lovers in bed are not necessarily both finding the experience of sexual intercourse to be equally pleasurable. One of them may even find it unpleasant. Pleasure cannot be shared. Only an authentic good can be shared.

At first glance, utilitarianism makes great sense. This author's consistent classroom experience has been that undergraduates who may struggle with other philosophers such as Plato or Aristotle, quickly grasp Mill's utilitarianism and accept it. It offers a common-sense approach to moral behavior and validates the morality by which they and most of their neighbors live. Nevertheless, these two principles—the principle of the result and subjectivism—render a true utilitarian ethics impossible. The favorable or positive result is never assured, and indeed may prove in the event to be unfavorable. The agent has only a probabilistic expectation that what he does will turn out well, as he expects. The root of the problem is that to achieve the result is simply to arrange or rearrange things in the world. A *Tatsachenbegriff* (fact-concept) is a concept about some "ontic" state of affairs, which can only be measured against some other *Tatsache* (facts). Besides the potentially difficult matter of evaluating competing states of affairs, there remains the fact that the agent is involved only as one of several factors affecting the ontic situation. In this respect, utilitarianism is a form of materialism that has no place for spiritual values.

One may argue that the moral value rests not on what *actually* occurs but rather on what the agent *intends* to occur. "I never expected it to turn out this way." But this does not meet Mill's standard. We may admire the intentions of a well-meaning agent who nevertheless causes harm, but we cannot call his actions good. Here the subjective disposition of the agent is called into play. More important and essential to our analysis is that utilitarianism demands that one's behavior aim at the subjective condition of those affected by the act. One must act to increase the general happiness, understood as the predominance of pleasure over pain. Mill (or any other consequentialist) may guess fairly accurately what will (or at least should) please most people; this is how utilitarianism is commonly understood. However, what is subjectively most pleasurable may well not be what is truly good for that person or persons. We may think here not only of mood-enhancing substances—let us remember that Mill's fictional contemporary Sherlock Holmes was an opium-user—but also of our contemporary reliance on electronic devices for amusement. Wojtyła writes: "But pleasure itself is not the only good; it is also not the proper end of man's action [...]. Pleasure in its essence is something collateral, accidental, something that may occur when acting."[33] Pleasure cannot be the appropriate end of an act.

God and morality

In the consequentialist or utilitarian conception, the person's relationship with God does not come into consideration. Such an ethics is entirely this-worldly, natural. To be sure, Mill thought that the greatest happiness principle does accord with God's will.

> If it be a true belief that God desires, above all things, the happiness of his creatures, and that this was his purpose in their creation, utility is not only not a godless doctrine, but more profoundly religious than any other. [...] [A] utilitarian who believes in the perfect goodness and wisdom of *God* necessarily believes that whatever God has thought fit to reveal on the subject of morals must fulfill the requirements of utility in a supreme degree.[34]

One may well argue—St. Thomas Aquinas does and at length—that God desires the happiness of his creatures, but this happiness cannot be construed as pleasure.[35] Indeed, if God's plan is that his

33 *Love and Responsibility*, 20.

34 *Utilitarianism*, 22.

35 *Summa Theologiae* Ia, IIae q. 2, a.6.

creatures are destined for pleasure, then the "problem of evil" becomes insoluble. Suffering is inevitable in the world he has created—a world with powerful storms, shifting tectonic plates, tigers and other predatory animals, as well as unforgiving gravity acting upon an unsupported human body. Furthermore, God plays no role at all in the utilitarian calculus of pleasure or in the consequentialist projection of results.

For his part, Knauer acknowledges forthrightly that the Christian faith is not directly connected with ethical thought.

> The foundation of ethics that we are seeking here is of the philosophical sort. For its comprehensibility it does not presuppose the Christian faith. However, as a theologian I also pose the question how such an ethics relates to the Christian faith: faith intends to free the human being from that fear that is the deepest root of all inhumanity.[36]

In short, faith in God has nothing to do with moral decision-making, but only with one's emotional response to fears. At the root of both classical utilitarianism and its contemporary derivatives is a conception of the good as something entirely subjective or this-worldly. As Hume had it over two centuries ago, in the world are only facts, but not values. The world consists of material objects or sensible events and states of affairs, which human beings can rearrange according to their wishes and intentions. The values by which moral decisions are made are not found in the world. Hence, our language can (and should) reflect this value-free character of the physical world. Knauer points to word-pairs: alienation of another's property–theft; killing–murder; false statement–lying; interruption of pregnancy–abortion; amputation–mutilation.[37] In each of these pairs, the first term expresses a

36 Peter Knauer. *Handlungsnetze,* 9 (Translation my own).

37 Peter Knauer, "Zu Grundbegriffen der Enzyklika *Veritatis Splendor.*" *Stimmen der Zeit,* (212 Band, Heft 1), 25.

fact-description (*Tatsachenbegriff*) and the second a value-description (*Wertbegriff*).[38] This fact-value distinction plays a major role in contemporary moral thought, because if values are not found in the world, in the objective order of things, then moral evaluations can depend only on subjective criteria—on human desires, intentions, and personal convictions.

We have gone into such detail on classical utilitarianism because, in one way or another, most revisionist moral theologies derive from philosophical utilitarianism. When Charles Curran and his eighty-seven signers for the *New York Times* essay refer to "natural law," it is to a variant of Locke's conception, as interpreted through Mill's principle of utility. This is not the notion of natural law found in *Veritatis Splendor*.

John Paul II's position

We have seen earlier in this work[39] how John Paul II infers the first great commandment from the truth that God is the Supreme Good and origin of all good and the second great commandment from the respect owed to each person in virtue of his dignity as a child of God, endowed with reason and will. These two primordial commands, to love God above all things and to love one's neighbor as oneself, constitute the foundation of the moral law. These are the truths about the fundamental goods from which we can infer the Great commandment.

> "You shall love the Lord your God with all your heart, and with all your soul, and with all your mind." This is the greatest and first commandment. And a second is like it: "You shall love your neighbor as yourself." (Matt 22:37–39)

38 Richard A. McCormick, S.J., *The Critical Calling: Reflections on Moral Dilemmas since Vatican II* (Washington, DC: Georgetown University Press, 1989), 58, 136.

39 Chapters 1 and 2 above.

The commandments of love of God and love of neighbor constitute the foundation of the natural law. The moral law is constructed around these two commandments and the truths from which they derive.

Pope John Paul II's conception of natural law builds on that of St. Thomas Aquinas, who writes,

> But supposing that God's providence rules the world, as I maintained in the First Part, his reason evidently governs the entire community of the universe. And so the governance of the world existing in God as the ruler of the universe has the nature of law. And since God's reason conceives eternally, [...] such law is eternal.[40]

Thomas's point is that the world is ruled by the wisdom of the Divine Architect who created it and the Divine King who rules of his handiwork. In creating the world, God acted intelligently, and his intelligent planning constitutes his providence.[41] Therefore there is a natural order of good and evil in the world, and created intelligence can know this providential order. That is, the human mind can know the laws by which the world is governed; it is the job of the sciences to discern the laws by which non-rational natures are governed. We call these the laws of nature.

Beyond the laws of nature, God's providence extends also to rational creatures, albeit in a different way. Thomas writes,

> But the rational creature is subject to God's providence in a more excellent way than other things, since a creature also shares in God's providence by providing for itself and others. And so it shares in the eternal plan whereby it has its natural inclination to its requisite activity and end. And we call such participation in the eternal law by rational creatures the natural law.[42]

40 *Summa Theologiae*, Ia, IIae q. 91, a. 1.
41 *Summa Theologiae*, Ia, q. 103.
42 *Summa Theologiae*, Ia, IIae q. 91, a. 2.

The rational creature is free, not entirely bound by the laws of nature as non-rational creatures are. As a body with physical properties, the human being is indeed subject to the laws of nature. However, he also enjoys a limited, but very real governance of himself. His behavior is not determined by his sensual appetites, but by his own will, his power to desire the good and to choose his acts. Sharing in God's providence by the powers of his own intellect, he is responsible to discern the laws governing his behavior. We can know the moral law.

John Paul II follows this same conception of natural law in *Veritatis Splendor*. Citing from the text we have just quoted from Thomas Aquinas, he writes,

> It also becomes clear why this law is called the natural law: it receives this name not because it refers to the nature of irrational beings but because the reason which promulgates it is proper to human nature.[43]

It is worth noting that Pope John Paul II tends not frequently to use the term "natural law." Rather he prefers the expression "moral law" and at times even "God's law." Here we see the essential personalism of Saint John Paul II's thought. He is alert to avoid the kind of abstract legalism of which moral theology and especially moral pronouncements by the Church's Magisterium are often accused. More importantly, however, is that the natural moral law *is* God's law. *All* men are obliged to honor God and love him, and similarly *all* are obliged to respect the dignity of their neighbors. For John Paul II the notion of a morality "as if God does not exist" is incoherent.[44]

A text from his theology of the body audiences is especially illuminating here. Speaking of Pope Paul VI's appeal to natural law in *Humanae Vitae* he writes:

43 *Veritatis Splendor*, §42.

44 *Veritatis Splendor*, §§37, 88.

> By "natural law" we understand here the "order of nature" in the field of procreation inasmuch as it is understood by right reason: this order is the expression of the Creator's plan for the human person. [...] [T]he virtuous character of the attitude expressing itself in the "natural" regulation of fertility is determined, *not so much* by faithfulness to an impersonal *"natural law," but to the personal Creator,* the source and Lord of the order that is shown in this law.[45]

The "natural law" is indeed the "order of nature," not simply as an expression of the laws of reproduction known to biology, but as an expression of the Creator's plan for the human person. An understanding of the natural law is not to be inferred simply from the regularities discovered by natural science. Were this so, then many common surgical interventions would be illicit—consider the implantation of cardiac pacemakers. John Paul II's point is clarified by an important text from his *Love and Responsibility*.

> The sexual drive has its objective greatness precisely because of this link with the divine work of creation, a greatness that almost completely disappears in the field of vision of a mentality influenced by the "biological order" alone. [...]
>
> The "biological order," as a work of the human mind separating some elements of this order from what really exists, has man as its immediate author. [...] The case is different with the "order of nature." It constitutes a group of cosmic relations that occur among beings that really exist. It is thus the order of existence, and the whole order present in existence finds its basis in the one who is the unceasing source of this existence, in God the Creator.[46]

45 *Theology of the Body*, 636 (124:6). Emphasis in the original.
46 *Love and Responsibility*, 41.

Karol Wojtyła here distinguishes between the *biological order* and the order of nature—more properly, the *order of existence* (or being).[47] He warns that if our thinking is inspired only by the biological order, then we lose sight of the Creator's plan and intention. Certainly, Wojtyła does not intend to deny the value and accuracy of the biological sciences. However, the "biological order," by which he means the body of biological theories and scientific understanding, is a human creation, the product of human beings—scientists—acting according to the canons of their science. According to those canons, this order prescinds from metaphysics, from the order of being. The scientist seeks, for example, to understand the mechanisms of natural selection, but refrains from addressing the questions of why it was good that there be dinosaurs and why their subsequent extinction was good—or, indeed, whether the existence or extinction of *any* species is good.

The species of rational animals transcends the order of biology. The Creator made the universe for the sake of human beings (see Isaiah 42: 5) that they may glorify him and share in his goodness. It is to this order of being that one must turn, argues Karol Wojtyła, correctly to understand the human reproductive capacity. In *Love and Responsibility,* he makes this argument to show why the person can and must acquire virtue (specifically chastity) to manage his sexual behavior. In the text cited above from his Theology of the Body John Paul II carries this reasoning further. Granting that the natural law (which is, nevertheless, not a law of biology) is, in a way, impersonal, the moral requirement stands in terms of a relationship with the *personal* Creator, "the source and Lord of the order that is shown in this law."

Pope Saint John Paul II repudiates the utilitarian approach and indeed every form of subjectivism by rooting his account in the relationship of the person with God. For him there is no "natural morality" independent of God. The moral law for him is God's law. Obedience to the moral law directly pertains to one's

47 Adrian J. Reimers, *The Truth about the Good*, 54–65.

relationship with God. The natural moral law is an authentic participation of the human person in the mind of the Creator. It is not merely a speculation based on hypotheses of what God might think. As one of the powers of the rational soul by which the human person is the image of God, reason is capable of sharing in God's government. This notion may resemble Kant's notion of the rational being's self-legislation, but it differs decisively. Kant's self-legislating autonomous mind is alone, legislating (in a way) for every rational being but sharing his responsibility with none. He is isolated. As a participant in the Divine Wisdom man participates in the legislation of the Divine Lawgiver. He is not bound to blind obedience to the Almighty. He is free.

Pope John Paul II emphasizes the intimate relationship between freedom and truth, denying that the moral law restricts human freedom.[48] If we regard the moral law only as a series of prescriptions and proscriptions, then the human person has no freedom. But this is a flawed conception of the moral law,[49] whose foundation is love. And love consists in the gift of oneself for the authentic good of the other, and such actions can be performed in an almost infinite variety of ways. To be sure, the Church specifies the first great commandment by commanding that every Catholic attend Mass on Sunday. However, the believer who seeks to love God with all his heart and soul and mind and strength can do so also by entering into chaste marriage, bringing children into the world and educating them in the ways of love. Or one can enter the consecrated religious life—and a wide variety of patterns of life are offered—or the priesthood, if one is a man. Similarly, love for one's neighbor can take a variety of forms from the total gift of self to a spouse in married life to shoveling snow from the elderly neighbor's driveway, to serving in public office. The law is love, and the options are almost infinite. What are precluded are those acts that violate the order of love by violating the dignity of the person.

48 *Veritatis Splendor*, §35.

49 See Servaise Pinckaers, O.P., *The Sources of Christian Ethics*, 193; also *Pour une lecture de Veritatis Splendor*, 27.

FREEDOM

A neuralgic issue in contemporary moral thought is the relationship between freedom and law. These two, freedom and law, stand in apparent opposition. On the one hand, it is reasonable that human beings be subject to law if societies are to function peacefully. On the other hand, modern man greatly treasures his freedom, which is taken to be a hallmark of human identity and dignity. Important as its purposes may be, law restricts freedom. From a scientific perspective, we find freedom and law to be contradictory.[1] Where the laws in question are those of nature, then human freedom seems to be restricted or even denied. A man cannot fly, and some day he will die. Many philosophers and scientists go so far as to maintain that freedom is an illusion, that all human behavior is determined by invariant natural laws. In the face of all this, we do well to examine what this term "freedom" means.

The Second Vatican Council writes:

> Only in freedom can man direct himself toward goodness. [...] For its part, authentic freedom is an exceptional sign of the divine image within man. For God has willed that man remain "under the control of his own decisions," so that he can seek his Creator spontaneously, and come freely to utter and blissful perfection through loyalty to Him. Hence man's dignity demands

1 Peter van Inwagen, *The Problem of Evil: the Gifford Lectures* (Oxford: The Clarendon Press, 2006), 170; see also Bernard Berofsky, *Determinism* (Princeton: Princeton University Press, 1971) for a detailed discussion.

> that he act according to a knowing and free choice that is personally motivated and prompted from within, not under blind internal impulse nor by mere external pressure.[2]

Noteworthy here is the opening sentence: "Only in freedom can man direct himself toward goodness." One can be directed by others toward goodness *in some respect*. By obeying the coach, one becomes a good player on the team. Obeying the teacher, one learns the subject. Freedom, according to the Council's conception, requires that one direct himself. This is clear from the continuation of the text, which cites the scriptural formula that the person remain "under the control of his own decisions," that is, by a "knowing and free choice" that arises from within. This formulation is very close to Karol Wojtyła's conception, which characterizes freedom in terms of self-determination.[3]

In *Veritatis splendor* St. John Paul II insists on the close relationship between freedom and truth. He writes: "Truth enlightens man's intelligence and shapes his freedom, leading him to know and love the Lord."[4] Later on, explaining the sources of dissent from the Church's moral teachings, he writes:

> At the root of these presuppositions is the more or less obvious influence of currents of thought which end by detaching human freedom from its essential and constitutive relationship to truth.[5]

Indeed, freedom depends on truth.[6] The theme of freedom is central to *Veritatis Splendor*; the word "freedom" appears 192 times in the document.

2 *Gaudium et Spes*, §17.
3 *Person and Act*, 217–18; *Love and Responsibility*, 97.
4 *Veritatis Splendor*, Prologue.
5 Ibid., §4.
6 Ibid., §34.

Freedom of alternatives and determinism

We begin by looking at the issue of scientific determinism, which effectively denies human freedom. An important aspect of the issue of freedom is what we can call the *freedom of alternatives*—a value or choice is either 1 or 0, plus or minus—or *freedom of indifference*.[7] The meaning of the freedom of alternatives is simply that a person is free if he could have done otherwise than he did. However, if one tries to judge after the fact whether an act was free or determined, there arises the logical problem of counterfactuals and affirming the consequent. This conception implies a "third person" perspective on the act and can lead to irresolvable controversies. We say, "If Jones were free, he would have stolen the money. Jones stole the money. Ergo, he is free." But similarly, "If Jones were determined, he would have stolen the money. Jones stole the money." Knowing what Jones has done can neither prove nor disprove his freedom.

The advent of the mathematical-experimental method of science—the scientific revolution—constituted a challenge to the notion of freedom, because freedom is necessarily written out of the modern scientific project. The genius of the scientific method lies in its reduction of physical reality to mathematical models. This was initially and most dramatically made clear by Newton's *Principia Mathematica*, in which the motions of the heavens are modeled by a system of relatively simple equations expressing the laws of motion and gravity.

The success and power of Newton's theories led almost immediately to a crisis concerning human freedom. If the motions of the planets—and, indeed, every object having mass—can be precisely located in space and time, if its behavior is determined by invariant mathematical laws, then there seems no room for freedom. Indeed, according to the mathematical-experimental paradigm of science, freedom is written out of science from the start. The scientific method itself precludes the notion of freedom.

7 Servais Pinckaers, O.P., *The Sources of Christian Ethics*, 330–42.

Pierre-Simon Laplace put this position starkly in 1820:

> We ought to regard the present state of the universe as the effect of its antecedent state and as the cause of the state that is to follow. An intelligence knowing all the forces acting in nature at a given instant, as well as the momentary positions of all things in the universe, would be able to comprehend in one single formula the motions of the largest bodies as well as the lightest atoms in the world, provided that its intellect were sufficiently powerful to subject all data to analysis; to it nothing would be uncertain, the future as well as the past would be present to its eyes. The perfection that the human mind has been able to give to astronomy affords but a feeble outline of such an intelligence.[8]

Within the context of the sciences so conceived, freedom is identified with unpredictability. The Third Antinomy of Kant's *Critique of Pure Reason* reads:

> We must, then, assume a causality through which something takes place, the cause of which is not itself determined, in accordance with necessary laws, by another cause antecedent to it, that is to say, an *absolute spontaneity* of the cause whereby a series of appearances [...] begins *of itself*.[9]

The idea at work here is that of "absolute spontaneity," unpredictable by any antecedent cause. An event or action is free, according to Kant, if it is not determined by a prior event according

8 Pierre-Simon Laplace, *The Stanford Encyclopedia of Philosophy*, January 21, 2016. Downloaded March 4, 2022, from https://plato.stanford.edu/entries/determinism-causal/.

9 Immanuel Kant, *Critique of Pure Reason* (New York: St Martin's Press, 1965), A446, B474.

to necessary laws. The Third Antinomy arises precisely because every event must have a cause, which excludes the absolute spontaneity necessary to originate a sequence of causes. Contemporary debates about freedom and necessity have generally focused on such a conception of freedom, even if less starkly stated. Kant's solution to the antinomy is to posit the laws of freedom, which govern morals but are unrelated to the realm of phenomena.

> Because these laws are either laws of nature or laws of freedom. The science of the former is called physics, while that of the latter is called ethics; they are also called doctrine of nature and doctrine of morals respectively.[10]

The upshot of this is that as far as one's own internal life is concerned, the decisions he makes according to his assessment of the Categorical Imperative, the person is free. He can and should choose what the universal moral law would dictate. However, if the observation of *another* person's behavior is under consideration, then his behavior is a phenomenon whose behavior falls under the necessary laws governing the phenomenal realm. So, if I am in straitened financial circumstances and can deceive my neighbor into lending me a sum of money which I have no intention of repaying, I can indeed reason to the morally correct decision. However, if called upon to predict another's behavior, I would have to study him, his background, possibly his brain-states, and other factors to determine what he may, in fact, do. Along the same lines, Peter van Inwagen writes:

> Anyone who has thought carefully about the problem of free will and who has come to a conclusion about free will that is detailed and systematic enough to be called a theory of free will must accept *some* proposition that seems self-evidently false. To choose what theory of free

10 Immanuel Kant, *Grounding of the Metaphysics of Morals*, 387.

> will to accept is to choose *which* seemingly self-evidently false proposition one accepts.[11]

Van Inwagen tries to resolve the conflict by saying that freedom means simply freedom to do what one wants,[12] but what one wants may well be determined by unseen or undetected forces. Therefore, one *feels free*, even though his behavior might well be determined.

It may be helpful to consider some examples of compromised or suppressed human freedom. In Stanley Milgram's famous shock experiments to test obedience to authority, 65% of his subjects obeyed to the point of (apparently) endangering the life of another person.[13] In his study of German police conscripted to kill Polish prisoners during World War II, Christopher Browning found that of those "ordinary men" drafted into the work of committing these wartime atrocities, approximately 20% refused to comply with orders to murder civilians.[14] These reports, along with several other studies, suggest that between 65% and 80% of a population can be expected to kill or endanger the lives of others when they are acting under authority. Does this tell us anything about freedom? The evidence seems to indicate that any random population is statistically predictable, that a large percentage of subjects will commit atrocious acts when some authority requires it. The question is whether human behavior is fully determined, whether in every case factors beyond or outside of the mind will determine a person's behavior.

Two consequences follow from determinism: First, moral responsibility disappears. Subjective feelings of guilt notwithstanding, strong determinism holds that one's behavior is beyond one's

11 Peter van Inwagen, op. cit., 70.

12 Ibid., 75.

13 S. A. McLeod, *Simply Psychology*, https://www.simplypsychology.org/milgram.html. February 5, 2017. Downloaded April 1, 2020.

14 Christopher Browning, *Ordinary Men: Reserve Police Battalion 101 and the Final Solution in Poland* (New York: Harper, 1992).

own control. Second, final causality—the good—is relativized and ultimately discredited as a concept. This holds even if we adopt van Inwagen's criterion of freedom as doing what one wants, because "what one wants" need not refer to an objective good but only to a subjective state.

In fact, strong determinism is a red herring. In every human decision, there is *something* that leads one to choose a particular act, but this need not imply that freedom is illusory. We need not be caught on the horns of van Inwagen's dilemma of having to deny a self-evident truth. Of course, human persons do not enjoy absolute freedom. We are indeed powerfully influenced by hereditary and environmental factors. However, there is no reason to adopt strong determinism at the cost of discarding free will. The theory of strong determinism of human acts is not indicated by data, evidence, or experience. The great challenge to teachers, governors, employers, advertising agents, and parents—indeed, anyone concerned to have others behave as they want—is precisely the freedom of those they hope to influence. We do not see human beings behaving inevitably in strictly predictable ways that demand an account. Rather we find people to be unpredictable, sometimes maddeningly so. Dictators go to great lengths to bring their subjects into line—and still some of their subjects resist. Strong determinism is not called for by the evidence, as though the persistent regularities in human behavior demand an account, but by an ideological commitment to mechanical causality and the rejection of final causation.

Freedom and the community

Locke and Mill

Beyond the issue of scientific determinism is that of political freedom, which was a major concern of the Enlightenment. John Locke writes,

> To understand political power right, [...] we must consider what estate all men are naturally in, and that is, a

> *state of perfect freedom* to order their actions, and dispose of their possessions and persons as they think fit, within the bounds of the law of Nature, without asking leave or depending upon the will of any other man.[15]

From this Locke moves quickly to affirm the right of the state to exercise power over its free subjects. The warrant for this right is the *consent of the governed*. Furthermore, this consent of the governed implicitly but necessarily implies the consent to decisions of the majority.[16] This conception of freedom was expressly written into the American "Declaration of Independence." The difficulties implicit in this account quickly became evident in the first eight decades of the country's existence, as the "consent of the governed" authorizing the adoption of the U.S. Constitution did not include the consent either of the black slaves or the native Indians. Arguably it was not until 1964 that black Americans acquired the full rights of citizenship, and in some respects the Indians' lack of consent was never addressed. Indeed, one may question the "consent" of the native-born citizen, who never expressly consented to the rules under which he lives[17]—a matter lampooned by Gilbert and Sullivan with a song from *HMS Pinafore*.

> For he might have been a Roossian
> or French or Turk or Proossian
> or perhaps Italian.
> But in spite of all temptations
> to belong to other nations,
> he remains an Englishman.[18]

15 John Locke, *Second Treatise of Government*, §4.

16 Ibid., §§95–98.

17 For a contemporary discussion of this issue, see Felix E Oppenheim, *Dimensions of Freedom: An Analysis* (New York: St. Martin's Press, 1961); also Isaiah Berlin, "Two Concepts of Liberty," in *Four Essays on Liberty* (Oxford: Oxford University Press, 1969), 166–217.

18 W. S. Gilbert, "He Is an Englishman," song from Gilbert and Sullivan, *HMS Pinafore*.

John Stuart Mill considers such issues in his *On Liberty*, where his concern is freedom, not in the metaphysical sense, but "civil, or social liberty: the nature and limits of the power which can be legitimately exercised by society over the individual."[19] His guiding principle reads:

> The sole end for which mankind are warranted individually or collectively, in interfering with the liberty of action of any of their number, is self-protection. [...] Over himself, over his own body and mind, the individual is sovereign.[20]

As long as he respects the rights of others, what one person does is only his own concern, even if his acts work against his own good. Of course, this issue is not simple, because an individual's act invariably affects others—consider the debates over smoking, recreational drugs, even prostitution. Mill must acknowledge that even freedom of expression must have some limits; consider the classic example of crying "Fire!" in a crowded theater.

The underlying value for Mill is especially important for our investigation.

> The grand, leading principle, towards which every argument unfolded in these pages directly converges, is the absolute and essential importance of human development in its richest diversity. [...] The only Freedom which deserves the name, is that of pursuing our own good in our own way, so long as we do not attempt to deprive others of theirs or impede their efforts to obtain it.[21]

Contrary to the Aristotelian-Thomistic position, it is not for

19 John Stuart Mill, *On Liberty*, 1, 6.
20 Ibid,. 9.
21 Ibid., 12.

laws or the state to make people good citizens.[22] Rather the individual is to seek his own good in his own way, to be hindered by society only when he actually harms others. He has no responsibility directly to benefit others or the community as a whole. Furthermore, Mill does not acknowledge, as do Aristotle and Aquinas, that there is a good for man as man, regardless of his personal impulses and genius. To Mill's mind, the great goal is to allow the individual to manifest his own individual strength of character, manifest in his inner impulses.

> Yet desires and impulses are as much a part of a perfect human being as beliefs and restraints; and strong impulses are only perilous when not properly balanced. [...] A person whose desires and impulses are his own—are the expression of his own nature, as it has been developed and modified by his own culture—is said to have a character.[23]

Mill's text here is remarkable on two points. First is that the individual's character is based not on reason but on "desires and impulses," which constitute his character. When allied with "conscience," which restrains strong impulses from harming others, such strong characters benefit society. The principal issue is the development of one's own genius. Custom, tradition, and conformity are the great evils to be avoided. Unwittingly, Mill has embraced a form of romanticism by which the inner energy of the human psyche lies at the root of creativity and freedom. An attentive reading of Mill's book, however, reveals the irreconcilable tensions implicit in the libertarianism with which the work begins. This romanticized inner energy, this character provides the foundation for the strongly held sign of conscience that Newman speaks of, "the right of self-will."[24]

22 *Summa Theologiae*, Ia, IIae, q. 92, a. 1.

23 Mill, *On Liberty*, 57.

24 John Henry Newman, *Newman Reader:* "Letter to the Duke of Norfolk," 250.

Here we should note that neither in Locke's nor in Mill's writing do we find any spiritual meaning to freedom. The freedom of Locke's individual whether in the state of nature or in civic society is the freedom to dispose of himself, his property, and his resources as he will. Mill expressly eschews any ontological account of freedom but considers only the relative freedom of one person vis-à-vis his fellows. If a social scientist (say) should propose that no person is free of the occult forces of biology and psychology, this would constitute no serious problem for either Locke or Mill. The point is that the person experiences himself as free. Whether he is freely ordered to a transcendent good is simply not a concern of these two thinkers.

Marxism

The issue of freedom arises from quite a different angle in Marxism, which ignores and indeed denies the freedom of the individual person. Because the principal agents in human history are not persons but classes,[25] the freedom of the individual person is irrelevant. One's place in history, which is to say the meaning and focus of one's life, depends entirely on his class membership. Freedom can be situated only in the class. The workers of the world must unite because, as proletarians, they have nothing to lose but their chains. Personal freedom of speech or religion, or even freedom from being cheated by his neighbor in a private dispute, is irrelevant. Within this framework the individual's behavior is, as it were, the result of the social and ultimately economic forces acting upon him. Not only does personal freedom disappear, but it is irrelevant.

John Paul II attributes the fall of Communistic systems in Central and Eastern Europe to the nature of Marxism itself. The problem is that Marxism is fundamentally materialistic and atheistic. Granting that the communist economic systems were inefficient, the principal reason for their failure lay in their inability to satisfy the fundamental spiritual needs of the human person.

25 Karl Marx, Friedrich Engels, *Manifesto of the Communist Party* in *The Portable Karl Marx* (New York: Penguin Books, 1981), 203.

> Socialism likewise maintains that the good of the individual can be realized without reference to his free choice, to the unique and exclusive responsibility which he exercises in the face of good or evil. Man is thus reduced to a series of social relationships, and the concept of the person as the autonomous subject of moral decision disappears, the very subject whose decisions build the social order.[26]

This was a theme he reiterated in the newly free and independent states after the end of Communism. "It seems to me possible to say that the among the ultimate, but not least reasons [for the fall of Communism] is the atheism that inspired Marxism."[27] Of course, until 1978 Karol Wojtyła had worked in Communist Poland, where engagement with Marxist principles was inevitable. It was during that period, in 1969, that he published *Osoba i czyn* [*Person and Act*] in which he analyzed in great depth and detail the roots of human subjectivity and with this the experience and meaning of freedom. He later comments,

> When I wrote the book *The Acting Person*, the first to take notice of it, obviously in order to attack it, were the Marxists. In fact, my book represented an unsettling element in their polemic against religion and the Church.[28]

Freedom and the dignity of the person are categories simply incompatible with Marxist thought.

26 John Paul II, Encyclical *Centesimus Annus* (Vatican City: Libreria Editrice Vaticana, 1991), §13.

27 John Paul II, *Discorse di Giovanni Paolo II al Mondo Accademico e agli intellettuali*, Vilnius Lithuania, 5 September 1993. Downloaded July 28, 2023, from https://www.vatican.va/content/john-paul-ii/it/speeches/1993/september/documents/hf_jp-ii_spe_19930905_universita-vilnius.html.

28 John Paul II, *Crossing the Threshold of Hope* (New York: Alfred A Knopf, 1994), 199.

Conditions on freedom: An historical example

As bodily creatures in space and time, human beings are not completely or perfectly free. Not only are we limited by nature, but psychological and social conditioning often restrict our freedom. We often seem unable to do what we should. St. Paul complains that even when he knows what is good, he does the evil that he would not do (Romans 7:19). Our acts are always (or almost always) conditioned, whether by law, custom, public opinion, or propaganda. In this condition, we are called to be morally responsible for our own good and evil. Let us consider a concrete historical example of freedom and the confrontation with evil.

From the end of World War II until 1989, Czechoslovakia was governed by a totalitarian Communist government subject to the Communist Party of the U.S.S.R. During that period, freedoms of speech, religion, the press, peaceful assembly, and even thought itself were sharply curtailed by the state through the arm of it secret police. The earlier years of this period were a time of Stalinist terror. After Stalin's death in March 1953, the terror was replaced by a gentler but still effective regime of control that Václav Havel called post-totalitarianism.

In his "Letter to Dr. Husák," General Secretary of the Czechoslovak Communist Party Havel attributes the Party's continued dominance of the populace to a different mechanism than sheer terror.

> We are concerned with fear in a deeper sense, an ethical sense if you will, namely the more or less conscious participation in the collective awareness of a permanent and ubiquitous danger; anxiety about what is being, or might be, threatened: becoming gradually used to this threat as a substantive part of the actual world. [...] Notoriously, it is not the absolute value of a threat which counts, so much as its relative value. It is not so much what someone objectively loses, as the subjective importance on the plane on which he lives, with its own scale of values. [...]

> Everyone has something to lose and so everyone has reason to be afraid.[29]

The fear referred to here is not that of the knock in the middle of the night when state authorities take the citizen off to an underground prison. The mechanism that enables this pervasive threat is the state secret police and its network of operatives and informants by which the state knows (or seems to know) everything about each citizen. Havel describes how this operates in his essay, "The Power of the Powerless,"[30] with particular emphasis on the importance of submission of one's mind to the regnant ideology. In that essay, Havel presents the image of the greengrocer who consents to affirm the Party's lie by doing what is expected of him. Along with the carrots and onions in the daily delivery, he receives a sign for his window: "Workers of the world, Unite!" He is expected to place it in his shop window. By this act he affirms the ideology he does not believe in. And if he does not display the sign? If he revolts? Havel writes,

> The bill is not long in coming. He will be relieved of his post as manager of the shop and transferred to the warehouse. His pay will be reduced. His hopes for a holiday in Bulgaria will evaporate. His children's access to higher education will be threatened [...].[31]

The greengrocer loses what the regime controls. As he gives the lie to the regime's ideology his life becomes much harder. Friends turn away from him and his family suffers. To live according to truth is rebellion that must be punished. Any ordinary Czech or Slovak of that period must live that lie if he hoped to have a decent life. He was required to participate in evil.

29 Václav Havel, "Dear Dr. Husák," in V. Havel, *Open Letters* (London: Faber & Faber, 1991), 53–54.

30 Václav Havel, "The Power of the Powerless," in V. Havel, *Living in Truth* (London: Faber & Faber, 1990), 36–122.

31 Václav Havel, "The Power of the Powerless," 146.

When the Communist regime fell in 1989, Václav Havel was elected president of a free Czechoslovakia. In his inaugural Address to the Nation, on 1 January 1990, celebrating his country's newly won freedom, he pointed to the *moral* harm that his people had suffered.

> The worst thing is that we live in a contaminated moral environment. We fell morally ill because we became used to saying something different from what we thought. [...] We had become used to the totalitarian system and accepted it as an unchangeable fact and thus helped to perpetuate it. In other words, we are all [...] responsible for the operation of the totalitarian machinery. None of us is just its victim: we are all also its co-creators.[32]

This is certainly an unusual statement by a politician—to tell his people that they are partly responsible for the evil done to them. Any savvy public figure would shift blame *away* from his audience. His people were in fact *deprived of their freedom*. Politically smarter is to identify the main culprits, go forward, and build a new future. Havel's point—and this applies to many other victims of oppression or seduction—was not that the Czechs and Slovaks should have risen in rebellion; even a modest rebellion in 1968 had been brutally crushed. In his address Havel told his countrymen:

> [W]e have to accept this legacy as a sin we committed against ourselves. [...] We cannot blame the previous rulers for everything [...] because it could blunt the duty that faces each of us today, namely the obligation to act independently, freely, reasonably, and quickly.[33]

32 Václav Havel, *Open Letters*, 391–92.
33 Ibid., 392.

Havel called the newly free citizens of Czechoslovakia to be responsible for themselves by acknowledging their participation in the regime of lies and by taking up the moral responsibility for their own lives and country. Even though they had been compelled to live in the lie, they were responsible for their acts.

> This digression into the challenges of a populace enslaved to an omnipresent ideology that warps the culture and hence the lives of the people, brings us again to the question of fundamental freedom. The citizens participate in and even propagate the lies—the exhortation, "Workers of the world, unite!" concludes the Communist Manifesto—while hoping to maintain their moral integrity.

This experience formed Karol Wojtyła's thought. Servais Pinckaers writes,

> To understand John Paul II's concern and determination on this point it is appropriate, in our opinion, to refer to the experience that he lived through under the Communist regime, under the threat of a veritable system of lies where one could not preserve oneself without adopting, with the Russian dissidents, the principle "never lie," never to touch the mechanisms of the lie. In this situation, it was clear that fidelity to truth was the necessary condition of freedom.[34]

Existential freedom

Jean Paul Sartre famously denied the reality of a human nature. If there is no human nature, according to which one can

34 Servais Pinckaers, *Pour une lecture de Veritatis Splendor, R*, 39.
35 Jean-Paul Sartre, "The Humanism of Existentialism," in J-P Sartre, *Essays in Existentialism* (Seacaucus, NJ: Citadel Press, 1999), 47.

know what it is to be human or what belongs to the human being as such, there is no preexisting standard of right and wrong.

> The doctrine I am presenting [...] declares, "There is no reality except in action." Moreover, it goes further, since it adds, "Man is nothing else than his plan; he exists only to the extent that he fulfills himself; he is therefore nothing else than the ensemble of his acts, nothing else than his life."[35]

In virtue of this conception, the individual is completely alone, left on his own to decide concerning his life and acts. He is forlorn.

> When I declare that freedom in every concrete circumstance can have no other aim than to want itself, if man has once become aware that in his forlornness he imposes values, he can no longer want but one thing, and that is freedom as the basis of all values. [...] It means that the ultimate meaning of the acts of honest men is the quest for freedom as such.[36]

Therefore, writes Sartre, "Man is a useless passion."[37] We do well to compare this with J. S. Mill's individual genius who is such, not by his specific accomplishments or knowledge and wisdom, but by the strength of his impulses and desires. Recent moral theologians (e.g., J. Fuchs, Böckle, J. B. Metz) have so emphasized the notion of human creative freedom as to hold that man *is* his freedom, a notion that Andrzej Szostek succinctly summarized: "Man is embodied freedom."[38] Underlying such conceptions is a notion

36 Ibid., 57.

37 Jean-Paul Sartre, *Being and Nothingness: An Essay on Phenomenological Ontology* (New York: Philosophical Library, 1956), 615.

38 Andrzej Szostek, *Natur-Vernunft-Freiheit*, 155.

of the human person as a kind of divinity. From a rejection of the empiricist or deterministic conception of the human being as merely a biological organism there arises a conception of the person as the source of truth and values. Therefore, the human being must sketch out his own structure. Absent teleology in nature (this according to Darwinism and contemporary philosophy of science), man must construct his own teleology from within himself.[39]

Fundamental Option

One of the most difficult issues, philosophically speaking, in contemporary moral theology is that of the *fundamental option* and its impact on the doctrine of sin. This notion calls seriously into question the Church's traditional distinction between mortal and venial sin by positing a third category, *serious* sin, which concerns grave matter but without the sin's being mortal. Concerning this fundamental option, Joseph Fuchs writes,

> Whereas freedom of choice is encountered within our reflective conscious experience, this is not true of the fundamental freedom. [...] So, awareness of *fundamental* freedom is not directly accessible to observation and verification. Necessarily athematic (that is, not conceptual and not reflectively conscious), it is also termed "transcendental."[40]

Only an act or decision touching one's fundamental freedom would truly constitute a mortal sin. Acts within one's ordinary "reflective conscious experience" involve a direct experience of the world, other persons, one's emotions and impulses—all the

39 Ibid., 143–47.

40 Joseph Fuchs, "Good Acts and Good Persons," in C. Curran and R. McCormick, S.J., *John Paul II and Moral Theology: Readings in Moral Theology No. 10* (New York, Mahwah NJ: Paulist, 1990), 49.

elements of immediate consciousness—but without touching the transcendental level of one's fundamental disposition toward goodness or evil. Therefore, an act limited by space and time within the finite capacities of one's existential situation can be seriously wrong in some respect without touching one's fundamental freedom. As in the example cited earlier, a discouraged salesman might fall into adultery on his business trip, or a Job might even curse God, without his act touching the disposition of his fundamental freedom. Richard McCormick sharpens this perspective further by maintaining that the fundamental freedom is more than simply the matter of a particular choice: "The turning away from God that results in the loss of charity must be a *self*-disposition, not merely freedom of choice."[41] Therefore, according to this theory it s almost impossible to conceive of an act that would change one's fundamental disposition for or against God.

Before addressing John Paul II's treatment of this issue in *Veritatis Splendor*, we do well to consider his conception of freedom in *Person and Act*. In the text just quoted, Richard McCormick contrasts "self-disposition" and "freedom of choice." Implicit to the latter is the notion of freedom as the freedom of alternatives, of choice between 1 and 0 or x and y, between "this and that." Unless they are determined by a flip of the coin, such choices are made based on factual relations within the ontic environment. The Samaritan can help the victim of robbers, which will alleviate the victim's suffering, or pass on the other side of the road, which will keep him safe as he pursues his own concerns. His choice of alternatives does not affect his self-disposition in charity. By contrast, Karol Wojtyła insists that the act does determine that person as good or evil, because a person's every act is efficacious, marked by the person's efficacy. This means that while exercising efficient causality (in the Aristotelian sense) the acting person makes himself to be the cause of the act. He not only effects changes in the world, but he also effects a change in himself. Therefore, the

41 Richard McCormick, S.J., *Critical Calling*, 182.

efficacy of the act marks the origin of morality within himself. Wojtyła writes,

> The fruit of this causation, the homogeneous *effect of the efficacy of the personal "I," is morality*—not as an abstraction, but as the strictest existential reality connected with the person as its proper subject. Through his acts, through conscious action, man becomes good or evil, good or evil in the moral sense. [...]
>
> This becoming, the *fieri* of man in the moral sense, the *fieri* most closely connected with the person, *determines the realistic character of good and evil, of the moral values themselves*. By no means are they contents of consciousness alone; they are contents of human, personal *fieri*.[42]

The coin, as it lands on the floor, has made no choice. Subject to the initial conditions and the laws of gravity and angular momentum, it comes up as "heads" or "tails." By contrast, the human person wills that one value should be realized rather than some others and decides to perform the requisite acts to realize that good (as he understands it). He *should* reflect upon the act before performing it, but even if he fails to reflect, the conscious choice of his own will to perform it makes it his own act. We may think of the seducer who invites a prospective partner in sex to his flat for a drink, thinking "whatever else might happen happens." Thoughtless as the subsequent act may be, nothing other than his own will chose the act for him.

Particularly important in this regard is Karl Rahner's concept of the *fundamental option* [*Grundentscheidung*], which is the consequence of the person's fundamental self-determination, the basic and definitive orientation of his life.[43] At the heart of this

42 *Person and Act*, 202.

43 Karl Rahner, *Grundkurs des Glaubens: Einführung in den Begriff des Christentums* (Freiburg im Breisgau: Herder, 1976), 35–121. See also Andrzej Szostek, *Natur-Vernunft-Freiheit*, 83.

conception is the primacy of the *will*. The freedom that is affirmed is not simply the free choice of the will, which is the will's power to choose between alternative options, but the freedom of the will to constitute the person himself by directing him toward the good.

This notion of conscience as a decision, rooted in the will, is philosophically and theologically developed in the notion of the *fundamental option*. Commenting on Karl Rahner's analysis in favor of this conception, Andrzej Szostek writes,

> The consequence of such a [Rahnerian] conception of freedom is, among other things, the view that sees the moral value of an act not only in its conformity with the objective norm of morality, [...] but also in this, that it *manifests one's freedom*.[44]

Further on, he adds,

> With this *the human being must freely decide who he will be* both because of its personal structure, which "demands" its own creative decision from the subject, and also because of the "normative inconclusiveness" of the given world; he has to decide *how he will understand himself*.[45]

Here the appeal to situationism becomes significant, for it leads to *nominalism* which makes the individual absolutely decisive with respect to good and evil.

> What Rahner finds particularly valuable about situationism is the emphasis on the individuality of the concrete moral subject and his decisions, an individuality

44 Szostek, op. cit., 87. Translation by the author. Emphasis in the original.

45 Ibid., 147. Emphasis in the original.

> that is not adequately grasped in the framework of the so-called essentialist ethics.[46]

The significance of this is that situationism—or the application of individual conscience to *determine what is good in this situation*—denies the universal. Therefore, good and evil are not knowable, but they are to be decided in the event. With this we are not far from Sartre's conception of the subject defining himself.

According to this conception of conscience, the transcendent good to which the person is called can consist only in the realization of one's own freedom. The true good for *me* is to live in conformity to the good as *I* conceive it, as *I* have chosen. If, on the other hand, there is a transcendent good to which the will is ordered, then how can the will be said to be free? Is it not bound to and limited by this good outside itself? Indeed, humans are embarrassingly susceptible to social pressures, as well as to personal manipulation through the exercise of power by others, sex, financial temptations, and threats—so much so that we might question whether anyone can truly call his acts his own. Can anyone be free of the factors that have conditioned him? This question lies close to the core of serious objections to John Paul II's arguments in *Veritatis Splendor*. What, if anything, constitutes a free act? If no act can be truly free, then the theological concept of mortal sin becomes unintelligible.

In his Apostolic Exhortation on Reconciliation and Penance, Pope John Paul II wrote,

> And when through sin, the soul commits a disorder that reaches the point of turning away from its ultimate end [*deordinatur per peccatum usque ad aversionem ab ultimo fine*], God, to which it is bound by charity, then the sin is mortal. [...] For mortal sin exists also when a person knowingly and willingly, for whatever reason, chooses something gravely disordered. In fact, such a

46 A. Szostek, op. cit. 70.

> choice already includes contempt for the divine law, a rejection of God's love for humanity and the whole of creation; the person turns away from God and loses charity.[47]

Two points are worth noting here. First, the soul commits a disorder that amounts to a turning away from God, its ultimate end. Implicit in this "turning" is the choice of an act, a turning *per peccatum*. Second is that the act is done "knowingly and willingly" [*etiam cum sciens ac volens*], an expression that, while clear, has been controverted in recent years. Commenting on this text, Richard McCormick writes,

> What does "knowingly and willingly" mean? If it refers to *freedom of choice* only, that is one thing, and most theologians would deny the statement. For mortal sin is precisely synonymous with the use of *fundamental freedom*. The turning away from God that results in the loss of charity must be a *self*-disposition, not merely freedom of choice.[48]

Here Fr. McCormick identifies an act done "knowingly and willingly" with an exercise of *freedom of choice*. Based on what he knows about nutrition and his own tastes, the diner chooses chicken rather than beef. The act of ordering the chicken is done knowingly and willingly. Presumably this choice will make him marginally healthier. Of course, John Paul II was not speaking of restaurants, but of acts gravely disordered; a popular example was of the wearied and discouraged traveling salesman who falls into an adulterous one-night stand at his hotel. To relieve

47 John Paul II, Apostolic Exhortation *Reconciliatio et Paenitentia* (Vatican City: Libreria Editrice Vaticana, 1984), §17.

48 Richard A. McCormick, S.J., *The Critical Calling: Reflections on Moral Dilemmas since Vatican II* (Washington, DC: Georgetown University Press, 1989), 182.

his feelings of failure and loneliness he goes to bed with a willing partner, forgetting his marital obligation. If his wife finds evidence of the dalliance (perhaps a condom pack in his pocket), she will be unhappy and there will be strife at home. This is a serious moral failing, but is it a choice against God? We can readily understand and even sympathize with his feelings of loneliness, amplified by failure, which can cloud his judgment. Who are we to condemn? Freedom of choice, so conceived, is ultimately nothing but a rearrangement of things in the environment or within one's own psyche, which may be advantageous or bad. In the moment, his downcast mind, clouded by two or three drinks, chooses comfort rather than fidelity to a distant wife. In the morning, he may well regret this choice.

Underlying this objection is the matter of one's consciousness of the moral character of his act. Might it not be argued that in some circumstances one who performs an act that is objectively wrong may be impeded by the situation or by psychological factors from recognizing the evil of the act and resisting it. Pope Francis addresses some of the factors surrounding this issue.

> A distinction is not always adequately drawn between "voluntary" and "free" acts. A person may clearly and willingly desire something evil, but do so as the result of an irresistible passion or a poor upbringing. In such cases, while the decision is voluntary, inasmuch as it does not run counter to the inclination of their desire, it is not free, since it is practically impossible for them not to choose that evil. We see this in the case of compulsive drug addicts.[49]

An act might be voluntary but not free. Hence, a voluntary act may well turn out not to be blameworthy and therefore not seriously sinful. The experience is fairly common for young

49 Pope Francis, Apostolic Exhortation *Amoris Laetitia* (Vatican City: Libreria Editrice Vaticana, 2016), 273.

adolescents just entering puberty, cigarette smokers, persons trying to lose weight, and others with strong compulsions. They know what they need and want to do, but they fall back into masturbation, smoking another cigarette, eating a box of cookies, or otherwise yielding to the compulsion. The addict (if we may use that term) feels himself subject to his compulsion. Nevertheless, because his behavior is voluntary—subject to his express decision—he may well not want to do it. The paradox arises from an inadequate understanding of the will and its freedom.

In the physical realm freedom is a measure of indeterminism. A railroad train has two degrees of freedom: forward and backward. An airplane has six: forward and backward (by turning around, of course), higher or lower, and to either side. The American shopper has a wider variety of choices—hence more freedom—concerning breakfast cereals than an Italian, but not so much freedom regarding pasta. The exercise of freedom of choice is governed only by the number of options and scope for action.

Human freedom involves more than this freedom of options because the human person governs his behavior and himself according to his understanding and will. The traveling salesman in our previous example is confronted with more than a choice of options as he faces the temptation presented by the woman at the bar. Is his mind a self-pitying nexus of emotion, seeking emotional relief from tough experiences? Or is he a faithful husband committed to the good of his wife and family? In making this choice, he also chooses how he will regard the woman in the bar, what she is to him, whether a congenial stranger or a source of relief for his lust. In making his choice he does far more than potentially to rearrange things in the world. He decides what and how he will love.

In *Veritatis Splendor*, Pope John Paul II correctly identifies the argument posed by the theorists of the fundamental option, writing,

> There is no doubt that Christian moral teaching, even in its biblical roots, acknowledges the specific

> importance of a *fundamental choice* which qualifies the moral life and engages freedom on a radical level before God. It is a question of the decision of faith, of the *obedience of faith* [...].[50]

But by his reference to fundamental choice, might John Paul II have missed the point of the fundamental freedom theorists, identifying the fundamental option as the choice to follow Jesus? Like any other, this is a categorical choice. Might one decline this option while maintaining his fundamental option for the Absolute Good? Does not even this choice fail to reach the level of the fundamental freedom? In fact, it does not, and the reason is both important and instructive. Concerning this theory, John Paul II writes,

> A *distinction* thus comes to be introduced *between the fundamental option and deliberate choices of a concrete kind of behaviour.* "Good" and "evil" are restricted to the moral, transcendental dimension, "right" and "wrong" to "innerworldly" behavior; hence "specific kinds of behaviour, which are judged to be morally right or wrong only on the basis of a technical calculation of the proportion between the "premoral" or "physical" goods and evils which actually result from the action. This is pushed to the point where a concrete kind of behaviour, even one freely chosen, comes to be considered as a merely physical process, and not according to the criteria proper to a human act.[51]

And from this he goes on to describe the call to discipleship, the *sequela Christi,* which is a concrete choice but one of eternal moment. Later in that same section, citing Galatians 5 with its warning that sin leads to slavery, he equates the act of faith with "a

50 *Veritatis Splendor,* §66 (emphasis added).
51 Veritatis Splendor, §65.

fundamental option." Might one not object that this act of faith, expressed by affirming the Creed or some similar formula, is precisely a categorical and not a transcendental decision? And might one not therefore maintain that even if a particular categorical act should implicitly constitute a denial of that faith that act need not necessarily reach to the transcendental level and therefore not constitute a repudiation of the fundamental option?

As we consider this, several crucial factors become clear. The first and surely most obvious is the *presumption that the sinner is in the state of grace in the first place or, in other words, that his freedom is already fundamentally ordered to the transcendent Good*. This presumption that one's fundamental option is towards the good arguably amounts to a denial of original sin. Indeed, it is difficult anthropologically to locate this fundamental freedom. Freedom is the will's capacity to love what is good and reject what is evil. The moral obligation is to love the good as presented to the rational appetite or will. Freedom is particularly manifest in the power of free choice by which one cognitively weighs alternative goods in order to choose one of them. One can choose between eating either vegetables or steak, between either accepting frustration of desire or using contraceptives. However, no state of affairs or object of proposed action that one can envision adequately embodies the transcendent good that is to be the object of the fundamental choice. This very fact implies a further problem, namely that the fundamental ordination to the absolute good is unaccounted for. What accounts for the person's transition from the state of original sin to fundamental goodness? This fundamental choice requires an account of the will.

If the transcendent good is to be found only in God, as fundamental option theorists agree, then it is not possible for human reason adequately to frame the choice, because in this life God himself cannot be known directly by human intellect. St. Thomas' treatment of the question is instructive. Under the conditions of this life, God cannot be known except in his effects. Therefore, it is conceivable that a person could turn away from God toward Zeus, or the promise of a life of earthly pleasure, or to the hope of the proletariat revolution.[52] What natural reason can know of God is only that he is the First Cause, perfect in his being, identical with his essence and existence, eternal, and perfect in goodness. Any mental image of God as an object of choice is inadequate. In this respect, the theorists of fundamental option are correct. One can never know whether he has directed his full being toward God. He can, however, direct himself toward the universal good, repudiating any limited good in the hope of finding his way to the ultimate and true good, conceived only abstractly.

In this life, the knowledge we can have directly of God can only be in faith. And faith is a theological virtue. In a text that Pope John Paul II found to be especially important, the Second Vatican Council teaches:

> The truth is that only in the mystery of the incarnate Word does the mystery of man take on light. For Adam, the first man, was a figure of Him Who was to come, namely Christ the Lord. Christ, the final Adam, by the revelation of the mystery of the Father and His love, fully reveals man to man himself and makes his supreme calling clear.[53]

The implications of this text are disconcerting, especially for the philosopher, because it clearly implies that any purely philosophical or scientific understanding of man is inadequate. "Only in the mystery of the Incarnate Word" can we make sense of the mystery of man. But the mystery of the Incarnate Word is accessible only through Revelation. It is Christ who reveals us to ourselves and makes our destiny and vocation clear. Of course, the Council Fathers did not intend to deny the value of philosophy nor of the other human sciences. What the Council tells us, however, is that the full depths of the human mystery are accessible only through Revelation. This is why that same document is able

52 *Summa Theologiae,* Ia, Iae q. 5, a. 4.
53 *Gaudium et Spes,* §22.

further on to affirm that "man, the only creature on earth that God has willed for itself, can realize himself only in the sincere gift of self," because the unity among God's sons and daughters is to be a participation in and imitation of the union of the divine Persons in the Blessed Trinity.[54]

Freedom is arguably at the heart of the mystery of man. On the one hand, the operation of freedom is perfectly clear. If the chess player positions his knight on the fifth rank, then he may open a file for his rook and achieve a decisive advantage. So, he chooses to move the knight rather than the bishop. On the other hand, we may ask if the emotionally fragile war hero, Othello, having been manipulated by a conniving subordinate, chose in complete freedom to murder Desdemona. Hamlet complains,

> Thus conscience does make cowards of us all;
> and thus the native hue of resolution
> is sicklied o'er with the pale cast of thought,
> and enterprises of great pith and moment
> with this regard their currents turn awry,
> and lose the name of action.[55]

Surrounded by the enemies of Christ and fearing for himself, Saint Peter, having boldly professed, "Lord, I am ready to go with you to prison and to death" (Luke 22:33), proceeds to deny Jesus three times. In the crucial moment as Jesus appeared before the High Priest, did Peter really love him or did he prove that he loved himself more? Freedom is a profound mystery that the theorists of fundamental option cannot resolve. Failing to account for the mystery, they cannot legitimately conclude that a specific categorical act performed by a specific person—such as for Peter to say "I do not know the man"—is not mortally sinful.

Indeed, if we consider the Gospel accounts of the trial and crucifixion of Jesus from the perspective of revisionist moral

54 Ibid., §24.
55 William Shakespeare, *Hamlet*, Act III, Scene 1, 84–88.

theology, it is possible to find plausible reasons to justify or at least excuse the actions of all the principal actors, from St. Peter to Judas, from the High Priest to Pontius Pilate. Peter was taken unawares in a threatening situation. Judas was confused about the Messiah. The High Priest was worried about the Temple, and so on. In the case of any of these principals, might one not say that although he had done serious wrong, his sin was not mortal, that he had not truly turned away from God? This specific sin, of course, was the gravest sin possible: the sin of deicide. God had come into the world as man in Jesus Christ, "true God from true God, begotten not made, consubstantial with the Father," as the Nicene-Constantinopolitan Creed states, and those to whom he came rejected him and had him killed. Pope John Paul II's argument is that Christ's words that Holy Spirit "will convince the world of sin and of righteousness and of judgment" (John 16: 8), mean that the world will be convinced of the sin of crucifying Christ. Furthermore,

> By convincing the "world" concerning the sin of Golgotha, concerning the death of the innocent Lamb, as happens on the day of Pentecost, the Holy Spirit also convinces of every sin, committed in any place and at any moment in human history: for *he demonstrates its relationship with the Cross of Christ*. The "convincing" is the demonstration of the evil of sin, of every sin, in relation to the Cross of Christ.[56]

In this way, the depths of every human heart are revealed by the Holy Spirit, the Counselor, the Third Person of the Blessed Trinity.

This analysis makes clear that *sin* is a theological and not merely a philosophical category. Aristotle's *Nicomachean Ethics* offers us an acute analysis of moral philosophy, accurately characterizing virtue and vice and providing a vision of the good life as one of virtuous activity culminating in contemplation of truth.

56 *Dominum et Vivificantem*, §32. Emphasis in the original.

What Aristotle does not provide is an account of the truly evil act. The closest he comes is in his discussion of virtue as the mean between excess and deficiency where he writes,

> But not every action nor every passion admits of a mean; for some have names that already imply badness [...] It is not possible, then, ever to be right with regard to them; one must always be wrong. Nor does goodness or badness with regard to such things depend on committing adultery with the right woman, at the right time, and in the right way, but simply to do any of them is to go wrong.[57]

Although Aristotle acknowledges that adultery is wrong to do—without arguing; he doubtless knew that his readers would recognize the reason why—he does not regard it as something that thoroughly corrupts one's relationship with the good itself. We see something similar in Plato, who regards sexual intimacy with boys as problematic but not as decisively corrupting.[58] Plato does acknowledge a kind of total corruption, which arises when a lower appetite rules over the rational part of the soul. Governed by a single overweening desire, the tyrannical soul has no rational control over its life but has become interiorly a slave to that desire.[59] We notice, however, that Plato has no account of the will. He does give an account of the degeneration of the soul into this state, but this decline from the pursuit of honors to that of pleasures to the tyranny of the one overweening lust lacks any account of freedom. Rather Plato proposes only that young people with the capacity for philosophical thought be trained in such a way that they not fall into such degradation. They must be carefully watched and guided. As the allegory of the cave indicates, the fulfillment and perfection of the person consists in philosophical

57 Aristotle, *Nicomachean Ethics*, Bk. II, ch. 6, 1007.
58 Plato, *Republic*, 402e–03; *Symposium*, 181–85b.
59 *Republic*, 572e–77.

contemplation of the Form of the Good. It is a purely intellectual salvation. Sin is a category beyond Plato and Aristotle.

As a choice against God, sin as such is irrational. One can ascribe various reasons for someone's wickedness. Of Hitler, W. H. Auden asked whether the evil of September 1, 1939, might be traced back to Martin Luther? Or is it Alois Hitler's poor parenting that is at fault? Auden wrote, "I and the public know / What all school children learn. / Those to whom evil is done / Do evil in return."[60] As his poem in its entirety shows, however, such accounts of the "psychopathic god" are inadequate. Ultimately, there is no reason that adequately explains evils. Nevertheless, they do make a certain sense. There is a logic behind them. The roots of the evil decision are hidden in the heart of the person. Precisely because of his dignity and exalted nature, the person can sin. In *Person and Act*, Wojtyła writes,

> Man is not only the agent of his action but *also its creator*. The task of evoking the coming to existing and the existence of the effect belongs to the essence of efficacy. However, the task of forming a work belongs to the essence of creativity.[61]

As elephants bathe in streams on the African plains, their huge bodies make ponds form, and other animals use these ponds for drinking and bathing. Although elephants make ponds, they do not create them, because creation is an intelligent act. The creator implements a plan that he has devised. Just as God the Creator has created the world according to his own intelligent plan, which originated from himself, the human person is, as it were, a co-creator. Gifted with his own intelligence, he acts according to his understanding and for the sake of a vision

60 W. H. Auden, "September 1, 1939" in Charles M. Coffin (editor), *The Major Poets: English and American* (New York: Harcourt, Brace and World, 1954), 518–20.

61 *Person and Act*, 171.

that he intends to implement. Karol Wojtyła writes, "We are by nature creators, not just consumers. We are creators because we think. [...] Creating as derived from thinking is so characteristic of a person that it is always an infallible sign of a person, a proof of a person's existence or presence."[62] Twenty years later, criticizing a materialistic approach to human work, Pope John Paul II wrote that:

> [...] *man is treated as an instrument of production*, whereas he—he alone, independently of the work he does—ought to be treated as the effective subject of work and its true maker and creator.[63]

The creative person—and every person acting by his intelligence is creative—is not only changing something in the external material world, but he is co-creating that world, imposing his own order upon a portion of the world and the human environment, deciding how the world shall be. This creation can be in harmony with the eternal law that God the Creator has impressed on his world, or it can be contrary to that law. And by acting contrary to the divine order, one has sinned. This is the key to our understanding of human evil.

Freedom in Karol Wojtyła's writings

At the Second Vatican Council, Archbishop Karol Wojtyła forcefully advocated for the freedom of the human person, especially for his religious freedom.[64] The Constitution resulting from those discussions states,

62 Karol Wojtyła, "Thomistic Personalism" in K. Wojtyła, *Person and Community: Selected Essays* (New York, San Francisco: Peter Lang, 1993), 171.

63 John Paul II, Encyclical *Laborem Exercens*, §7.

64 Robert Skrzypczak, *Karol Wojtyła: na Soborze Watykańskim II* (Warsaw: Centrum Myśli Jana Pawła II, 2011), 309–31.

> For its part, authentic freedom is an exceptional sign of the divine image within man. [...] Hence man's dignity demands that he act according to a knowing and free choice that is personally motivated and prompted from within, not under blind internal impulse nor by mere external pressure.[65]

This freedom includes but does not reduce to the freedom of choice discussed above. Rather, it is deeply personalistic, falling as it does in the first chapter of the Pastoral Constitution, titled "The Dignity of the Human Person." Let us consider its elements.

First and fundamentally, freedom is a sign of the divine image. The human being has a definite nature, "created 'to the image of God' and [...] capable of knowing and loving his Creator."[66] Freedom is intrinsically linked to the dignity that derives from this capacity to know and to love God himself. Gifted with the power of free choice he has a conscience, "Always summoning him to love good and avoid evil, the voice of conscience when necessary speaks to his heart: do this, shun that."[67] Furthermore, the free choice arises from personal motivation prompted from within and not compelled by blind impulse or external pressure.

This first point directly contradicts the radical existentialism of Jean-Paul Sartre. Man does have an essence, a plan for his own being, and Sartre is not the only thinker to have seen this as problematic. Some others complain that to affirm something like an "Aristotelian essentialism" would deny or at least significantly diminish human freedom, because the action of a thing flows from its nature or essence. This is a significant point in the revisionist proposals arising from the Pontifical Council for Life, many of whose members maintain that an "essentialist" ethics fails to capture the ethical situation of the individual person is her

65 *Gaudium et Spes*, §17.

66 Ibid., §12.

67 Ibid., §16.

richness and the complexity of her lived experience.[68] To know the essence of a thing is to know what to expect of it. This is closely related to the second point. If every human person, "from the very circumstance of his origin," is destined and called to communion with God, then might not this compromise his freedom? This problem seems to be acute if seen in terms of St. Thomas' account of the will's necessary desire for the perfect end. If our hearts are restless until they rest in God, does this not entail that no one can turn away from God?

The most important question for the contemporary thinker concerns the third point. How can a person securely make his decision his own? What does "prompted from within" really mean, especially in a context when the environment is filled with consumerist messages and advertisements, when governments, corporations, and the press use powerful methods of communication to form the thinking of those under their power? Indeed, if we pay careful attention, we see that much of what we hear from our neighbors—and even from our own tongues—has originated in some mass communication. We do repeat what we hear. And we do what is expected of us far more than we want to admit. If our minds are formed by others, then freedom would seem to be impossible—an illusion. We may be as susceptible to renunciation of our freedom as were the Czechs of Havel's time.

The key to Karol Wojtyła's conception of freedom is *self-determination*, a notion already implicit in Kant. Like Kant, Wojtyła emphasizes the person's *rational* character. However, although Kant greatly values reason, he places it not in relation to truth but in relation to law. That is, the role of practical reason is to "legislate for human nature" by determining how practical maxims cohere with the categorical imperative.[69] Wojtyła, on the other hand, maintains that reason is the key to the inner life by which the person forms his life.

68 Vincenzo Paglia, (ed.) *Etica teologica della vita*, 38, 136, et passim.
69 Immanuel Kant, *Grounding of the Metaphysics of Morals*, 406.

> This interior life is the spiritual life. It focuses on truth and the good. [...] [W]hat is the final cause of everything, and how to be good and possess the fullness of the good.[70]

An immediate implication of this is that reason forms one's life not according to imperatives but according to goods and ultimately the highest good. This differentiates Wojtyła's position from that of those who speak of self-determination as a matter of applying the autonomous will to assert or define one's own individuality. We may think of Mill's ideal of the man of character "whose desires and impulses are his own—are the expression of his own nature, as has been developed and modified by his own culture."[71] Or the autonomous or atomized individual as conceived by much contemporary thought.[72] This autonomous, self-defining, self-affirming approach is not Karol Wojtyła's position.

Wojtyła characterizes fundamental freedom of choice

We need not accept the premises of the fundamental option theorists. *Gaudium et Spes* speaks of "knowing and free choice that is personally motivated and prompted from within." What is this "within" that is truly the person's own and not some factor that is not his own? Karol Wojtyła points to the "inner life," and he says that this centers on truth and goodness. We must examine this more closely.

> *The history of freedom*, which the Creator gave to man as a being in his image and likeness, has developed—in the words of Augustine of Hippo—in the direction of

70 *Love and Responsibility*, 5.

71 J. S. Mill, *On Liberty*, 57.

72 O. Carter Snead, *What It Means to Be Human: The Case for the Body in Public Bioethics* (Cambridge, MA: Harvard University Press, 2020), 76–77.

> two extremes antithetical to each other: "*amor sui usque ad contemptum Dei*" on the one hand, and "*amor Dei usque ad contemptum sui*"[73] on the other.[74]

Although this choice certainly implies and depends on particular choices, it transcends them. Exhorted by his mother, the child decides to love God and hears the catechist cite the first great commandment. One immediate consequence of this is that upon entering church the child genuflects. Furthermore, he is to avoid blasphemous expressions he may hear on the playground. As he proceeds through life, different decisions will accord or conflict with this fundamental decision to love God to the contempt of self. So it is with any decision for one's life. If he chooses to be a scientist, then he must study and overcome his distaste for mathematics. To spend his time playing and watching TV will undermine his prospects for a scientific career.

To choose an ideal, be it an earthly project or a decision to love God above all things, is to transcend the material plane. This choice cannot be simply the effect of physical or material factors. This is because an ideal does not function physically. To be sure, the image of a successful scientist and the attractive prospects for rewarding future work may stimulate the young person's enthusiasm for attaining that goal. He may imagine himself in a doctoral cap and gown receiving his PhD or thanking the Nobel committee for his prize. However, these imaginings do not affect his engagement to read further, to solve unforeseen problems in the laboratory, and so on, because the appropriate behavior is related *logically or meaningfully* with his objective. This is why an inspiration or realization may completely change a plan of action, even one that is underway.

The fundamental choice between love of God to the contempt of self and love of self to the contempt of God is a choice of an ideal. The person does not, as it were, need to see himself before

73 See *De Civitate Dei*, 14, 28.

74 John Paul II/Karol Wojtyła, *Teachings for an Unbelieving World*, 53.

God and a set of procedures for loving him, which impel him to say, "Yes, I choose this" or "No, I reject this." He may perceive imaginatively a compelling vision of rewards and punishments—the rewards of heaven and the pains of hell—relating to his love of God, and these may move him to respond. However, it is necessary to note two points about this. First, one may further examine and evaluate these imagined consequences and find them less convincing or compelling. Second, any reasonably mature consideration of the notion of love leads to the conclusion that a love based on cost-benefit analysis is not truly love. Hence, we may conclude that this fundamental choice between love of God and love of self is not and cannot be physically determined. What is decisive is not power but truth.

Spirituality and transcendence

In *Person and Act* Karol Wojtyła links the notion of spirituality[75] directly with transcendence. In a phenomenological sense, transcendence of the person is manifest horizontally, in his engagement with the objects of his experience outside his own mind or imagination. Vertical transcendence "is connected with self-governance and self-possession as a specific structural property of the person."[76] This is the transcendence toward the good as such, by which the person transcends values presented to him in experience, evaluating them in terms of the good. The person can always question whether this or that object of desire is truly good, questioning the basis of its purported goodness. In virtue of vertical transcendence, the person's act cannot be determined by environmental or organic factors alone, because the appetitive impulse is subject to the evaluation of intellect and choice by the will.

75 By *spirituality* we mean the interiority of the person by which she is a spiritual being. This does not refer to the form a person's religious devotions may take.

76 *Person and Act*, 234.

Implicit in transcendence is the intellect's power to know the truth. The reference of the will to truth is intrinsic to decision: "To choose means above all to decide about the objects presented to the will in the intentional order on the basis of a certain truth. In no way can we understand choice without reducing the will's proper dynamism to truth as the principle of volition."[77] Choice of the will transcends sense desire, which exactly parallels the *appetitus rationalis* that St. Thomas speaks of. This latter is connected with and dependent upon sense perception. The freedom of the human person is based on the transcendence of intellect over sensation, and this necessarily implies the transcendence of will over impulse and instinct.

Two apparent difficulties arise from this claim that freedom depends on truth. The first is that the reference to truth seems to restrict choice. If we consider this problem more closely, however, the difficulty vanishes, for if the choice is at all meaningful, if it serves any purpose, then it needs to be linked to the truth. If one chooses to walk to Megara, then he needs to know the road to take and to start walking.[78] In other words, as the conformity of thought with reality, by knowing the truth one can act according to reality and can avoid specific errors. Without the truth, the agent literally does not know what he is doing.

The second difficulty is that truth, properly understood, is objective and interpersonal, while freedom seems of all things to be most intimately personal. Would it not be the case that the more one knows, the more determined he is by the contents of his mind and memory? Such an objection is based on a misconception of the human mind and intellect as analogous with the processing and memory storage of a computer. However, the human mind does not simply receive and store facts that are input from an external source. To be sure, the mind does indeed receive information through the senses, and this information is received in the form of data from the senses—electromagnetic signals impinging

77 *Person and Act*, 240.

78 Aristotle, *Metaphysics*, Book IV, 417b15–17.

on the retina, sound vibrations striking the eardrum, and so on. These data are transmitted by nerves to the brain, where they are further processed by the network of neurons. None of this, however, constitutes understanding, nor is it truth. In a way, this is Hume's conception, according to which the images of the mind, reserved in words and other symbols, do not—cannot—relate directly to reality. Thus, thought and desire are sharply distinguished.

Once information is received, the intellect's project is to understand it, which is to form concepts or ideas by which the object is known. The physical form of a visible object is indeed replicated on the retina, but the intelligible form of the object understood is composed by the intellect according to the data received from sensation *and* its own principles of reason. Confronted with the same real thing, many persons may understand it in the same way. However, as the realities of disagreement, debate, continued investigation and research show, different persons may arrive at very different understandings. The formation of understanding is the work of one's own mind, specifically of the agent intellect.[79] This activity is not—cannot be—physically determined but arises from within the soul of the thinking person. Of course, a particular individual may decline to seek to understand the truth, accepting instead the interpretation given by another. To do so, however, is his own choice.

During one's own life and experience of the world, reality constantly proposes, as it were, different values, particularly through the senses and sense appetites. This is evident in the process of maturation. To the infant, the good appears in the form of comfort and the satisfaction of hunger. As he outgrows his need for mother's milk, he learns of the sweetness of fruit and candy, but also—at mother's insistence—the health benefits of spinach. The process of maturation is revealed to be a process of coming more accurately (it is hoped) to identify what is truly good and not just apparently so. The good is an object that must

79 Thomas Aquinas, *De Veritate*, q. 1, a. 2; q. 10, a. 6.

be understood. The mind can, however, turn to false or illusory goods by choosing as one's principle of understanding a false criterion, such as the satisfaction of sense appetite or of vainglory. Freedom arises from the capacity to investigate and grasp the nature of the true good.

Conditions on freedom

Besides the reality of spiritual transcendence, human behavior is conditioned by temporal and physical factors. To have recognized one's moral obligations in thought does not ensure that one will fulfill them in action. Human behavior is often conditioned by factors external to personal interiority. As is most dramatically evident in addiction, physical and sense appetites can impel a person almost irresistibly toward destructive behavior. The addict can remind himself and insist that he is in control of his drinking, but then in a vulnerable moment fall into another drunken binge. The couple who have resolved to refrain from inappropriate physical intimacy find themselves overcome by lust in passionate embraces. Similarly, habits, especially those developed from childhood, and customs (social habits) can form one's character so that certain actions become almost "automatic." We see this in racism and other social prejudices. As our earlier example of life in Communist Czechoslovakia illustrates, external forces often induce persons to perform immoral actions, such as to inform the secret police of their neighbors' movements. This is indeed the situation that many martyrs have faced when obliged to worship some idol under penalty of torture or execution. The reality of these conditions suggests that freedom may not be enjoyed fully at any moment, that one's freedom must be won.

Virtue and the acquisition of freedom

Virtue is necessary to attain governance of one's bodily impulses and appetites. The function of virtue is to subordinate spontaneous emotivity to self-determination.[80] To acquire virtue is to grow in the skill of managing one's own emotivity so that the will can effectively govern one's behavior. The fruit of virtue is one's perfection as a moral agent, as the bodily responses are subordinated to reason.[81] Such development necessarily occurs over time—it is not an angelic, instantaneous affair—and this implies that the acquisition of freedom is a process, whose full attainment may not be immediate. A person having trouble managing his or her appetites may even need the help of others to overcome some impulses. This principle is used in such groups as Alcoholics Anonymous, where the person addicted to drink finds help and support from others in his efforts to control his behavior.

As we saw earlier, social, economic, political, and cultural pressures can tend to deprive persons and entire populations of freedom. The intense danger of the battlefield may overwhelm a person's intentions faithfully to defend his country. For this reason, he undergoes training beforehand in which he faces battlefield simulations and is trained to respond to his commanders. As with the bodily appetites, virtue is required, specifically the virtues of wisdom and courage.

Virtue is the key to managing oneself reasonably and not being managed by appetites, and social pressures. In his analysis of the essence of virtue, Aristotle acutely remarks, "In every situation one must guard especially against pleasure and pleasant things, because we are not impartial judges of pleasure."[82] We know, if we are honest with ourselves, that pleasures can surprise us, take us off guard and lead us into wrongdoing. Only a virtuous human being can be truly free. A virtue is a habit formed by repeating good acts in relation to an end. Wojtyła writes, "The fully-mature virtue is a habit that consists in keeping constantly in balance the concupiscent power by habitual relation to the true good (*bonum honestum*), which is defined by

80 *Person and Act*, 364.

81 *Love and Responsibility*, 178–79.

82 Aristotle, *Nicomachean Ethics*, Book II, 1109b9–10.

reason."[83] The virtue does not, therefore, stand on its own, as it were, as though temperance consists simply in declining to drink alcohol or chastity were to be a refusal to engage in sex. Karol Wojtyła writes,

> Because of this erroneous view of the essence of chastity, a purely negative character of this virtue is suggested: Chastity is only a "no." However, chastity is first and foremost a "yes," from which a "no" then proceeds.[84]

The end of any virtue, its *raison d'etre,* is the realization of some further good. To attain a virtue, one performs acts in accord with that virtue and resists influences that militate against the exercise of that virtue. In defense of his moral innocence, Job affirms, "I have made a covenant with my eyes; how then could I look upon a virgin?" (Job 31:1). He has developed a habit of chastity by disciplining his eyes not to "check out" the attractive forms of young women.

At stake here is the problem mentioned above of compulsive behavior. The habitual sinner in confession must adopt a firm purpose of amendment, which does consist in a promise never to perform the act again. Rather he undertakes the project of rooting out the sinful behavior, even at the cost of significant effort and ascesis. The acquisition of a virtue is not simply the adoption of a pattern of behavior, but it is more fundamentally the adoption of a belief about a good for which one lives and forms his own life.[85] Addressing the moral maturity necessary for virtue in married life, Karol Wojtyła wrote of a *propaedeutic for* marriage, or the ethical formation for the couple preparing to enter into marriage.[86] This propaedeutic must include ethical formation for the

83 *Love and Responsibility*, 153.

84 Ibid., 155.

85 Adrian J. Reimers, *The Soul of the Person*, 153–72.

86 Karol Wojtyła, "Myśli o małżeństwie," [Reflections on Marriage] in

future spouses ethically to confront the specific pressures they will face from their social environment. Writing in Poland of 1957, Karol Wojtyła was quite aware of the severity of these pressures as the government sought to undermine Christian values, especially moral values. He speaks of a certain "heroism" that may be required to resist these pressures. The point is that for a person to embrace his freedom he must be formed in the virtue necessary to exercise the freedom he wants to claim. Therefore, the virtuous person does not have to rely on sheer willpower to overcome temptation. Indeed, to a great extent he is not tempted because his embrace of a path to the good is, as it were, written into his heart. Being in constant control of his fears and appetites, he can govern his own behavior and freely pursue the good as he knows it.

For Karol Wojtyła, the performance of an act—whether it be good or bad—is a matter of freedom, which is experienced as "I can, but I do not have to."[87] What I do lies within my power, even if after the fact, I may excuse myself as being "unable to help doing it." The origin of the act is not "from outside"; it is the will. Wojtyła writes,

> Freedom seems to occur and to be manifest precisely, and more than anywhere else, in the ability to choose. For this ability confirms the will's independence in the intentional order of volition: here the will is not restricted by the object, by the value as an end. *The determination of this object belongs exclusively to the will itself.*[88]

There is no deeper or more transcendent power within the person than the will. If the person is free—by this meaning not governed by blind instinct or external forces but by his own

K. Wojtyła, *Aby Chrystu się nami posługiwał [That Christ would use us]* (Krakow: Wydawnictwo Znak, 2009), 452.

87 *Person and Act*, 203.

88 Ibid., 234–35.

rational choice—then his act is a determination of himself in relation to his higher values. Our notorious discouraged salesman chooses comfort and sense pleasure above any higher value precisely by the act of engaging in adultery. He may wish he were better than that. He may even think that he loves his wife. In fact, he has chosen to act against that love and for his own satisfaction. There is no deeper or more fundamental freedom than that which he exercises in choosing his act in the hotel bar on that night.

In *Veritatis Splendor,* Pope John Paul II affirms that this fundamental orientation toward or away from God can be and is determined by particular acts.[89] The fullest explanation of how this is so is found not in *Veritatis Splendor*, but in his earlier encyclical on the Holy Spirit, where sin and our ultimate knowledge of sin is necessarily linked to the cross of Christ.

> Beginning from this initial witness at Pentecost and for all future time the action of the Spirit of truth who "convinces the world concerning the sin" of the rejection of Christ is linked inseparably with the witness to be borne to the Paschal Mystery: *the mystery of the Crucified and Risen One*. And in this link the same "convincing concerning sin" reveals its own salvific dimension.[90]

89 *Veritatis Splendor*, §70.
90 *Dominum et Vivificantem*, §31.

INTRINSECE MALUM

Object of the act

One of the most—if not, indeed *the* most—neuralgic issues in *Veritatis Splendor* is John Paul II's insistence that some human acts can be intrinsically evil, so marked by evil that no intention, no circumstance, no interpretation can redeem and make them good. John Paul II writes:

> Reason attests that there are objects of the human act which are by their nature "incapable of being ordered" to God, because they radically contradict the good of the person made in his image. These are the acts which, in the Church's moral tradition, have been termed "intrinsically evil" (*intrinsece malum*): they are such *always and per se,* in other words, on account of their very object, and quite apart from the ulterior intentions of the one acting and the circumstances.[1]

Notice John Paul II's reference to "objects of the human act," that these objects are by their very nature "incapable of being ordered" to God. The concept of the *object* of an act is decisive. John Paul II explains:

> *The morality of the human act depends primarily and fundamentally on the "object" rationally chosen by the deliberate will.* [...] In order to be able to grasp the object of an act which specifies that act morally, it is therefore necessary

1 *Veritatis Splendor*, §80.

> to place oneself *in the perspective of the acting person.* The object of the act of willing is in fact a freely chosen kind of behavior. [...] By the object of a given moral act, then, one cannot mean a process or an event of the merely physical order, to be assessed on the basis of its ability to bring about a given state of affairs in the outside world. Rather, that object is the proximate end of a deliberate decision which determines the act of willing on the part of the acting person.[2]

The *object* of the act is not a thing, but a "freely chosen kind of behavior." Therefore, the object of the act of stealing is not the money, but the choice to take what is not one's own—to steal—just as the object of the act of adultery is not the woman or man, as the case may be, but the choice to have sexual relations with some person other than one's spouse. Furthermore, the object is not simply the motion or action as such but the kind of behavior that the person has chosen. The police recruit points his pistol at a paper target and fires. Aaron Burr pointed his pistol at Alexander Hamilton and fired. Although both aimed pistols and discharged them, the objects of their respective acts were decidedly different. The recruit acts to improve his proficiency with firearms. Burr acted to kill Hamilton.

John Paul II specifies that to grasp the moral species of the act, it is necessary to place oneself in the "*perspective of the acting person.*" By this he does not mean that one should try to put oneself in the other person's shoes, as if to say "what would I do in this situation?" Rather, it means that to grasp the moral species one must know what the acting person proposes to do. If a man complains about the "slings and arrows of outrageous fortune" we must know whether he is rehearsing a line from Shakespeare or melodramatically referring to his own sorrows. To slice into another's throat with a sharp knife seems to be a wicked thing, but the person slicing may well be performing an emergency

2 Ibid., §78.

tracheotomy. We cannot come to an adequate moral evaluation of an act from a third-person perspective, as though by observing someone's actions we can know what he has decided to do. As noted earlier, efficacy is intrinsic to the act of the person. Every act arises from within the person, not from some action upon the person or that happens within him, but from the person himself—from his will, to use St. Thomas' terminology. The person dynamizes himself, sets himself into action, in order to realize his efficient causality and to bring about some change. Thus, the acting person is *acting* precisely because he has made a conscious decision to dynamize himself, to behave in such and such a way to achieve a particular end.

Particularly important in the text quoted above from *Veritatis Splendor* is the phrase "objects of the human act which are by their nature 'incapable of being ordered' to God." If the human person can create or author his own acts, then John Paul II's text implies that he can author acts that are incapable of being ordered to God. A direct violation of one of the Ten Commandments would seem to be such an act. God commands, "Do not commit adultery." It follows, then, that to commit adultery is an act that cannot be ordered to God, because God himself has commanded that it not be done. At issue, however, is more than the direct disobedience of a divine command. As Creator, God has a plan for his creation. According to this plan he brought the creation into being, and it is according to his plan that he governs it.[3] In his governance of the whole he has given rational creatures a share in the governance by empowering theme with reason and free will.

> Now among all others, the rational creature is subject to Divine providence in the most excellent way, in so far as it partakes of a share of providence, by being provident both for itself and for others. Wherefore it has a share of the Eternal Reason, whereby it has a natural inclination to its proper act and end: and this participation

3 *Summa Theologiae*, Ia, IIae q. 93, a. 1.

of the eternal law in the rational creature is called the natural law.[4]

From here St. Thomas goes on to show that the fundamental precept of this natural law is this: "Good is to be done and pursued, and evil is to be avoided."[5] In order to know what is good to be done, the human being is to use his power of reason. Indeed, St. Thomas repeatedly turns to reasonableness as the touchstone of good human behavior, such that acts according to reason are good and those contrary to reason are evil.[6] From this it follows that the natural law participates in the law of God. Indeed, we may note that in *Veritatis Splendor* Pope John Paul II uses "natural law," "moral law," and "law of God" almost interchangeably.

If the natural law participates in God's providence for his creation, it follows that the human intellect participates in God's own mind. We read in the Pastoral Constitution from Vatican II, "Man judges rightly that by his intellect he surpasses the material universe, for he shares in the light of the divine mind."[7] This means that the human mind is not and cannot be only "natural," that it is adapted only to analysis and understanding of relationships among perceptible things in this world as Hume maintained and as Kant sought to show in his first *Critique*. The panther leaves her den at night and goes out in search of prey because she is a panther. It is her nature to hunt living animals as prey. In this quest she is guided by her senses and remembered experience of prior hunts. Every human act is ordered to some good known to reason, which is the object of the act. As John Paul II insists, it is not merely a process or event in the physical order that may bring about some change in the physical world. The automobile engine that will not start on a frigid morning is not "trying to ruin the start of the day." Even in our frustration, we do not believe that

4 *Summa Theologiae*, Ia, IIae q. 91, a. 2.
5 Ibid., Ia, IIae. q. 94, a. 2
6 Ibid., Ia, IIae q. 94, aa. 3, 4; q. 95, aa. 1, 2, 3, etc.
7 *Gaudium et Spes*, §15.

this is the case. Rather, the machine is malfunctioning because of some flaw. The human being, however, does not malfunction. He acts, and every act is for some good.

The teleology of acts

The act—every human act—is ordered to some good. At issue is whether the act is capable of being ordered to God, and this question lies at the heart of the controversy concerning intrinsically evil acts. Let us approach this issue in stages. The first stage concerns the knowledge that the human mind can have of the order of God's creation, the order of nature. By scientific investigation the human mind can penetrate the secrets of nature, and sometimes it can fall into error. The history of science is, to a great extent, the history of systematically correcting mistakes and reconstructing our vision of reality. Aristotle attributed thunder to the quenching of fire in the clouds.[8] Given the evidence that he had to work with, namely, the experience of thunderstorms, and the complete ignorance of static electricity in ancient Greece, his hypothesis was reasonable. However, as Benjamin Franklin and others came to realize two millennia later, thunder was the result of a powerful discharge of static electricity. The point of this is that man can gain knowledge of the created order—the order of God's plan—and that the ignorance of this order can have unfortunate or even tragic consequences. The destruction of the North American prairies in the early twentieth century in order to expand croplands proved to be disastrous, as the predictable drought conditions caused huge dust storms that rendered a large part of the continent infertile, resulting in serious social and economic dislocations.[9] Ignorance of science and failure to respect the order of nature can yield bad results. The next stage of the analysis is more serious. We do not find

8 Aristotle, *Posterior Analytics*, Book II, 93b 8–15.

9 Timothy Egan, *The Worst Hard Time: The Untold Story of Those Who Survived the Great American Dust Bowl* (Boston, New York: Houghton Mifflin Company, 2006).

Aristotle morally at fault for his flawed account of thunder. Our knowledge of the world is imperfect. However, God created us to live not only in an ordered physical environment, but also to live in a social environment with other human beings. Because of our mutual personhood we are obliged to love one another. To understand this commandment more deeply we can investigate that most intimate human relationship of love, that between wife and husband.

The "beginning" and theology of the body

From the outset of his theology of the body audiences, Pope John Paul II insists on the importance of the *beginning*, by which he means the creation as God had intended.[10] The question of the beginning arises when John Paul II recounts the story of Jesus' conversation with the Pharisees, who ask him whether a man may divorce his wife (Mt 19:3–9). Jesus responds by saying that "because of the hardness of your hearts," Moses allowed for divorce, but "from the beginning it was not so." John Paul II notes that Jesus does not appeal to his command as king and first Legislator, but that Jesus points instead to "the beginning."

> Yet, that significant expression, "from the beginning," repeated twice, clearly leads the interlocutors to reflect about the way in which, in the mystery of creation, man was formed precisely as "male and female," in order to understand correctly the normative meaning of the words of Genesis.[11]

The words of Genesis are "normative," meaning that they contain a fundamental truth about the nature of male and female and about their good. As John Paul II observes, this is not a case of divine legislation, like the command to Adam not to eat of the tree

10 *Theology of the Body*, 131–33.
11 *Theology of the Body*, 133.

of the knowledge of good and evil. Rather, it was evident that the human race, which God had created, consists of male and female who could unite sexually, so as to "become one flesh." From this John Paul II argues that certain ethical content derives concerning marriage. He begins his extended argument:

> Man enters into the world […] with the consciousness of the spousal meaning of his own body, of his masculinity and femininity. Original innocence says that this meaning is conditioned "ethically." […] The understanding of the fundamental meanings contained in the very mystery of creation, such as the spousal meaning of the body […] is important and indispensable for knowing who man is and who he ought to be, and therefore how he ought to shape his activity.[12]

We need to unpack this important text. Man—created both male and female—is conscious of the "spousal meaning" of the human body. In part, this means that man and woman can unite sexually, but clearly this is not the fundamental or even primary sense of "spousal meaning." John Paul II refers here to the "original innocence" of the first couple. The creation narrative tells us that although the man and woman were both naked, they "were not ashamed" (Gen 2:25). Shame arose only after the sin of eating the fruit of the tree. The implication of this is that there is far more to the sexual differentiation than physical sex. John Paul II's term "spousal meaning" means that the body is intended to and ordered to express love. Although we who live after the Fall do not experience the sexual encounter in "original innocence," that is, without concupiscence bordering on lust, there is within this encounter an element that transcends the physical. Here we may note the common association of falling in love with beauty; the embodied personhood of the other is found to be beautiful. Romeo speaks of Juliet's "beauty too rich for use, for earth too

12 Ibid., 200.

dear."[13] Admiration of the beloved's beauty instills the desire for union with that person. When one's own fascination, even if merely infatuation, is reciprocated there is found the basis for a relationship of love. If that love is mature and realized in marriage, then the experience of receiving the beloved's body in the conjugal embrace is to experience the unexpected riches of the gift of another. The normal and natural experience is gratitude. Granted that many people may regularly engage in impersonal sexual encounters, one has to have allowed himself to become calloused and jaded if he is to experience sex as just a physical encounter. This spontaneous admiration of beauty and gratitude for the gift are marks of the spousal meaning of the body. Hence, John Paul II writes, "Man appears in the visible world as the highest expression of the divine gift, because he bears within himself the inner dimension of the gift."[14] This spousal meaning, present even after the sin of the Fall, is a continual element of human experience and not something directly revealed by God.

In virtue of the original innocence, this meaning of the body is conditioned ethically. The very term "spousal meaning" implies a gift given and received, because spouses give themselves to each other and mutually receive each other's gift. To be sure, throughout history, this spousal relationship has been abused in practices such as polygamy, forced marriages, concubinage, and prostitution. Nevertheless, such practices can be identified as abuses precisely because of their failure adequately to reflect the spousal nature of the sexual encounter itself. In other words, when two persons encounter each other, whether sex is a factor or not, the encounter is determined not only physically but spiritually as well. The very discovery of beauty is metaphysically based.[15] Therefore, from this fact of experience that the man and woman can unite to become one flesh, there follows a series of ethical consequences, beginning with that which Jesus, and John

13 William Shakespeare, *Romeo and Juliet*, Act I, Scene V.
14 *Theology of the Body*, 203.
15 Adrian J. Reimers, *The Soul of the Person*, 79–85.

Paul II after him, identified as the indissolubility of marriage. This involves not only the exclusivity of the sexual union, but also the mental attitudes to adopt concerning others where sex is concerned.[16]

Indeed, much of the rest of John Paul II's theology of the body is an exploration of the ethical consequences of the spousal union. The basis for this richly developed argument is Jesus' appeal to the *beginning*, by which John Paul II understands the Creator's intention for his creation. This can and should be discerned by the human intellect. As is the case with the sciences, the human mind, especially insofar as it can be and is influenced by concupiscence, can err concerning the requirements of the natural law. King David, who was a king after the Lord's own heart, had multiple wives. The historical process of developing a just understanding regarding the employment of labor by other human beings involved a painful wrestling with the institutions of slavery, chattel bondage, and even wage-labor. On the other hand, the most common moral truths—we may think of those concerning murder, theft, and adultery—are readily known, just as the most basic scientific truths are known—such as gravity, sunrise, our need for air. By seeking the truth, the human mind can know the essentials of the order of divine providence, and therefore is able to act in accord with that order.

It is also the case, however, that a person can act in ways that are "incapable of being ordered to God." Here we are not talking about mistaken applications of one's knowledge of the laws of nature as might happen when human activity unwittingly upsets a local ecosystem. We may think here of an overly aggressive effort to eliminate predators which can result in an over-population of other species, which become pests destructive of vegetation. When John Paul II writes of "objects of the human act which are by their nature 'incapable of being ordered' to God, he affirms that some acts radically contradict the good of the person made in his image."[17] The first great commandment is to love God with

16 See *Theology of the Body*, Chapter Two, 225ff.

17 *Veritatis Splendor*, §80.

all one's heart and soul and mind and strength, because God is the Good itself from which all goods flow. To turn away from God is to turn away from good as such and hence from all that is good. St. Thomas Aquinas characterizes the natural law as "simply rational creatures' participation in the eternal law."[18] John Paul II explains,

> God calls man to participate in his own providence, since he desires to guide the world [...] through man himself, through man's reasonable and responsible care. The natural law enters here as the human expression of God's eternal law.[19]

Because he shares in God's providence as, indeed, a rational being responsible to guide the world, the human being is responsible to act according to the truth about the good of God's providence. The point, therefore, is that there are *actions* that are incapable of being ordered to God. Perhaps the clearest example of such an act is willful murder, which is constituted by the direct, intentional killing of another person. By this we exclude the killing of enemy soldiers in war, killings by police to protect the public, lethal self-defense, and the like. Concerning murder, the *Catechism of the Catholic Church* teaches:

> Human life is sacred because from its beginning it involves the creative action of God and it remains forever in a special relationship with the Creator, who is its sole end. God alone is the Lord of life from its beginning until its end: no one can under any circumstance claim for himself the right directly to destroy an innocent human being.[20]

18 *Summa Theologiae*, Ia, IIae q. 91, a. 2.
19 *Veritatis Splendor*, §43.
20 *Catechism of the Catholic Church*, 2258.

This is exactly to the point. God created human life, as the Scriptures testify (Gen 1:26–27), and even without divine Revelation, human reason can validly infer that human life is sacred, that the life of a human being is his own (however often this principle may be violated in practice), that it is a serious violation to deprive him of it. The decision to kill is effectively to judge and decide that the world (or this part of the world) is better without this person. For instance, if an heir kills his rich uncle, then his financial woes are solved. In fact, after the murder, the world might, in some ways, be a better place. The uncle may well have been cruel man who used his wealth to harm others. The heir might well use his inheritance to right some wrongs in the broader family. Arguably, the murderous heir could be "making the world a better place." Such scenarios often turn out worse than hoped, but in some cases good may well result from the crime. Nevertheless, the nephew who kills has done murder. Arguably a little part of the world may be a better place with the uncle gone. The difficulty is that God has created the uncle out of love specifically for him. Further, Jesus has redeemed this same uncle by his own sacrifice on the cross. The heir has murdered him in defiance of God's claims on the uncle and his life. Furthermore, the term "murder" is warranted not by some value judgment extraneous to the killing, but by the act itself. Whether there was hatred in the nephew's mind or greed or a sense of benevolence—here we might think of the Raskolnikov in Dostoevsky's *Crime and Punishment*—his act was one of murder, the direct and intentional killing of another human being. This murder, and any other murder, cannot accord with the order of God's providence but rather stands in opposition to it. In a very real sense, the one who performs such an act is "playing God."

Responsibility for reason

Implicit in all this is the requirement that the human person use his power of reason. John Paul II writes, "Although each individual has a right to be respected in his own journey in search of the truth, there exists a prior moral obligation, and a grave one at that, to seek the truth and to adhere to it once it is known."[21] Our nature is to be rational, which means that the power of reason is not an additional characteristic added on to the constitution of a particular species *homo sapiens*. Rather, reason, the power of intellect, forms every aspect of the human person's life and activity. We are rational to the tips of our fingers. This truth profoundly affects our moral responsibility. In his Apostolic Exhortation on sin and penance, John Paul II wrote, "For mortal sin exists also when a person knowingly and willingly, for whatever reason, chooses something gravely disordered."[22] This accords exactly with his own analysis of the nature of the act of a person in his *Person and Act*.[23] Much has been made, especially in the wake of Pope Francis' Apostolic Exhortation *Amoris Laetitia*, of the impact of imperfect knowledge, ignorance, or temporary mental incapacity on the subjective guilt of an agent. Certainly, despite the Catholic Church's clear teaching on contraception, many Christians—mostly Protestants—continue to use them. Good, devout Jews refrain from turning to Jesus as the promised Messiah. Granting such cases and their significance, we must also insist on the person's responsibility to be conscious and aware of the truth about the good of his acts. He is responsible to know the truth as best he can and to *adhere to it* once it is known.

Out of regret one may disavow an act—we may think of a very imprudent action under the influence of alcohol or lust—but this disavowal does not nullify the responsibility for the act, because the acting person chooses the one act (or even non-action) rather than another. Even if one is "carried away" with the experience, perhaps an act performed out of anger or lust, he knew what he intended to do—he knew the object of the act—as he began to perform it and indeed as the act proceeded, even if later he maintains that he "could not help himself." The truth concerning the act is that as a rational being, the human person knows

21 *Veritatis Splendor*, §34.

22 John Paul II, *Reconciliatio et Paenitentia*, §17.

what he is doing when he chooses to act. And he is responsible to seek the truth about the good and to act on it. This is why it is essential for a person who has done wrong clearly to acknowledge his sin, to confront the evil that he has done. We may remark here that even Pope Francis confuses (perhaps inadvertently) the significance of this:

> I said, "be merciful." Mercy. Always forgive. When a member of the faithful comes for confession, he or she comes to seek forgiveness, to seek the Father's caress. And we, pointing an accusatory finger, say: "How many times? And how did you do it?" [...] No, not this. Forgive. Always. "But I don't know [...] because the code tells me [...]." We have to observe the code, because it is important, yet the heart of the shepherd goes beyond! Take a risk. Take a risk on the side of forgiveness. Always. Always forgive in the Sacrament of Reconciliation.[24]

The "code" to which Francis refers is the canonical requirement that the penitent acknowledge specifically what he has done. The shepherd must also observe this code, but that is not all that he does. One who has done wrong cannot excuse his act by denying his own responsibility for it. Even if his will was somehow compromised, the act is his, and it is for him to acknowledge his responsibility.

Some might also plead that a truly human act is one that arises from the interior emotional depths of the person, which are deeper than reason's cold calculations. One application of this notion is found in James Martin, S.J.'s objection to the phrase "disordered affection" in the discussion of homosexuality in the *Catechism of the Catholic Church*. To refer to homosexual desires as

23 Karol Wojtyła, *Person and Act*, 11, 147–48.

24 Pope Francis, Meeting with Bishops, Kinshaasa, 3 February 2023. Downloaded 14 August 2023 from https://www.vatican.va/content/francesco/en/speeches/2023/february/documents/20230203-vescovi-repdem-congo.html.

"disordered" is hurtful and erroneous because it allegedly disparages that part of the person that loves.[25] Fr. Martin is not necessarily reducing love to sexual desires alone. As we have noted above, the experience of love includes also the experience of beauty, the warmth of human closeness, gratitude for another's gift of affection and contact, and simply the joy of interacting with another person. It is inaccurate, however, to assert that this nexus of desire and emotion irresistibly or inevitably compels a person to perform certain sexual acts. He may call them "love," but, as Karol Wojtyła insists, love must be formed in truth, and reason is the power by which the person attains to truth.[26] As our discussion of the "heart" shows, the depths of one's interiority can become so formed that he has an almost "instinctive" sense for what it good and what is evil. Such a formation of the heart, however, needs to be formed reasonably, that is, by the use and under the guidance of reason. To abandon or disregard reason, even this abandonment is done thoughtlessly, does not relieve one of the responsibility to be guided by reason. Joseph Ratzinger writes,

> For *Logos* means a reason that is not simply mathematical but is at the same time the foundation and guarantee of the good. Faith in God as Logos is also faith in the Creative power of reason; it is faith in God the Creator, which means that man is created in the image of God and that he therefore shares in the inviolable dignity of God himself.[27]

The Holy Spirit

> The primary and decisive element for moral judgment is the object of the human act, which establishes

25 James Martin, S.J., *Building a Bridge* (New York: Harper Collins, 2014), 47.

26 *Love and Responsibility*, 47, 61, 225.

27 Joseph Ratzinger, *Western Culture: Today and Tomorrow*, 120.

> whether it is *capable of being ordered to the good and to the ultimate end, which is God.*[28]

The human act, which has the person as its author and creator, must be ordered to God as the person's ultimate end, but by the very nature of the act, this implies that the person himself must be ordered to that end, which is God.[29] In John Paul II's vision of the moral life, the acting person does not stand as simply an earthly being under the gaze and judgment of a distant and somewhat abstract God whose aims he must decipher. Rather, as is evident from the opening pages of the encyclical, the relation between the human person and God is personal. At the end of his conversation with the rich young man, Jesus says, "Follow me." John Paul II continues:

> Jesus asks us to follow him and to imitate him along the path of love, a love which gives itself completely to the brethren out of love for God: "This is my commandment, that you love one another as I have loved you" (Jn 15:12). [...] Jesus' way of acting and his words, his deeds and his precepts constitute the moral rule of Christian life.[30]

The measure of a human life is love. Freedom exists for love.[31] The central reality, the standard for our freedom is the Cross of Christ by which Jesus freely gave his life in love for human beings.

The existential problem we face—and this problem seems particularly acute at present—is that of even recognizing sin. A person can be blind to his own sin, to the sinfulness of his own acts. In his farewell discourse, Jesus explained the mission of the Holy Spirit.

28 *Veritatis Splendor*, §79.
29 *Person and Act*, 171–73.
30 *Veritatis Splendor*, §20.
31 *Love and Responsibility*, 117.

> When [the Holy Spirit] comes, he will convict the world of sin and of righteousness and of judgment: of sin, because they do not believe in me; of righteousness, because I go to the Father, and you will see me no more; of judgment because the ruler of this world is judged. (John 16:8–11)

Pope John Paul II expands on this.

> In the mind of Jesus, sin, righteousness, and judgment have *a very precise meaning*. [...] "*Sin,*" in this passage, means the incredulity that Jesus encountered among "His own," beginning with the people of His own town of Nazareth. Sin means the rejection of his mission, a rejection that will cause people to condemn him to death.[32]

What John Paul II tells us here is that the good Jewish people of Nazareth were culpable of unbelief when they rejected Jesus' preaching to them. Their incredulity was "sin." For us in the 21st century, with centuries of preaching on and representations of the life of Jesus, the incredulity of Jesus' contemporaries who witnessed his healings and miracles, who came from the towns and villages to the Sea of Galilee to hear him preach, and who cut down palm branches to pave his triumphal entry into Jerusalem, strikes us as odd. The man they saw was a striking public figure, who today would count as a kind of celebrity. He was exciting, and he met the serious needs of very needy people. But his dramatic healings notwithstanding, illness was still widespread. Jesus fed five thousand, but the next day all were hungry again. Indeed, Jesus himself remarks, "Truly, truly, I say to you, you seek me not because you saw signs,[33] but because you ate your fill of the loaves" (Jn

32 *Dominum et Vivificantem*, §27.

33 In John's Gospel, "signs," beginning at Cana, were more than miracles or extraordinary events. They were acts to evoke the faith of

6:26). It was not enough to have seen and heard Jesus to believe in him. John Paul II identifies this incredulity as "sin," and it was the work of the Holy Spirit to convict the incredulous of their sin. In proof of this we may look to the events of the first Christian Pentecost, when having heard Peter talk about the crucifixion of Christ, many of his hearers were "cut to the heart" and repented (Act 2:37).

Here we must beware, or better, become aware of the extent to which we have naturalized our conception of the human being. The hearers of St. Peter's Pentecost sermon learned nothing new that day. On hearing Peter's words, however, they were cut to the heart. Why? We tend to think of ourselves "naturalistically" as intelligent beings who receive information through our sense experiences and the communications of others, and who process intellectually what we experience and hear. Having done so, we may reach the point that we can judge that something is true. The gift of the Holy Spirit is something that is added in baptism and confirmation, and by it we may receive special graces to understand spiritual matters. More accurately, we receive the sevenfold gifts of the Holy Spirit. But according to John Paul II this is too simplistic. Rather, we are, from creation itself, related to the Holy Spirit. He writes,

> It [the self-giving of God in Christ] is a *new beginning* in relation to the *first, original* beginning of *God's salvific self-giving*, which is identified with the mystery of creation itself. [...] This biblical concept of creation includes not only the call to existence of the very being of the cosmos, that is to say the *giving of existence*, but also the presence of the Spirit of God in creation, that is to say the beginning of God's salvific self-communication to the things he creates. This is true first of all concerning man, who has been created in the image and likeness of God.[34]

those who saw them. Recall that after the raising of Lazarus, some went off to find ways to kill Lazarus (Jn 12:10).

34 *Dominum et Vivificantem*, §12.

This is a continuation of the insight that John Paul II presents in his theology of the body that the creation itself is an act of love on the part of the Creator.[35] The very act of creation itself is God's self-communication to the creation, an act of love. As such the creation indicates the presence of the Holy Spirit. To be sure, this self-giving is perfected and made clearly manifest in the Redemption, but it is already present from the beginning of creation. Because man is created in the image and likeness of God, he constitutionally adapted, as it were, to respond to thc Holy Spirit. To put this more bluntly, the human person is not a value-neutral material entity, a sensing organism that makes its way through the world as best it can to survive as comfortably as possible.

To maintain that a human act is intrinsically evil is to maintain that the agent—a human person—can set himself directly against God, to deliberately direct himself toward some other good than God as his ultimate good and in doing so to set himself in opposition to God. Because we are bodily beings with especially powerful brains, we can create our own mental realities—fantasies—by which we can weave alternative narratives to the truth about the good. The Redemption shed light on sin.

> The revelation of the mystery of the Redemption opens the way to an understanding in which every sin, wherever and whenever committed, has a reference to the cross of Christ—and therefore indirectly also to the sin of those who "have not believed in him" and who condemned Jesus to death on the cross.[36]

Human beings condemned Christ and crucified him. Every one of us is a human being. Through Jesus's sacrifice of himself on the cross, our capacity for sin is revealed.

35 *Theology of the Body*, 191, 205.
36 *Dominum et Vivificantem*, §29.

GOD AND THE MEANING OF LIFE

The project of formulating a post-Christian morality, a moral system *etsi Deus non daretur* (as if God did not exist) has collapsed. After the terrorist attacks of September 11, 2001, the United States used "enhanced interrogation. techniques" against suspected terrorists, generally in foreign countries outside the jurisdiction of American laws. In February 2022, Russia launched an unprovoked attack on its peaceful neighbor that dared to defend its own independence. Although within any given society or moral community, we may indeed find consensus concerning some moral rules—murder is proscribed, as is deliberate cruelty to children; ingratitude is frowned upon, as is disloyalty to one's benefactors—these social norms prove to be vulnerable to rejection when circumstances change. We have seen the photos of employees of the Auschwitz Concentration Camp enjoying Sunday outings with their families not far from the crematoria. Photos show smiling white American men and women beneath the tree from which hangs a black man. If moral behavior is that which maintains the peaceful consensus of members of a particular population, then some moral norms do find widespread acceptance. Stephen Pinker argues plausibly that the moral sense, which every human being shares to a greater or lesser extent, arises from certain shared values or attitudes that enable us to live in relative harmony.[1] The most common and rhetorically potent argument for a thoroughly secular morality is that which points to ordinary people, who can be good without having any religion at all. Not only do religious people—those who believe explicitly in God—

1 Stephen Pinker "The Moral Instinct," *New York Times Magazine*, January 13, 2008, p. 632.

do moral wrongs, but many (most?) non-believers are fine upstanding citizens. There is a sense in which human beings do not need God in order to be good. This is true, but it is a dangerously weak argument.

Like our primate cousins, the chimpanzees and gorillas, we are social animals that cooperate in order to maintain the survival and relatively agreeable life of the social groups we find ourselves in. At issue here is what we call a cultural ethos—conventional morality, the nexus of moral codes and values by which people in our culture structure their lives, sanction offenders, and rear their children. The standards of our conventional morality tend to reflect the Judeo-Christian morality expressed in the Ten Commandments. However, the experiences of history—including that of the century just ended—have shown that conventional morality is weak, shallow. The proscription against taking the Lord's name in vain has all but disappeared, and reverence for the divine has markedly diminished. Observance of the Fourth Commandment is reduced to a general admonition to be considerate of aging parents. The decay in conventional morality from the full understanding of the Decalogue is most evident where sexual issues are at stake. Abortion is widely regarded as a procedure to which every woman has a right. The word "fornication" has almost completely disappeared from the common vocabulary, and premarital sex is no longer subject to social disapproval. Insofar as it may involve elements of deception and betrayal, adultery is morally suspect, but the wrong tends to attach more to the deception than the sexual activity itself. No moral stigma attaches to homosexual practices, and today, for the first time in the history of our civilization, both law and custom recognize the right and legitimacy of persons of the same sex to marry. In contemporary culture few forms of sexual interaction—save those involving children—are considered morally wrong. Indeed, Stephen Pinker's article cited above seriously raises the question why a brother and sister, having taken contraceptive precautions and far from family and relatives, may not enjoy sexual intercourse together. Of course, we may find pockets where a stricter, more traditional morality holds sway. Nevertheless, it is safe to say that the governing moral standards within our civilization are generally as described above. In a society governed morally by utilitarian norms each person has the right to pursue his own pleasures, especially personal pleasures, so long as he does not interfere with the rights of others. Utilitarianism and its public manifestation in consumerism (made possible by the existence of a reasonably prosperous middle class) provides the governing ethos of our civilization. Within the context of this ethos the moral proscriptions of traditional Christianity are seen as practically indefensible.

The full meaning of life

In *Veritatis Splendor,* John Paul II begins his analysis of the moral life not by asking which acts are moral, but with the question of life's ultimate meaning. The rich young man addresses Jesus as "good teacher," and Jesus immediately challenges his use of the term "good": "Why do you call me good? None is good but God alone." We use the term "good" as though it were not problematic, as though we know what goodness is. Jesus' jarring response, which fails even to address the rich young man's question, reminds him and us of the foundations of the entire discussion. The Law of Moses is good, and the young man affirms that from his youth he has obeyed the commandments, given by God who is good. He obeys the Law of Moses. But he realizes that there is something more that he lacks if he is to be perfect. (Mt 19:20) He is not, like the Pharisees, asking subtle questions about the permissibility of divorce or the application of the Jewish hygienic code (see Mk 7:3–5). Nor is he asking about sacrifices he might offer at the festival. Jesus, who, "looking upon him loved him," reads the deeper desire of his heart and the real intent of his question. John Paul II explains:

> For the young man, the *question* is not so much about rules to be followed, but *about the full meaning of life.* [...]

> This question is ultimately an appeal to the absolute Good which attracts us and beckons us; it is the echo of a call from God who is the origin and goal of man's life.[2]

The question of the meaning of one's life is central. Indeed, John Paul II begins his later encyclical on philosophy and theology with precisely this consideration. Citing Israel's Scriptures, as well as the Veda and Avesta, Confucius and Lao-Tze, the Buddha, and the ancient Greeks (especially Plato and Aristotle), he writes:

> They are questions which have their common source in the quest for meaning which has always compelled the human heart. In fact, the answer given to these questions decides the direction which people seek to give to their lives.[3]

What a human being loves gives meaning to his life, because this phrase, "the meaning of life" connotes the important truths and values by which he lives his life. This implies that the meaning of life has to do with an implicit conception of the highest good. In this John Paul II follows St. Thomas Aquinas, as well as the Fathers and Doctors of the Church. John Paul II cites the history of human cultures and their search for meaning and the ultimate good of life. Like truth, the good is a spiritual reality.

One might immediately object that there is no such meaning or perhaps that the question is itself meaningless. But the young man asked the question as, in one way or another, does everyone else: What must I do to have a full life? What do I lack? In real life, persons do ask in one way or another where their lives are going. Whether one believes that there is anything transcendent to life or to his being, he asks the question what more there might be to life than what he experiences. Contemporary answers to this

2 *Veritatis Splendor*, §7.

3 John Paul II, Encyclical *Fides et Ratio* (Vatican City: Libreria Editrice Vaticana, 1998), §§1–4.

question are characteristically formulated in terms either materialistic or subjectivistic. The materialist sees the challenge was one of possessing more or maintaining one's possession more securely, as though one can guarantee his life by providing adequately for a comfortable retirement. The subjectivistic approach is closely related, that the meaning of life is to discover who one *really is,* to develop one's own identity. Therefore, the answer to the question of eternal life inevitably lies within oneself.

The rich young man is not of the 21st century. He has approached Jesus, a noted rabbi of his own time. He does not realize the fullness of the Lord's identity as God Incarnate. However, Jesus' response to the young man's question challenges everything that the young man understands about his life. "You lack one thing; go, sell what you have, and give to the poor, and you will have treasure in heaven; and come, follow me" (Mk 10:21). Jesus' reply has two parts, which take the young man and his question to a completely different plane. The question about the good he must do has unexpected depths for the young man. First, Jesus calls him to sell what he has and give to the poor, that is, to divest himself of all he has hitherto depended on for his life. He may have expected Jesus to suggest that he disciple himself to a Pharisee to learn the Law more perfectly or to take a vow to offer a holocaust at the next feast in Jerusalem. But Jesus tells him to sell everything and give to the poor.

To be sure, this is an unexpected revelation to the young man, and its consequences are transformative. Jesus completes this invitation to renounce all by calling the young man to follow him. The point here is that Jesus did far more than shed some marginal clarity on the demands of morality. His call appears to be unreasonable, indeed, impossible. Immediately after this episode, when told that it is hard for a rich man to enter the kingdom of God, Jesus's own astonished disciples asked, "Then who can be saved?" (Mk 9: 26). Jesus has called into question the foundations of the young man's understanding of what the good life is. The rich young man's question is therefore religious. Jesus directs the young man's attention to God, who

> [I]s the source of man's happiness. Jesus brings the question about morally good action back to its religious foundations, to the acknowledgment of God, who alone is goodness, fullness of life, the final end of human activity, and perfect happiness.[4]

After calling the young man to the humanly impossible—"sell all and give to the poor"—Jesus invites the young man to follow him. "What man is and what he must do becomes clear as soon as God reveals himself."[5] In this exchange between Christ and the rich young man, we find the basis of the entirety of *Veritatis Splendor*. Here the young man has learned God's true prerogatives in relation to the goods of this life—including the good of Torah—and the one who has taught him is God himself in Christ.

In this story, Jesus offers the young man a specific meaning for his life. The invitation to follow Christ is a transformative and all-encompassing embrace of a new life. By teaching the young man about the fullness of God's goodness in relation to the Decalogue, Jesus had effectively interpreted for him the meaning of his life as a Jew. "*Acknowledging the Lord as God is the very core, the heart of the Law,* from which the particular precepts flow and towards which they are ordered."[6] The invitation to "follow me" is an offer to enter *even now* into the eternal life that the young man was seeking.

> Consequently, after making the important clarification: "There is only one who is good," Jesus tells the young man, "If you wish to enter into life, keep the commandments" (Mt 19:17). In this way, a close connection is made *between eternal life and obedience to God's commandments*: God's commandments show man the path of life and they lead to it.[7]

4 Ibid.
5 *Veritatis Splendor*, §10.
6 *Veritatis Splendor*, §11.
7 Ibid., §12.

Declining Christ's invitation and the demands of discipleship

The young man declined Christ's invitation to sell everything and follow him because he "had great possessions" (Mk 10:22; Mt 19:22), and so he went away sorrowing. The Scriptures do not tell us what became of him. John Paul II notes that his response is understandable, because even the disciples are taken aback. "Then who can be saved?" (Mt 19:25). The Pope continues: "*But the Master refers them to God's power:* 'With men this is impossible, but with God all things are possible'" (Mt 19:26). If we insist on maintaining the conventional conception of ethics and the good Christian life, we are faced with an impossible conundrum, because the standards have changed radically. The rich young man is a good person, one who has obeyed the Commandments all his life. Because he approached Jesus with the question about perfection and eternal life, he was clearly a serious person and not one drifting thoughtlessly. Socrates would have approved: "the unexamined life is not worth living."[8] But, at this point of his life at least, he was not willing to accept the invitation to become a follower of Christ. He chose to remain within the context of the Old Law.

The disciples themselves put the question to the Lord. Peter asked him, "Lord, we have left everything and followed you," and Jesus promised to return all that they had sacrificed one-hundred-fold, but "with persecutions." We now know what they did not know then, namely that many—indeed, most—of Christ's disciples were destined to painful, untimely deaths as martyrs. Jesus called Peter and his brother Andrew, promising that instead of fish they will catch men, but it was some time before he began to communicate to them what their discipleship would cost. They were apparently beginning to grasp this when Jesus encountered the rich young man, but even then they seemed unsure how to understand the cost of their discipleship. What they did know was that their response to Christ was an absolute, total commitment. Indeed, the young man's refusal makes this evident. He

8 Plato, *Apology*, 38a.

went away sorrowing because he could not let go of his possessions, of the things that had defined his life to that point. (It may be fair to hope that the young man later may have regretted his refusal and returned to Jesus. Others have done so.)

John Paul II does not allow us to regard this young man as an exceptional case, as though Jesus were inviting him to a life of heroic sanctity beyond the ordinary goodness constituted by obeying the commandments. On the contrary, John Paul II regards the rich young man as a kind of Everyman.

> This vocation to perfect love is not restricted to a small group of individuals. *The invitation,* "go, sell your possessions and give the money to the poor," and the promise "you will have treasure in heaven," *are meant for everyone,* because they bring out the full meaning of the commandment of love for neighbour, just as the invitation which follows, "Come, follow me," is the new, specific form of the commandment of love of God.[9]

John Paul II adds, "Jesus' conversation with the rich young man continues, in a sense, *in every period of history, including our own.*"[10] It follows, therefore, that Christian morality is truly a new way of life, and furthermore, not an individualized life. This life of following Christ (*sequela Christi*) is found in the Church. "*Christ's relevance for all times is shown forth in his Body, which is the Church.*"[11]

The interior life

One further factor remains for us to investigate. We have seen that John Paul II insists on the one hand that the moral life is ultimately the religious life, not to be separated from the life of faith, and on the other hand that it requires an intimate union with Christ: "come

9 *Veritatis Splendor*, §18.
10 Ibid., §25.
11 Ibid.

follow me." On the other hand, philosophical ethics (curiously excepting Kant) seldom addresses the interior life, because the concern of ethics is external behavior, whether it is good or bad. To be sure, a virtue ethics will maintain that one is not truly virtuous unless and until the virtue or virtues are somehow engrained in the person's character. And John Stuart Mill maintains that it is necessary to develop a conscience, understood as an internal psychological sanction, that aligns with the greatest happiness principle.[12] Nevertheless, the ethical concern is always (again excluding Kant) with the performance of good acts. We distinguish Kant from other ethicists and ethical theories, because his primary—indeed, only—concern is with the formation of a good will. He does not concern himself with good versus bad acts. Nor does he allow any concern with a person's ultimate destiny or meaningfulness of life.

For John Paul II the interior life is essential, as important as one's exterior behavior. Indeed, the moral worth of one's external acts is intimately related to the interiority of the agent. Christ concludes his conversation with the rich young man with the invitation, "come, follow me." John Paul II makes clear that this is more than a mere physical following, as though Jesus was simply asking the young man to join the group that accompanied him in his travels. Jesus invited this young man to follow him in his own life of self-giving love. John Paul II writes:

> *Following Christ is thus the essential and primordial foundation of Christian morality*: just as the people of Israel followed God who led them through the desert towards the Promised Land (cf. Ex 13:21), so every disciple must follow Jesus, towards whom he is drawn by the Father himself (cf. *Jn* 6:44).[13]

This "following" means to live according to Christ's own life of love. It means conformity to Christ: "*Following Christ* is not an

12 J. S. Mill, *Utilitarianism*, 29–31.
13 *Veritatis Splendor*, §19.

outward imitation, since it touches man at the very depths of his being."[14] This "following" has direct moral implications, as John Paul II's comparison of it with the covenant with Israel makes clear. Indeed, we have seen exactly this same pattern in the interchange with the rich young man, who obeyed the Mosaic Law. We have already noted how demanding this is, how the young man turned away because he had many possessions. Not only did the disciples have to renounce riches, but Christ had also insisted that divorce was morally illegitimate, a requirement that the disciples also found unsupportable.[15] By their own powers, it appears that human beings are not capable of following the new law of Christ.

John Paul II affirms this, adding that to follow Jesus' law of love something more is required.

> Love and life according to the Gospel cannot be thought of first and foremost as a kind of precept, because what they demand is beyond man's abilities. [...]
>
> And so we find revealed the authentic and original aspect of the commandment of love and of the perfection to which it is ordered: we are speaking of a *possibility opened up to man exclusively by grace,* by the gift of God, by his love.[16]

To follow Christ, a gift is needed, a gift of grace, which strengthens the person interiorly. Certainly, one can follow Christ by striving to follow his teachings. Having come across a victim of assault, beaten and bloody, the Christian should recall the good Samaritan and care for the victim. We should forgive when offended and go the extra mile with those who would impose their will upon us. In these ways one can indeed and should strive to

14 Ibid., §21.
15 *Veritatis Splendor*, §22.
16 Ibid., §23, §24.

follow Christ. The human will is generally capable of following the example of a model and a set of instructions. However, there are two reasons why this natural human power is insufficient for the *sequela Christi*.

The first insufficiency of nature arises from the weakness of the human heart. Every people and every person lives by an *ethos*, a nexus or configuration of values and consequently of habits that form a family or a culture. We can speak of a Jesuit or Franciscan *ethos*, or of an Amish *ethos*. In his theology of the body, Pope St. John Paul II writes at length of the *ethos* of Christian marriage. An *ethos* is a nexus of habits formed around particular related values. To a great extent, each person's heart is formed by an *ethos*. As a nexus of habits, every *ethos* is formed by repetition, imitation, and examples, which are interiorized as one enters into the life of the group. The social *ethos* is helpful—very helpful—for the Christian life. However, because a social *ethos* develops naturally by natural powers (and the nature of the social and physical environment), it cannot adequately conform the soul to the model of Christ himself. This is evident in the differences between the Commandments and the Beatitudes. One commandment requires, "Do not steal," and whenever the rightful property of another is at stake, one is required not to violate his ownership. We learn this at mother's knee, and it is written into civil law. By contrast, the Beatitudes enjoin no specific behavior. The poor in spirit and the meek are blessed; theirs is the kingdom of heaven, and they will inherit the earth. We are told that these Beatitudes provide a kind of portrait of Christ himself and as such invite us to the imitation of Christ.[17] However, the Beatitudes, nor even the entire Sermon on the Mount with all its instructions, provides a kind of recipe, a pattern of life and behavior the obedience to which suffices to make one a follower of Christ. The conformity with Christ must needs be interior.

The second insufficiency arises from the sinfulness of the human heart. Not only are we weak, but we are constantly

17 *Veritatis Splendor*, §16.

inclined to turn away from God and his love. The original sin in the Garden has become the pattern of all human sin.[18] Of his own resources, man is incapable of overcoming sin. We see this most clearly, perhaps, in St. Peter's denial of Christ. Here was a good man, a strong and resolute man, the one to whom the Father entrusted the secret of Jesus' identity as "the Christ, the Son of the living God" (Mt 16:16–17). He had lived with Jesus and heard his teachings—*all* his teachings. Then on the night of the last supper, Jesus went into the garden of Gethsemane to pray. Knowing what was to befall him, the sufferings he was to endure, Jesus needed to bring his own human heart before his Father. "Abba, Father, all things are possible to thee; remove this cup from me; yet not what I will, but what thou wilt" (Mk 14:36). Having prayed, he was able serenely to undergo his arrest and trial and passion, not with the inhuman detachment of a super-Stoic, but as a man whose heart and will were in perfect harmony with God the Father. He also asked Peter, James, and John to watch and pray with him. They fell asleep. Perhaps this was understandable. It was late, and they had eaten and drunk shortly before. In any case, they slept. Because they slept, they were unprepared, and when the betrayer came along with the soldiers and guards carrying swords and clubs to seize Jesus, Peter could not stand. He was a brave man who could endure danger, but in the Garden on that terrible night, his courage was no match for the evil that was unfolding. The powers of hell were about to undo the Incarnation, to strip the God-man of his human flesh and to give the lie to all Jesus had done and taught. The lesson we learn is not that the first pope had feet of clay, but that even Jesus' most trusted friend was incapable of confronting evil without having received the help that only the Father could give.

The drama of the personal encounter with evil rests on an even deeper drama, which is the conformity with Christ implicit in the *sequela Christi*, which is, as we noted above, more than a simple exterior following. It means being conformed to Christ.

18 Ibid., §35; *Theology of the Body*, 237.

"*Following Christ* is not an outward imitation, since it touches man at the very depths of his being."[19] In addition to the natural knowledge that forms the intellect, the follower of Christ needs the theological virtue of faith, which is a grace given directly by God himself. That is, faith is far more than the intellectual affirmation of a series of propositions such as those found in the Creed. The rich young man asked for eternal life, which can be "attained in its perfection only after death," acknowledges John Paul II, but let us note well the continuation of that same sentence: "*but in faith it is even now a light of truth*, a source of meaning for life, an inchoate share in the full following of Christ."[20] This means that even now in this life, the follower of Christ is able *in faith* to know the truth that he will eventually see in the glory of the Beatific Vision.

St. Paul speaks of the "obedience of faith" (Rom 1:5). To obey is an act of will, not intellect. The scientist affirms the propositions of physics or history or animal husbandry based on knowledge acquired by study and experiences that he and others have carried out. The follower of Christ, however, whose intellect is enlightened by faith cannot justify his beliefs in the normal human way. Rather he must affirm what has been given him or revealed to him by God. The believer has no personal scientific warrant for affirming in the Creed that Jesus of Nazareth is "God from God, light from light, true God from true God." His affirmation of this element in the Creed is an act of obedience to the One whose grace of faith enables him to follow a way that is inchoate in this life.

This does not imply, of course, that the operational activities of the mind are irrelevant to faith, that where faith is involved, reason has no standing. Jesus, having affirmed to his disciples that he has come to do what the Father does (Jn 5: 19–32) and that the Father is greater than he (Jn 14:28), told his disciples, "The Father and I are one" (Jn 17:20). From these seemingly contradictory

19 *Veritatis Splendor*, §21.
20 Ibid., §12 (emphasis added).

statements and many others from the Gospels and the writings of St. Paul, the Fathers at the Council of Nicaea concluded that Jesus is "God from God, light from light, and true God from true God" and indeed "consubstantial with the Father." This formula and others in the Church's credal statements were the fruits of subtle and disciplined reasoning by churchmen and theologians in (often heated) discussions about the expressions of faith. As Christians confess, Jesus is God incarnate, and therefore his statements about himself can be received (by Christians, at least) as authoritative. But when a Council introduces a new term, such as "consubstantial" (*homoousias*), which appears nowhere in the Scriptures and which Christ certainly never uttered, how can the Christian believer accept it? On what grounds? Let us not forget that the Nicene Creed, with the term "consubstantial," must be repeated every Sunday in the Western Church. Let us recall the contrary comment of the Superior General of the Jesuits concerning Christ's words, "what God has joined, let no one put asunder." "You need to start by reflecting on what exactly Jesus said," [Fr Arturo] Sosa told Rusconi. "At that time, no one had a tape recorder to capture the words."[21] Father Sosa proposes that even the words of Scripture may be insufficient to establish a truth of faith.

Something more than the tools of the historian, the psychologist, the literary analyst, or a tape recorder is needed. What is needed is precisely the light of the Holy Spirit, which is the gift of faith, by which the scholar—the theologian—can accurately interpret propositions concerning Christian belief. No science, not even mathematics, can be reduced only to a set of propositions, logically related to each other so that the truth of any one of them can be derived logically from the fundamental propositions of the science. In other words, no nexus or system of symbols can, on

21 Crux Staff, "Jesuit chief rejects charges of 'heresy' for views on Gospels," *Crux*, April 10, 2017. Downloaded 22 June 2022 from https://cruxnow.com/vatican/2017/04/jesuit-chief-rejects-charges-heresy-views-gospels.

its own, logically entail all the truths of a science.[22] Indeed, proportions constructed of logically related terms cannot adequately represent any science. The symbolic system, even one within mathematics, must admit of an interpretation by some model constructed of real things. This is why even the mathematician must be able to "visualize" the realities he studies. The chemist cannot proceed only on his knowledge of the periodic table and the definitions of electron levels. If this is the case with the exact sciences—as I have simplistically represented it—then much more so is it the case with the human sciences, whose founding premises cannot be so well defined. Our subject here is theology, whose fundamental premises or axioms, if you will, must come from God himself.[23] It is not possible readily to find these premises and then systematize them into anything resembling a deductive system. A model, some contact with the reality under investigation is required.

Faith provides that model, that contact. In an admittedly inchoate way, faith forms the intellect of the believer with the truths that will be grasped directly only in the afterlife. Without faith, one who would do theology may cleverly connect concepts expressed in Revelation and relate them to human knowledge, but without assurance that these investigations can even approach the truth. On the other hand, the faith-filled believer knows, albeit imperfectly, his way around the Christian beliefs. He has a sense for the truth that will lead him steadily, even if uncertainly, toward that truth. He becomes increasingly able to recognize the utterances and expressions of others as accurate or erroneous. More important, with a mind formed by faith, he becomes increasingly clear about the truth of the good, about what is more deserving of his love. His soul formed by the grace of faith, the Christian believer has a sense for God.

22 Torkel Franzén, *Gödel's Theorem* (Wellesley, MA: A. K. Peters, 2005), 16 ff; Angelo Margaris, *First Order Mathematical Logic* (Waltham, MA: Blaisdell Publishing Co., 1967), 187–90.

23 See *Summa Theologiae*, Ia, q. 1.

From this it follows that the entirety of the moral law consists in the human person's response to the God who has revealed himself to him. "*The moral life presents itself as the response* due to the many gratuitous initiatives taken by God out of love for man. It is a response of love [...]."[24]

What a life means

Every symbol and every human action can be interpreted by other symbols and acts. Symbols interpret other symbols. The driving instruction manual explains that a diamond-shaped sign with a black arrow bending to the right *means* that the road bends to the right. Sometimes it is necessary for a person to explain to another what he means by a particular utterance. Symbols are related to each other logically. Human acts are so related, too. Every act expresses a belief which can be expressed symbolically.[25] Furthermore, every belief (not necessarily every utterance that appears to express a belief) will or can issue in action. In other words, thoughts interpret actions and actions realize or contradict thoughts. One may advocate thrift in argument with friends while charging frivolous purchases to a credit card. We say that such a one does not truly appreciate or understand the virtue of thrift. He is *lying to himself* if he thinks he does. In principle this implies that all one's acts and stated beliefs stand in some sort of interpretive relationship with one another. In this respect the human mind in the totality of its manifestations is a sign. Therefore, C. S. Peirce maintains "the mind is a sign, developing according to the laws of inference.[26]

If the mind, understood to be the totality of one's beliefs expressed symbolically (as in an express set of symbols, such as a

24 *Veritatis Splendor*, §10.

25 Adrian J. Reimers, *The Soul of the Person* (Washington, D.C.: Catholic university of America Press, 2006), 92.

26 Charles S. Peirce, *Collected Papers, Volume V: Pragmatism and Pragmaticism* (Cambridge, MA: Harvard University Press, 1965), §313. See also A. Reimers, op.cit., 147.

creed, or in maxims such as the Golden Rule), develops according to the laws of inference, then the person is compelled more or less forcefully to bring his ideas into logical harmony. Of course, we must allow that many expressed beliefs are insincere, and some may be lies. Solzhenitsyn says that Josef Stalin never believed anything that anyone said, not even himself, because Stalin used words as instruments of power. Solzhenitsyn writes of him, "Another strength was his habit of disbelieving what others said and attaching no importance to his own words. Say not what you mean to do (you may not know it until the moment comes) but what puts the other at ease."[27] The compulsion toward logical consistency, although real, may not come to the fore in some particular person's life. One may well not become conscious of his personal inconsistencies until challenged by others or by circumstances. The overarching principle governing the compulsion to consistency is the reality of the *good*. As noted earlier in this work, an essential part of anyone's personal project is to determine what is truly good and ultimately what is the good one lives for.

Among all the animals on earth, human beings are unique in having vocations. Whether explicit or not, every human being is challenged to discern his own vocation. To be sure, some persons—think of slaves or the extremely poor—have few options for their lives. But even these must make up their minds how to live in their own situations. Most of us must decide what to do with our lives, whether to marry or not, what kind of work they might do, how they shall express themselves in their leisure, and so on. Ursa, a cat I once knew, had her life plan dictated by circumstances and the plans of her owners. She did not plan to be taken in, nor did she choose to live in the house she grew up in. Every human being, however, needs to determine to the extent possible how to live and what to live for. One's life is guided by his conception of what is good for him.[28]

27 Aleksandr I. Solzhenitsyn, *In the First Circle*, trans. Harry T. Willetts (New York, London: Harper, 2009), 118.

28 A. Reimers, *The Soul of the Person*, 199 ff.

Of course, one's plans for his life need to accord with reality, both the physical reality of the world and the social reality. It does not suffice, therefore, that one's personal vision of the world be consistent. Writers of fantasy and science fiction create imaginary worlds, which are consistent to a certain extent. They cannot be completely consistent, however. The reader must suspend his analytical judgments to a certain extent. So much more is it that no one can live in his own reality. And just as the spacecraft in *Star Wars* does the impossible by travelling faster than the velocity of light, a person's inner visions of his own life can eventually come a cropper against the facts of the world around him. We must live by truth.

By doing science we come to know the truth of the physical world. We can also know moral truths about the nature of the human person and his rights and about God and his prerogatives. The mind is to be formed in part by its interactions with the world. Sense perception is one avenue of cognition. Like other animals, we humans can learn from repeated experiences as we encounter obstacles and challenges. By these means we gain our knowledge of the physical world and its spatial and temporal conditions. The human mind, however, is more than a kind of receptacle for sense-data and memories of successful and futile interactions with the environment. The logic of human mental development is decisively formed by its capacity for hypothetical reasoning. Only by its power to *form hypotheses*, can the human mind transcend the physical realm of space and time. Hypothetical reasoning is the capacity to form universal concepts by which diverse experiences are ordered. One might characterize hypothesis as the mental power to see what is not there. This is the ability that the high school geometry teacher tries to foster in her students as they learn to do geometrical proofs and demonstrations, the key to which lies in the student's positing (for instance) a line through the apex of the triangle and parallel to its base. Only by "seeing" such a line can the student show that the sum of the angles equals one straight angle (or 180 degrees). Similarly, but on a much more sophisticated level, Albert Einstein posed for himself the hypothesis that the fundamental invariant property in physics is not the conservation of matter and energy, respectively, but the velocity of light in every frame of reference. His development of this idea resulted in the special theory of relativity, which transformed the science of physics.

The capacity to advance hypotheses, which is to form new ideas, enables the mind to reach beyond space and time and to reach for God. The animal can often recognize patterns of behavior in its world, as Pavlov's famous dog learned to associate the ringing of a bell with the serving of dog food. Pet owners rely on this principle to train their animals. Human persons can do more than learn from repeat experiences. A hypothesis is a principle that gathers many disparate things into unity. Thus, the human mind can posit a *cause* for things and events. From repeated experiences, the turkey comes to expect food when the farmer enters the pen. A human mind can ask *why* the man is so generous to provide unearned food every day (until mid-November). A cause is an explanation of phenomena that may appear to be unrelated. This principle opens the door to metaphysics. Karol Wojtyła says that this is how we know the rational human soul, through its "acts, experiences, and manifestations of life." "The whole of our knowledge of the human soul is therefore tightly based on the principle of causality."[29]

Here we are concerned with our ultimate goal, with what is worth living for and what we should desire in life. And this takes us back to the story of the rich young man and his encounter with Jesus. We direct ourselves toward many things in our lives—toward food, shelter, and clothing, toward honest work and pleasurable leisure, toward acquisition of wealth and freedom from fear. Yet we know that whatever we attain is not enough. Wealth is insecure, even if it is great. We know that to gain and preserve wealth, disreputable means are often used. Bad men can become very wealthy, but this raises the question whether wealth is a

29 Karol Wojtyła, *Considerations on the Essence of Man/ Rozważania o Istocie Człowieka,* trans. John Grondelski (Lublin-Roma: Polskie Towarzystwo Tomasza z Akwinu, 2016), 31.

worthy goal for anyone. We enjoy pleasures but when indulged they go sour and flat. Because no physical and temporal good suffices to meet our needs, we search for something higher. Indeed, the mind posits a higher reality that can satisfy human longings permanently and reliably. Plato posited such a being, the Form of the Good, and Aristotle argued that there is indeed a highest being, a First Mover, that is perfect in its beauty and desirability. But although these thinkers and others intuited that there is a highest being, a God, they had no way to attain to it. (Neither of these philosophers recognized the God as a personal being.)

When, after seventy years, the Soviet Union collapsed and Aleksandr Solzhenitsyn was asked for the cause of the tragedy of Soviet totalitarianism, he answered, "Because men have forgotten God."[30] Inspired by Marxist materialism, the Bolshevik Revolution proposed to build a society, indeed a new world, based on a utopian science of history. By any standard that science was badly flawed. Its fundamental flaw, however, was what Solzhenitsyn pointed out. It had eliminated God. Man was to be perfected and saved by establishing a new social and economic order. On its own humankind could determine the structure of reality and therefore the rules by which men could live in peace and harmony. This was a blind alley. Having eclipsed God, mankind disappeared. If God has no prerogatives, neither has the human person. Human dignity goes lost. The ancient philosophers did not claim such knowledge. This is why their philosophy was unable to displace the mythic religions of their time. Indeed, after proving to his satisfaction that his soul is immortal (and urging his unconvinced friends to continue their own inquiries), Socrates offered a mythical account of the soul's journey to the afterlife and its perpetual fate therein.[31]

30 Aleksandr Solzhenitsyn, "Templeton Prize: Acceptance address by Mr. Aleksandr Solzhenitsyn," May 10, 1983, downloaded August 16, 2023, from https://www.templetonprize.org/laureate-sub/solzhenitsyn-acceptance-speech/.

31 Plato, *Phaedo*, 107c–115a.

We need an account of reality, not only of the causes of things and of the universe as a whole, but also the significance of our lives, especially the significance of suffering. A child is bitten by a snake and dies; the parents are grief-stricken. Grandma, the *abuela,* turns her palms upward and says, "*Dios quiere*" (God wills it). *Abuelita* may be right, but what comfort is that? If all truth and the pattern of all goodness is in God, and if in his mind is the ultimate explanation of everything, then the vision of him and the eternal conversation with him[32] will satisfactorily respond to this and other mysteries. For human beings to attain to such knowledge we need a teacher, someone to fill in the knowledge of the being that we suspect is there but cannot lay hold of by the power of our minds. The hypothesis that we want to make, toward which the reflective mind inclines and which it intuits, is proposed to us for belief by one who loves us. John Paul II writes,

> [M]en and women are on a journey of discovery which is humanly unstoppable—a search for a person to whom they might entrust themselves. Christian faith comes to meet them, offering the concrete possibility of reaching the goal which they seek.[33]

That truth is revealed in Jesus Christ. This is the truth that John Paul II develops in the first chapter of *Veritatis Splendor*. As much as we may admire the taut arguments of Aristotle in the *Nicomachean Ethics* (and this author does) and their deep connection with book XII of his *Metaphysics,* we are left empty-handed. The promise of an ultimate good is there, but we cannot attain it. We may admire the crystalline logic of Kant's system, but he allows us only to glimpse the Ideal of whose reality we have no assurance. John Stuart Mill offers common-sense answers for our everyday lives, but his system works only if its followers are lucky enough to live in peace and prosperity.

32 See *Gaudium et Spes,* §19.
33 John Paul II, Encyclical *Fides et Ratio,* §33.

If God is the ultimate good, as John Paul II argues in the first chapter of *Veritatis Splendor*, then he stands as the ultimate interpreter of human life. That is to say, whatever a human person decides to do should harmonize coherently with the plans and prerogatives of God, to the extent that these can be known. To fail to do this is to live in unreality.

CONCLUSION

> You shall love the Lord your God with all your heart, with all your soul, with all your mind, and with all your strength. [...] You shall love your neighbor as yourself. (Mark 12:30–31)

Veritatis Splendor is about the moral law, and the foundation of the moral law is the twofold law of love. Hence, Pope Saint John Paul's encyclical *Veritatis Splendor* is about love, about the requirements for living a life of love for God and neighbor. As its title indicates, the encyclical is about truth, the splendor of truth. The moral life is a life of love according to truth. From its first pages, the encyclical repudiates the notion that morality can be divorced from reference to God, that it is possible and reasonable to do moral theory as if God does not exist.

We philosophers and theologians, who busy ourselves with morality and ethics, tend to focus our analyses on the moral properties of single acts. There is a point to this. The human person engages with his fellows, with society, and with the world in single acts that can be good or bad. It is a mistake, however, to reduce morality to the evaluation of single acts because these acts inevitably fall within a larger and more comprehensive context. The moral challenge is not simply to perform good acts and to avoid bad ones. Indeed, most of one's life consists of acts that have no immediately apparent moral value. To tend the tomatoes in the garden or to prepare a peanut butter and jelly sandwich involves no moral imperative. As Aristotle taught us, the moral life is about the formation of character by fostering virtue and eradicating vices. A chaste man ignores the prostitute on the street-corner, impervious to her allure and suggestive posturing. A slave to his vice, the alcoholic unthinkingly pours another drink. The moral challenge that faces every person is to become good, and this implies that one has some standard of goodness by which he can measure the success of his life. *Veritatis Splendor* is structured around the ultimate standard of what is good for the human being. And that standard is God. God is *the* good.

Visiting his homeland in 1991, after the fall of Communism and Poland's reattainment of her independence from the Soviet Union, John Paul II addressed the representatives of Polish culture. This was a moment of moral crisis for Poland. Following the Second World War, Poland's Russian overseers had imposed on the Polish people a totalitarian system based on an atheistic and materialist ideology. During those years of suppression, the Catholic Church, led by the Primate of the Millennium, Cardinal Stefan Wyszyński, stood up for the people, their national values and culture. Poles enjoyed more freedoms than did many of their counterparts elsewhere in Central Europe. Under Communist economic mismanagement, however, they were a poor nation, suffering shortages of food and other necessities. With the fall of Communism, Poles had to reform their political institutions, to rebuild their economy and to learn to live in freedom. In a very real sense, the soul of Poland was at stake. Pope John Paul II, a Polish patriot raised in the traditions of Polish patriotism, recognized the need to speak to his compatriots of how they were to live under dramatically new circumstances, to live so as to realize their freedom. The lesson he delivered to the Polish world of culture in Warsaw constituted the core of the message that he was to deliver to the Church two years hence in *Veritatis Splendor*.

He structured his address around the Conciliar text: "Man, being the only creature on earth which God willed for itself, cannot fully find himself, except through the disinterested gift of self."[1] Of this John Paul II said, "This saying from the Council can rightly pass as a *synthesis of the Christian truth about man*."[2]

1 *Gaudium et Spes*, §24. (Translated from the Pope's Polish text.)
2 John Paul II, "Discourse to the World of Culture," Saturday, 8 June

A consequence of this Conciliar saying is that the human person is to live in communion with his fellow human beings, a communion ultimately realized through the "complete gift of self," following the pattern of the relationships among the Persons of the Blessed Trinity. "This constitutes the true key for the *entire Christian anthropology in the Christian sense*."[3] He reminded his audience, which had just recently gained their freedom from a soul-crushing materialist regime, of the priority of "being" over "having," and he warned against falling into the materialism of wealthier Western consumer societies. To realize its true cultural values, Polish society needed to develop its moral strength only in love, through sincere gift of self. Post-Communist morality was not primarily about setting up transparent free markets, eradicating corruption, and establishing representative political institutions (important as these are). It was about restoring a society worthy of man.[4] The Polish Pope did not address himself to the institutions of the newly independent state but to its people, challenging them to live in a way that reflects their destiny to transcendence marked by the gift of self to God and their neighbors.

This study has examined some of Karol Wojtyła's principal philosophical interlocutors of the modern era, philosophers whose conceptions have formed most contemporary approaches to ethics and therefore to moral theology. Specifically, we considered Kant's rationalist deontology, which eventually reduced religion to morality, as evidenced in his subsequent *Religion within the Limits of Reason Alone*. Kant saves morality, in a sense, but at the cost of condemning the individual to the loneliness of his own rationality, in a loveless kingdom of ends relating not to other persons in love but to universal laws instantiated in the phenomena they encounter. Scheler's moral world is emotionally warm and

1991. Downloaded February 6, 2023 from www.vatican.va/content/john-paul-ii/pl/speeches/1991/june/documents/hf_jp-ii_spe_19910608_moondo-cultura.html.

3 Ibid.

4 *Gaudium et Spes*, §§9, 51, 81.

allows for the loving encounter with other persons. It is, however, a world without sharp demands of truth. Such love is without responsibility, because its only requirement is that it be authentic to experienced emotion. A further point, crucially important, is that Scheler's emotionalism leaves no room for a transcendent good. Plato challenges us to leave the cave of images and shadows, to come out into the life of truth and the vision of the Form of the Good. Aristotle holds up the ideal of the philosopher who, having served the *polis* in a noble and virtuous life, retires to a life of philosophical contemplation of truth, particularly of the most divine truths. Scheler lacks all transcendent teleology and leaves only the hope of emotional appreciation of sublime values.

Most significant of the moral theories have been the variants of utilitarianism. As we have noted already, Mill's *Utilitarianism* offers a remarkably prescient vision of contemporary Western societies marked by democratic ideals, economic prosperity, and relatively free market economies. The possibilities that John Stuart Mill envisioned for Victorian England were realized in the 20th century, not only in Great Britain but in North America, Western Europe, and beyond. When asked for a summary of the good for human beings and societies, most reasonably educated persons (and the members of these societies are at least modestly educated—as Mill had hoped) will speak in utilitarian terms of generalized happiness of life and the reduction of suffering. Utilitarianism is the *de facto* moral philosophy of the West. It is, however, on the verge of collapse and with it too the cultures that it informs.

And here we do well briefly to consider the Marxist alternative. Strictly speaking, Marx does not offer a moral theory but a theory of society. Marxism does not offer an account of good or bad behavior for individuals. Of course, Marxist regimes have behavioral requirements, but these vary according to the immediate requirements of the regime. Persons who behave wrongly are not bad or evil; they are counter-revolutionary or "wreckers." They need not be called to repentance but to be punished or re-educated. Marxism does not see the person as a moral being but only as a material being to be treated according to the needs of the revolution.

Technological revolution

Human desire and its attendant pleasure is enhanced, in a way, by fantasized anticipation. It has doubtless always been so as lovers dream of the ecstatic realization of their love in each other's arms and as rivals relish the bloody and satisfying revenge they will wreak. The great problem with such fantastic anticipations is the intrusion of reality. The 20th century, however, brought the photographic and cinematic technologies to portray those dreams and to suggest the possibility and, in a way, the likelihood of their realization as beautiful actors fulfill their hopes of love or victory and go on to live satisfied lives. The presence of television sets in almost every home has magnified the impact of video technologies. Beyond this, other technologies have apparently made possible the realization of these fantasies. The United States developed a weapon that in an instant destroyed a Japanese city and brought victory in war. The world could watch as men walked on the moon. Telephones became computers and televisions. The advent of contraceptive pharmaceuticals made possible unrestrained sexual exploration without the consequence of pregnancy, and effective antibiotics and antiviral medications relieved the sexually adventurous of much of the risk of pathologies associated with unrestrained sexual activity. Improvements in plastic surgery and further understanding of the operation of hormones suggest the possibility that a person dissatisfied with her sex may change it. In short, we can change the vision of the world and our roles in it via the tools of audio-visual communications, while contemporary sciences offer the promise that whatever we imagine can be realized. This means that the scope of pleasures that one may desire to realize personal happiness has expanded far beyond Mill's conception.

Writing about materialistic philosophies of society—and materialism is becoming the philosophical basis of our civilization—Jacques Maritain writes, "It has been frequently noted that bourgeois liberalism with its ambition to ground everything in the unchecked initiative of the individual, conceived as a little God […]."[5] Note Maritain's use of the phrase, "a little God." God is the supreme being, the Author of all truth, the exemplar of all that is good, and the criterion of reality. If the individual human being is the ultimate judge of all truth and his desires the standard for goodness, then he is a god—perhaps not the Almighty God, but a god nevertheless. The being that does these things is a god, and the prerogatives of this god are his rights. And because different autonomous persons have different rights, their perceived rights will inevitably conflict.

Because the state is precluded from recognizing any substantive value as a common good, its judgments concerning rights—especially when rights are in conflict—must be formal, almost mathematical. Decisions cannot be made with reference to a transcendent common good but only according to neutral procedures accepted as fair to all so that each person enjoys reasonably unfettered access to the good as he or she conceives it. With this, the utilitarian standard collapses into chaos. We can no longer agree on what is authentically good.

Sin and the presence of evil

Veritatis Splendor is far more than a critique of consequentialism and proportionalism in contemporary moral theology. Rather, the encyclical is an extended examination of the foundations of the human person's relationship with God and other human beings. As such it expresses the anthropological fruit of four decades of Karol Wojtyła's philosophical reflection. That being said, however, *Veritatis Splendor* does present a strong critique of erroneous approaches to moral theology, erroneous because they undermine the bases of human (and specifically Christian) morality. John Paul II writes,

5 Jacques Maritain, *The Person and the Common Good* (Notre Dame: University of Notre Dame Press, 1966), 91–92.

> The specific purpose of the present Encyclical is this: to set forth, with regard to the problems being discussed, the principles of a moral teaching based upon Sacred Scripture and the living Apostolic Tradition, and at the same time to shed light on the presuppositions and consequences of the dissent which that teaching has met.[6]

At its publication, *Veritatis Splendor* triggered—and continues to trigger—strong, and even angry reactions. As one moral theologian expressed it to this author, "We're mad as hell." This comment is, perhaps, to the point, for hell is precisely what is at stake. Even though *Humanae Vitae* uses the term "sin" or "sinner" each only twice (in sections 19, 25, and 29) and never with the adjective "mortal," it was clear immediately upon its publication that the use of contraceptives as described in the Encyclical constituted mortal sin. *Veritatis Splendor*, however, treats the question of mortal sin directly and at some length (sections 68–69). What this encyclical makes clear is that any person who performs certain kinds of acts risks the possibility of eternal damnation. Of course, as both *Humanae Vitae* and *Veritatis Splendor*, as well especially as *Dominum et Vivificantem* and *Reconciliatio et Paenitencia*, are at pains to make clear, every sin, no matter how serious, can be forgiven. One who has offended God need only approach him contrite and repentant to be forgiven. Catholics have known this for years.

The problem today is not that Catholics do not believe in forgiveness but that many do not accept the notion of sin and with this the notions of guilt and judgment. If *Veritatis Splendor* is right, then every human person, no matter how ordinary, no matter how socially agreeable, stands under the judgment of God. Ordinary Catholics in the pews on Sunday may well include some who will be eternally damned if they die unrepentant of hidden sin. Shortly after the publication of *Amoris Laetitia* one commentator in the religious press raised the polemical question whether

6 *Veritatis Splendor*, §5.

it is just or rather hurtful to label as an adulteress a woman (for instance) in an "irregular" second marriage. Fr. James Martin, S.J., regularly appeals for the virtues of "respect, compassion, and sensitivity" in the Church's dealing with homosexual persons while ignoring the fact that to perform homosexual acts is grievously wrong and that by engaging in them, one endangers his salvation.

The root difficulty we face is the problem of evil. Because we no longer accept the reality of evil, we no longer know how to cope with it. This is evident in the work of Peter Knauer, S.J., whose notion of evil depends on non-moral (or ontic) evils such as earthquakes, broken bones, and kidney disease. This conception, however, is rooted in the Enlightenment and subsequent utilitarian thinking. In Hume's realm of sense experience, as in Kant's realm of *phenomena,* is found no possibility of any form of evil. Evil is discerned only by the emotions or, in Kant's case, in the will of the agent. Mill tells us that evil is found in pain or the absence of pleasure; it is God's will that his creatures be happy in the sense that Mill conceives.[7] If evil is constituted by a more or less unfortunate or painful arrangement of things in the world, then the person responsible for the evil may be more accurately described as ignorant or careless, imprudent or mean—or even thoughtless, nasty, unkind, misguided, or sick. We may dislike or even restrain him, but we do not condemn him as wicked as though he should be identified with his evil. This author has heard undergraduates in the classroom maintain that even the terrorists who crashed airplanes into skyscrapers on September 11, 2001, or who have bombed nightclubs in Israel, are not truly wicked, because they believed in what they were doing. On a more homely level, where the sexual abuse of a child or adolescent is concerned—here it does not matter whether we are speaking of the acts of a priest or clergyman, of a public-school teacher, a coach, or a family member—those closest to the victim and the event are very often unwilling to face the evil and to acknowledge its reality. Ordinary good people are often blind to evil around them.

7 J. S. Mill, *Utilitarianism*, 22.

Even more serious than our inability to acknowledge the reality of evil is our ignorance of the good. John Paul II writes:

> According to the witness of the beginning, God in creation has revealed himself as omnipotence, which is love. At the same time he has revealed to man that, as the "image and likeness" of his Creator, he is *called to participate in truth and love*. This participation means a life in union with God, who is "eternal life."[8]

Much can be made of God's omnipotence, that God can do anything he wants, that he can damn any one of us to hell with a simple flick of his almighty hand. This is manifest in the famous words of Jonathan Edwards.

> The God that holds you over the Pit of Hell, much as one holds a Spider, or some loathsome Insect, over the Fire, abhors you, and is dreadfully provoked; his Wrath towards you burns like Fire; he looks upon you as worthy of nothing else, but to be cast into the Fire; he is of purer Eyes than to bear to have you in his Sight; you are ten thousand Times so abominable in his Eyes as the most hateful venomous Serpent is in ours.[9]

In the Great Awakening Pastor Edwards was indeed effective in moving his hearers to repentance, and his sermon does evoke a strong sense for the wickedness of sin. Edwards is right in this, that sin offends God far more grievously than we realize and that our wickedness deserves a severe response. However, his conception of God's attitude toward human beings is dreadfully wrong.

8 *Dominum et Vivificantem*, 35.

9 Jonathan Edwards, "Sinners in the Hands of an Angry God. A Sermon Preached at Enfield, July 8th, 1741." DigitalCommons@University of Nebraska - Lincoln, downloaded 7 July 2022, from https://digitalcommons.unl.edu/cgi/viewcontent.cgi?article=1053&context=etas.

At the core of Pope John Paul II's consistent teaching is that God is love and that his love for us continues despite our sin. He wants so much that we participate in his love and thereby enjoy eternal life that he became man and subjected himself to our wickedness. In other words, everything that Jonathan Edwards found horrifying about human sin is there. It is truly real. If the evil of human sin were constituted only by ignorant, stupid, or even selfish choices about the arrangement of temporal affairs that consequently turned out badly, then it would not be necessary that Jesus die on the cross. Nor would we need an outpouring of the Holy Spirit. However, the essential core of *Veritatis Splendor* is that we are called to participate in God's love forever, that we are called to be like God. This is achieved by grace, but it is blocked and indeed denied by human acts that are incompatible with God's love. If by our choices we, like Lucifer,[10] choose love of self rather than love for God, then God allows this choice. This amounts to a rejection of God's way of loving and the consequence of falling under the reign of his enemy, Satan, and the inevitable sentence, "Depart from me, you cursed, into the eternal fire prepared for the devil and his angels." (Matt 25:41)

If *Veritatis Splendor* is unacceptable to so many contemporary thinkers, it is because it constitutes a rejection of the received modern paradigms of philosophical and moral thought. Speaking to a conference on moral theology in May 2022, Julio Martinez, S.J., remarked,

> *Veritatis Splendor* introduced a very profound development in moral theology with the introduction of the concept we call intrinsic evil. This is a controversial philosophical concept that brought serious difficulties for moral theology in the development of the path of dialogue and discernment [...].[11]

10 Adrian J. Reimers, *Hell and the Mercy of God* (Washington, DC: The Catholic University of America Press, 2017), 18–22.

11 Gerard O'Connell, "Spanish priest: 'Amoris Laetitia' allows the

Father Martinez proceeds to argue that this concept of intrinsic evil (*intrinsece malum*) undercuts the possibility of a mature formation of conscience by holding the acting person to a strict obedience to the Church's magisterial pronouncements. More serious in his eyes is that this concept, *intrinsic evil*, is a philosophical concept, allegedly introduced into moral theology by John Paul II in this encyclical. That is simply not true. In his philosophical writings prior to his election to the papacy, especially in his central works, *Love and Responsibility* and *Person and Act*, Karol Wojtyła does indeed address the issue of moral evil and human acts. Indeed, *Person and Act* might be read as a preliminary philosophical groundwork for *Veritatis Splendor*. Contrary to Father Martinez, he does not introduce the notion of intrinsic evil in these or any other philosophical works for the simple reason that the intrinsic evil is that which is "incapable of being ordered to God."[12] This is a *theological* notion. The rich young man who is seeking eternal life is not the subject of the investigations in *Person and Act*. With the notion of intrinsic evil and the possibility of mortal sin—acts that are intrinsically evil—Pope John Paul II has brought to the fore an essential element in Christian moral thinking.

In this study we have examined the philosophies that Karol Wojtyła frequently addressed in his own works. His early lectures in the Catholic University of Lublin[13] manifest a deep appreciation for and understanding of Aristotle's thought, especially in relation to Saints Augustine and Thomas Aquinas. As this present study shows, John Paul II bases his thought and argumentation on a careful study of modern and contemporary currents in philosophy, currents that he also examined carefully in his encyclical *Fides et Ratio*. Engaged with post-Enlightenment philosophy, Pope

church to 'untie the knots' in Catholic morality since 'Humanae Vitae,'" *America: The Jesuit Review*, May 27, 2022, accessed 31 May 2022 from https://www.americamagazine.org/faith/2022/05/27/amoris-laetitia-pope-francis-rome-julio-martinez-sj-243066

12 *Veritatis Splendor*, §79.

13 Karol Wojtyła, *The Lublin Lectures/ Wykłady Lubelskie*.

John Paul II has personally and profoundly addressed our contemporary culture, calling it back to love of God and full acceptance of the dignity of the human person. The encyclical *Veritatis Splendor* is offensive and unacceptable—a "knot" in the words of Luis Martinez—not because it falsifies the proper understanding of human act, nor because it amounts to an imposition of impossible demands from a distant magisterium, but because it insists that the human person is called to a demanding life, not of asceticism imposed, but of holiness and communion with God. No, we are not destined to the impossibly happy life of post-industrial consumerism sketched out by contemporary utilitarianism. We are destined to eternal bliss, a sharing in God's own happiness.[14] Therefore, Pope John Paul II devotes the third chapter of the Encyclical to the cross of Christ and inevitable reality of martyrdom.

> *Jesus asks us to follow him and to imitate him along the path of love, a love which gives itself completely to the brethren out of love for God.*[15]

14 On this see also, Servais-Th. Pinckaers, *Pour une lecture de Veritatis Splendor*, 67.

15 *Veritatis Splendor*, §20.

BIBLIOGRAPHY

Alighieri, Dante. 1980. *The Divine Comedy of Dante Alighieri: Inferno*. Translation by Allen Mandelbaum. New York, Toronto, London: Bantam Books.

Aquinas, Thomas. 1964. *Commentary on the Nicomachean Ethics.* Translation by C. I. Litzinger, O.P. Vol. I. II vol. Chicago: Henry Regnery Company.

—. 1951. *Disputed Questions on Truth.* Vol. I. Chicago: Henry Regnery.

—. 1952. *Summa Theologiae.* Great Books of the Western World. Translation by Fathers of the English Dominican Province. Vols. 19–20. Chicago, London, Toronto: Encyclopedia Britannica.

Aristotle. 1956. *Metaphysics.* Vol. I, in *The Works of Aristotle: Volume I.* Edited by Robert Maynard Hutchins. Translation by W. D. Ross. Chicago, London: Encyclopaedia Britannica.

—. 1976. *Nicomachean Ethics.* Translation by J. A. K. Thompson and Hugh Tredennick. London: Penguin Books.

Aristotle, and Thomas Aquinas. 1961. *Commentary on the Metaphysics of Aristotle.* Translation by John P Rown. Vol. II. Chicago: Henry Regnery Company.

—. 1951. *De Anima and the Commentary of St. Thomas Aquinas.* New Haven: Yale University Press.

Auden, W. H. 1954. "September 1, 1939." In *The Major Poets: English and American*. Edited by Charles M. Coffin. New York: Harcourt, Brace & World.

Augustine of Hippo. 1952. *City of God.* Edited by Robert Maynard Hutchins. Translation by Marcus Dods. Chicago, London: Encyclopedia Britannica, Inc.

—. 1960. *Confessions.* Translation by John K. Ryan. New York: Image Books.

Ayan, Steve. 2018. "There Is No Such Thing as Conscious Thought." In *Scientific American*, 20 December.

Benedict XVI. 2006. "Faith, Reason and the University: Lecture of the Holy Father." *The Holy See.* 12 September. Downloaded on June 6, 2021. https://www.vatican.va/content/benedict-xvi/en/speeches/2006/september/documents/hf_ben-xvi_spe_20060912_university-regensburg.html.

Bentham, Jeremy. 2017. *An Introduction to the Principle of Morals and Legislation.* Edited by Jonathan Bennett.

Berlin, Isaiah. 1969. "Two Concepts of Liberty." In *Four Essays on Liberty*. Oxford: Oxford University Press.

Berofsky, Bernard. 1971. *Determinsim.* Princeton, NJ: Princeton University Press.

Bishops of Canada. 1968. "Canadian Bishops' Statement on the Encyclical *Humanae Vitae.*" Winnipeg, Manitoba. Accessed on July 25, 2014.

Browning, Christopher. 1992. *Ordinary Men: Reserve Police Battalion 101 and the Final Solution in Poland.* New York: Harper.

—. 1939. *Gone with the Wind.* Directed by Victor Flemin. Performers, Vivien Leigh, Clark Gable.

Curran, Charles. 2004. "Conscience in the Light of Catholic Moral Tradition." In *Conscience Readings in Moral Theology, No. 14,* Edited by Charles Curran. New York: Paulist Press.

—. 2004. *Conscience: Readings in Moral Theology No. 14.* Edited by Charles Curran. New York: Paulist Press.

Curran, Charles, Fr., and 87 others. 1968. "Text of the Statement by Theologians." In *New York Times*, 31 July: 16.

Darwin, Charles. 1981. *The Descent of Man: and Selection in Relation to Sex.* Princeton: Princeton University Press.

Descartes, René. 1993. *Meditations on First Philosophy.* Third Edition. Translation by Donald A. Cress. Indianapolis: Hackett.

Egan, Timothy. 2006. *The Worst Hard Time: The Untold Story of Those Who Survived the Great American Dust Bowl.* Boston, New York: Houghton Mifflin Company.

Eliot, Thomas Stearns. 1935. *Murder in the Cathedral.* New York: Harcourt, Brace & Co. https://archive.org/stream/in.ernet.dli.2015.86641/2015.86641.Murder-In-The-Cathedral_djvu.txt.

Francis. 2016. Apostolic Exhortation *Amoris Laetitia.* Vatican City: Libreria Editrice Vaticana.

—. 2022. "Discorso del Santo Padre Francesco ai Partecipanti ai Convegno Internazionale di Teologia Morale." *The Holy See.* 13 May. Downloaded on October 9, 2023. https://www.vatican.va/content/francesco/it/speeches/2022/may/documents/20220513-convegno-teologia-morale.html.

Franzen, Torkél. 2005. *Gödel's Theorem: An Incomplete Guide to Its Use and Abuse.* Wellesley, MA: A. K. Peters.

Fuchs, Joseph. 1990. "Good Acts and Good Persons." In *John Paul II and Moral Theology: Readings in Moral Theology No. 10,* Edited by Charles E. Curran and Richard A. McCormick. New York, Mahwah, NJ: Paulist.

General Assembly of the United Nations. 1948. "Universal Declaration of Human Rights." *United Nations.* 10 December. Downloaded on June 25, 2021. https://www.un.org/en/about-us/universal-declaration-of-human-rights.

General Congress of the United States of America. 1776. "Declaration of Independence." *American's Founding Documents.* 4 July. Downloaded on June 6, 2021. https://www.archives.gov/founding-docs/declaration-transcript.

Gula, Richard. 2004. "The Moral Conscience." In *Conscience: Readings in Moral Theology, No 14,* Edited by Charles Curran. New York: Paulist Press.

Häring, Bernard. 1998. "A Distrust That Wounds." In *John Paul II and Moral Theology,* edited by Charles E. Curran and Richard A. McCormick, S.J., 42–46. Mahwah, NJ: Paulist Press.

Havel, Václav. 1991. "Dear Dr. Husák." In *Open Letters*, edited by Václav Havel, 50–83. London: Faber & Faber.

—. 1991. *Open Letters: Selected Prose 1965–1990*. London: Faber & Faber.

—. 1990. "The Power of the Powerless." In *Living in Truth*, edited by Václav Havel, 36–122. London: Faber & Faber.

Holy See. 1995. *Catechism of the Catholic Church*. New York: Image Books.

Howorth, Henry H. 2008. *History of the Mongols from the 9th to the 19th Century*. New York: Cosimo.

Hume, David. 2019. *A Treatise of Human Nature*. Overland Park, KS: Digireads.com Publishing.

—. 1965. *An Enquiry Concerning the Principles of Morals*. In *Hume's Ethical Writings*, edited by David Hume and Alasdair MacIntyre. London: Collier Books.

—. 1955. *An Inquiry concerning Human Understanding*. Indianapolis: Bobbs-Merrill.

International Theological Commission. 2009. The Holy See. *In Search of Universal Ethic: A New Look at the Natural Law*. Downloaded on June 2, 2021. https://www.vatican.va/roman_curia/congregations/cfaith/cti_documents/rc_con_cfaith_doc_20090520_legge-naturale_en.html#2.2._Moral_experience:_%E2%80%9Cone_must_do_good%E2%80%9D.

Jobs, Steven. 2011. "Find what you love." In *Wall Street Journal*. 6 October. Accessed August 22, 2016. http://www.wsj.com/articles/SB10001424052970203388804576613572842080228.

John Paul II (Karol Wojtyła). 2020. *Teachings for an Unbelieving World: Newly Discovered Reflections on Paul's Sermon at the Areopagus*. Notre Dame, Indiana: Ave Maria Press.

—. 1984. Apostolic Exhortation *Reconciliatio et paenitentia*. Vatican City: Libreria Editrice Vaticana.

—. 1984. Apostolic Letter *Salvifici Doloris*. Vatican City: Libreria Editrice Vaticana.

—. 1988. Apostolic Letter *Mulieris Dignitatem.* Vatican City: Libreria Editrice Vaticana.

—. 1994. *Crossing the Threshold of Hope.* Edited by Vittorio Messori. New York: Alfred A. Knopf.

—. 1980. "Discours du Pape Jean-Paul II a l'UNESCO." *The Holy See.* 2 June. Downloaded June 25, 2021. https://www.vatican.va/content/john-paul-ii/fr/speeches/1980/june/documents/hf_jp-ii_spe_19800602_unesco.html.

—. 1991. "Speech to Representatives of the World of Culture." *The Holy See.* https://www.vatican.va/content/john-paul-ii/it/speeches/1991/june/documents/hf_jp-ii_spe_19910608_mondo-cultura.html. 8 June. Downloaded May 28, 2012.

—. 1986. Encyclical *Dominum et Vivificantem.* Vatican City: Libreria Editrice Vaticana.

—. 1981. Encyclical *Laborem Exercens.* Vatican City: Libreria Editrice Vaticana.

—. 1998. Encyclical *Fides et Ratio.* Boston: Pauline Books & Media.

—. 1993. Encyclical *Veritatis Splendor.* Vatican City: Libraria Editrice Vaticana.

—. 2006. *Man and Woman He Created Them: A Theology of the Body.* Edited by Michael Waldstein. Translation by Michael Waldstein. Boston: Pauline Books & Media.

—. 1987. "Omelia di Giovanni Paolo II." *The Holy See, Viaggio Apostolico in Polonia.* June. Downloaded April 24, 2017. http://w2.vatican.va/content/john-paul-ii/it/homilies/1987/documents/hf_jp-ii_hom_19870609_celebraz-parola-lublino.html.

Kant, Immanuel. 1965. *Critique of Pure Reason.* Translation by Norman Kemp Smith. New York: St. Martin's Press.

—. 1993. "Grounding of the Metaphysics of Morals." In *Grounding of the Metaphysics of Morals with On a Supposed Right to Lie because of Philanthropic Concerns*. Edited by James W. Ellington. Indianapolis: Hackett.

—. 1911. *Grundlegung der Metaphysik der Sitten.* Vol. 4: Kant's gesammelte Schriften. Berlin: Georg Reimer.

Knauer, Peter. 2002. *Handlungsnetze: Über das Grundprinzip der Ethik.* Frankfurt am Main: Books on Demand.

—. 1980. "Teleologische als deontologische Normenbegründung." *Theologie und Philosophie* (55: 3): 321–60.

—. 1994. "Zu Grundbegriffen der Enzyklika 'Veritatis Splendor.'" In *Stimmen der Zeit (212 Band, Heft* 1): 14–26.

Krąpiec, OP, Mieczysław A., and Andrzej Marynirczyk, SDB. 2010. *The Lublin Philosophical School.* Translation by Hugh McDonald. Lublin: Towarzystwo Tomasza z Akwinu.

Kupczak, Stanisław. 2021. *Before Amoris Laetitia: The Sources of the Controversy.* Translation by Grzegorz Ignatik. Washington, DC: The Catholic University of America Press.

Laplace, Pierre-Simon. 2016. *Stanford Encyclopedia of Philosophy.* 21 January. Downloaded March 4, 2022. https://plato.stanford.edu/entries/determinism-causal/.

Locke, John. 1980. *Second Treatise of Government.* Indianapolis: Hackett.

Margaris, Angelo. 1967. *First Order Mathematic Logic.* Waltham, MA: Blaisdell Publishing.

Maritain, Jacques. 1966. *The Person and the Common Good.* Translation by John J. Fitzgerald. Notre Dame, Indiana: University of Notre Dame Press.

Martin, S.J., James. 2014. *Building a Bridge.* New York: Harper Collins.

Marx, Karl, and Engels, Friedrich. 1983. "Manifesto of the Communist Party." In *The Portable Karl Marx*. Edited by Eugene Kamenka. New York: Penguin Books.

McBrien, Richard P. 1994. *Catholicism.* New York: Harper Collins.

McCormick, S.J., Richard A. 1998. "Some Early Reactions to *Veritatis Splendor*." In *John Paul II and Moral Theology*. Edited by Charles E. Curran and Richard A. McCormick, S.J. Mahwah, NJ: Paulist Press.

—. 1989. *The Critical Calling: Reflections on Moral Dilemmas since Vatican II*. Washington, D.C.: Georgetown University Press.

McLeod, S. A. 2017. *Simply Psychology*. 5 February. Downloaded April 1, 2020. https://www.simplypsychology.org/milgram.html.

Mill, John Stuart. 1978. *On Liberty*. Indianapolis: Hackett Publiching Co.

—. 2001. *Utilitarianism*. Cambridge, Indianapolis: Hackett.

Moore, George Edward. 1968. *Principia Ethica*. Cambridge: Cambridge University Press.

Murphy, Jr., William F. 2022. "Reflections on Fundamental Morality, Conscience, Norms, and Discernment." In *Etica Teologica della Vita*. Edited by Vincenzo Paglia. Vatican City: Libreria Editrice Vaticana.

Nagel, Thomas. 1975. "Sexual Perversion." In *Moral Problems: A Collection of Philosophical Essays*. Edited by James Rachels. New York: Harper & Row.

Newman, John Henry Cardinal. 1955. *An Essay in Aid of a Grammar of Assent*. Garden City, NY: Image Books.

Newman, John Henry. 2001. "A Letter Addressed to the Duke of Norfolk on Occasion of Mr. Gladstone's Recent Expostulation." In *Newman Reader*. Downloaded January 23, 2023. https://www.newmanreader.org/works/anglicans/volume2/gladstone/index.html.

O'Connell, Gerard. 2022. "Spanish Priest: '*Amoris Laetitia*' allows the Church to 'untie the knots' in Catholic morality since '*Humanae Vitae*.'" *America: The Jesuit Review*. 27 May. Downloaded May 31, 2022. https://www.americamagazine.org/faith/2022/05/27/amoris-laetitia-pope-francis-rome-julio-martinez-sj-243066.

Owne, James. 2007. "Modern Humans Came Out of Africa, 'Definitive' Study says." In *National Geographic*. 18 July. Downloaded March 29, 2022. https://www.nationalgeographic.com/history/article/modern-humans-came-out-of-africa-definitive-study-says.

Paglia, Vincenzo. 2022. *Etica teological della vita: Scrittura, tradizione, sfide practiche.* Vatican City: Libreria Editrice Vaticana.

Papal Commission for the Study of Problems of the Family, Population, and Birth Rate. 1966. "Majority Report of the Papal Commission for the Study of Problems of the Family, Population, and Birth Rate." In *Agathon Associates.* Downloaded September 18, 2014. http://www.bostonleadershipbuilders.com/0church/birth-control-majority.htm.

Paul VI. 1968. Encyclical Letter *Humanae Vitae.* Vatican City: Libreria Editrice Vaticana. Downloaded July 24, 2014. http://www.vatican.va/holy_father/paul_vi/encyclicals/documents/hf_p-vi_enc_25071968_humanae-vitae_en.html.

Pinckaers, Servais. 2001. *Morality: The Catholic View.* Translation by Michael Sherwin, O.P. South Bend: St. Augustine's Press.

—. 1995. *Pour une lecture de Veritatis Splendor.* Paris: Editions Mame.

—. 1995. *The Sources of Christian Ethics.* Translation by Mary Thomas Noble, O.P. Washington, D.C.: The Catholic University of America Press.

Planned Parenthood of Southeastern Pa. v. Casey, 505 US 833 (U.S. Supreme Court, 29 June 1992).

Plato. 2011. "Apology." In *The Complete Works of Plato*. Translation by Benjamin Jowett. New York, Oxford: Oxford University Press.

—. 1969. "Euthyphro." In *The Collected Dialogues of Plato*. Translation by Lane Cooper. Princeton: Princeton University Press.

—. 1969. "Phaedo." In *The Collected Dialogues of Plato.* Edited by Huntington Cairns and Edith Hamilton. Translation by Hugh Tredennick. Princeton: Princeton University Press.

—. 1961. "Republic." In *The Collected Dialogues of Plato*. Edited by Edith Hamilton and Huntington Cairns. Translation by Paul Shorey. Princeton: Princeton University Press.

—. 1961. "Symposium." In *The Collected Dialogues of Plato*. Edited by Edith Hamilton and Huntington Cairns. Princeton: Princeton University Press.

Rahner, Karl. 1976. *Grundkurs des Glaubens: Einführung in den Begriff des Christentums.* Freiburg im Breisgau: Herder.

Ratzinger, Joseph (Benedict XVI). 2019. *Western Culture: Today and Tomorrow.* Translation by Michael J. Miller. San Francisco: Ignatius Press.

Reimers, Adrian J. 2017. *Hell and the Mercy of God.* Washington, DC: The Catholic University of America Press.

—. 2020. *The Good Is Love: The Body and Human Acts in* Humanae Vitae *and John Paul II.* South Bend, IN: St. Augustine's Press.

—. 2006. *The Soul of the Person.* Washington, D.C.: Catholic University of America Press.

—. 2011. *Truth about the Good: Moral Norms in the Thought of John Paul II.* Ave Maria, Florida: Sapientia Press.

—. 1995. "Truth and the Open-Endedness of the Natural Order." Edited by Niels H. Gregersen, Michael W. S. Parsons, and Christoph Wassermann. *Studies in Science and Theology, Part I* (Labor et Fides, S.A.): The Concept of Nature in Science and Theology.

Rescher, Nicholas. 1995. "American Philosophy." In *The Oxford Companion to Philosophy.* Edited by Ted Honderich. Oxford, New York: Oxford University Press.

Rhonheimer, Martin. 2008. *The Perspective of the Acting Person: Essays in the Renewal of Thomistic Moral Theology.* Washington, DC: The Catholic University of America Press.

Sartre, Jean-Paul. 1956. *Being and Nothingness: An Essay on Phenomenological Ontology.* Translation by Hazel Barnes. New York: Philosophical Library.

—. 1999. "The Humanism of Existentialism." In *Essays in Existentialism.* Secaucus, N.J.: Citadel Press.

Scheler, Max. 1966. *Der Formalismus in der Ethik und die materiale Wertethik: Neuer Versuch der Grundlegung eines ethischen Personalismus.* Bern and Munich: Franke Verlag.

Searle, John R. 1992. *The Rediscovery of the Mind.* Cambridge, Mass., London: MIT Press.

Secretariat of State of the Holy See. 2020. *Report on the Holy See's Insitutional Knowledge and Decision-Making Related to Former Cardinal Theodore Edgar McCormick (1930–2017).* Vatican City: Holy See – Secretariat of State.

Shakespeare, William. 1919. "Hamlet: Prince of Denmark." In *The Complete Works of Shakespeare*. New York: Oxford University Press.

—. 1919. "Julius Caesar." In *The Complete Works of Shakespeare*. New York: Oxford University Press.

Singer, Peter. 1979. *Practical Ethics.* Cambridge: Cambrige University Press .

Skrzypczak, Robert. 2011. *Karol Wojtyła: na Soborze Watykańskim II.* Warsaw: Centrum Myśli Jana Pawła II.

Snead, O. Carter. 2020. *What It Means to Be Human: The Case for the Body in Public Bioethics*. Cambridge, Massachusetts: Harvard University Press.

Solzhenitsyn, Aleksandr. 1983. "Acceptance address by Mr. Aleksandr Solzhenitsyn." *Templeton Prize.* 1983 May. Downloaded August 16, 2023. https://www.templetonprize.org/laureate-sub/solzhenitsyn-acceptance-speech/.

Sperry, Roger Wolcott. 1987. "Consciounsess and Causality." In *The Oxford Companion to the Mind*. Edited by R. L. Gregory. Oxford – New York: Oxford University Press.

Spohn, William. 2004. "Conscience and Moral Development." In *Conscience: Readings in Moral Theology No. 14*. Edited by Charles Curran. New York: Paulist Press.

Stonestreet, Erica Lucast. 2023. "Review of Markus Gabriel, Moral Progress in Dark Times: Universal Values for the Twenty-First Century." In *Notre Dame Philosophical Reviews,* 7 April. Downloaded July 7, 2023. https://ndpr.nd.edu/reviews/moral-progress-in-dark-times-universal-values-for-the-twenty-first-century/.

Szostek, Andrzej. 1992. *Natur-Vernuft-Freiheit: Philosophische Analyse der Konzeption "Schöpferischer Vernunft" in der zeitgenössischen Moraltheologie.* Frankfurt am Main: Peter Lang.

Taylor, Charles. 1992. *The Ethics of Authenticity.* Cambridge, MA: Harvard University Press.

van Inwagen, Peter. 1993. *Metaphysics.* Boulder, San Francisco: Westview Press.

—. 2006. *The Problem of Evil: The Gifford Lectures Delivered in the University of St. Andrews in 2003.* Oxford: Clarendon Press.

Vatican Council II. 2009. Constitution on the Liturgy *Sacrosanctum Concilium*. In *The Documents of Vatican II*. Staten Island, NY: St. Paul Publications.

—. 2009. Declaration on Religious Freedom *Dignitatis Humanae*. In *The Documents of Vatican II*, 391–402. Vatican City: St. Paul Publications.

—. 1965. Pastoral Constitution on the Church in the Modern World *Gaudium et Spes.* Vatican City: Libreria Editrice Vaticana.

Waldstein, Michael Maria. 2021. *Glory of the Logos in the Flesh: Saint John Paul's Theology of the Body.* Ave Maria, Florida: Sapientia University Press.

Wojtyła, Karol. 2016. *Considerations on the Essence of Man/Rozważania o Istocie Człowieka.* Translation by John Grondelski. Lublin – Roma: Polskie Towarzystwo Tomasza z Akwinu.

—. 2000. "Człowiek jest osobą." In *Osoba i czyn – oraz inne studia antropologiczne*. Lublin: Towarzystwo Naukowe KUL.

—. 2013. *Love and Responsibility.* Translation by Grzegorz Ignatik. Boston: Paulist Press.

—. 1981. *Lubliner Vorlesungen.* Translation by Anneliese Danka Springer and Edda Wiener. Stuttgart-Degerloch: Seewald Verlag.

—. 2003. "L'uomo nel campo della responsibilità." In *Metafisica della persona*. Rome: Bompiani.

—. 2009. "Myśli o małżeństwie [Reflections on Marriage]." In *Aby Chrystu się nami posługiwał [That Christ would use us]*. Krakow: Wydawnictwo Znak.

—. 2000. "Osoba i czyn." In *Osoba i czyn: oraz inne studia antopologiczne*. Lublin: Towarzystwa Naukowe KUL.

—. 2021. *Person and Act.* Vol. 1, in *Person and Act and Related Essays*, Karol Wojtyła, Translation by Grzegorz Ignatik. Washington, D.C.: The Catholic University of America Press.

—. 1993. *Person and Community.* Translation by Theresa Sandok, O.S.M. New York, Berlin, Vienna: Peter Lang.

—. 1993. "Person: Subject and Community." In *Person and Community: Selected Essays*. Translation by Teresa Sandok, O.S.M., 219-61. New York: Peter Lang.

—. 2003. "Persona e atto." In *Metafisica della persona: Tutte le opere filosofiche e saggi integrativi.* Translation by Giuseppe Girenti and Patricja Mikulska. Milan: Bompiani.

—. 1993. "Separation of Experience from the Act in Ethics." In *Person and Community: Selected Essays*. Translation by Theresa Sandok. New York, San Francisco: Peter Lang.

—. 1979. *Sign of Contradiction.* New York: The Seabury Press.

—. 2020. *The Lublin Lectures/Wykłady Lubelkie.* Translation by Hugh McDonald. Lublin: Polskie Towarzystwo Tomasza z Akwinu.

—. 1993. "Thomistic Personalism." In *Person and Community: Selected Essays*. Translation by Theresa Sandok. New York, San Francisco: Peter Lang.

—. 2003. "Valutazione sulla possibilità di costruire l'etica cristiana sulle base del sistema di Max Scheler." In *Metafisica della persona*. Milano: Bompiani.